ISLAMIC RESISTANCE
TO IMPERIALISM

ISLAMIC RESISTANCE TO IMPERIALISM

Eric Walberg

Clarity Press, Inc

© 2015 Eric Walberg
ISBN: 978-0-9860731-8-2
EBOOK ISBN: 978-0-9860731-8-5

In-house editor: Diana G. Collier
Cover: R. Jordan P. Santos

ALL RIGHTS RESERVED: Except for purposes of review, this book may not be copied, or stored in any information retrieval system, in whole or in part, without permission in writing from the publishers.

Library of Congress Cataloging-in-Publication Data

Walberg, Eric.
 Islamic resistance to imperialism / Eric Walberg.
    pages cm
 Includes bibliographical references and index.
 ISBN 978-0-9860731-8-2 (alkaline paper)
 1. Middle East--Politics and government--1979- 2. Government, resistance to--Middle East. 3. Anti-imperialist movements--Middle East. 4. Islam and politics--Middle East. 5. Jihad--Political aspects--Middle East. 6. Radicals--Middle East--Biography. 7. Geopolitics--Middle East. 8. Middle East--Relations--Western countries. 9. Western countries--Relations--Middle East. I. Title.

DS63.123.W35 2015
322'.10956--dc23
                                                  2015007327

Clarity Press, Inc.
2625 Piedmont Rd. NE, Ste. 56
Atlanta, GA. 30324 , USA
http://www.claritypress.com

TABLE OF CONTENTS

Glossary / 8

Preface / 10

Introduction: The Logic of Resistance / 16
    Geopolitics: Great Games I & II / 16
    Great Game III: Resistance and Reform / 21
    Saudi/ Pakistani 'Islamic States': Terrorism as
        Blowback / 25

PART I
TOWARDS A THEORY OF POLITICAL ISLAM

1 Political Spirituality and Jihad / 33
    Political and Social Thinking Embedded in
        Human Nature / 34
    Jihad / 36

2 Sunni Failure in Egypt / 40
    Banna and Political Spirituality / 42
    Qutb Emphasizes the Cultural Divide / 46

3 Shia Success in Iran / 53
    Ayatollah Khomeini / 54
        Vilayat-e faqih / 56
        Peaceful revolution / 58
    Comparing Iranian and Egyptian Experience
        in Context / 64

4   Uniting the Ummah / 68
   Re-assessing Strategy based on Islamic Principles / 80

PART II
THE EXPANDING PARAMETERS OF POLITICAL ISLAM

5   From Salafi to Kharijite / 87
   Salafis' Personal Integrity / 92
   Kharijite Revival / 95
   Internationalizing Jihad / 98
   Retail Terrorism: Suicide Bombers, Hijackers,
      Kidnappers / 100

6   Azzam: Violence Against Invaders / 108

7   Bin Laden: Violence in the Imperial Center / 111
   Early life / 111
   From Sudan to Afghanistan / 113
   Reaching America / 115
   Bin Laden's Fatwas / 117

8   Zawahiri: Violence Against Client Regimes / 123
   Early Life / 123
   Assassinations as a Catalyst / 124
   From Faraj to 'Anything Goes' / 126
   Bin Laden as 'Moderate' / 130

9   Many al-Qaedas: The Legacy / 139
   Both al-Qaeda and the US Miscalculate / 139
   New Theorists on Jihad / 143
   Islamists Confront Jihadists / 150

10 Terrorism: 9/11 and After / 157
   Who Dunnit? / 157
   Saudi-Pakistani Conspiracy / 161
   US Plans: LHOP? / 165

   Post-9/11 Terrorism / 167
   US Chicken and Jihadist Egg / 169
   Appendix: Al-Qaeda Spin-offs / 173

11 Perils of Cooperation / 183
   Saudi Arabia / 183
   Qatar / 185
   Pakistan / 188
   Turkey / 189

12 Perils of Implementation / 197
   Afghanistan / 197
   Iraq / 201
   Lebanon / 207
   Gaza / 209
   Tunisia / 214
   Morocco / 217
   Sudan / 220
   Libya / 221
   Egypt / 223
   Iran / 234

13 Return of the Caliphate / 251
   A Rump Caliphate / 255
   Rump Caliphate II / 257
   From Many Into One? / 261
   Other Forms of Unity / 265
   Color Revolutions and the Arab Spring / 268

14 The Ummah in the 21st Century / 274
   Striving for a New Modernity /
   Muslim-Christian-Jewish Understanding / 278
   Postmaterialism / 281

GLOSSARY

bid'a	"innovation, novelty, heretical doctrine, heresy" (Hans Wehr, Arabic-English Dictionary), generally having a negative connotation (something new in opposition to the Quran and sunna)
dawa	invitation to/ proselytizing Islam
fard ayn	a personal obligation for all Muslims.
fard kifaya	collective religious obligation.
hadd (hudud)	fixed penalty established in the Quran/ sharia (rights of God, God's law)
hadith(s)	documented sayings and traditions of the Prophet
haram	forbidden
ijtihad	independent reasoning, legal interpretation based on tajdid
imam	prayer leader (Sunni), spiritual leader (Shia)
ISI	Pakistani Inter-Services Intelligence
ISIS/ISIL/IS	jihadist group (Islamic State in Iraq and Syria/ the Levant), since June 2014 Islamic State, Arabic acronym Da'ish to its adversaries
jahiliya	state of ignorance of divine guidance, referring to the condition Arabs found themselves in prior to the revelation of the Quran, now referring to backsliders and non-Muslims in the absence of the rule of sharia
Jamaat-e Islami	Islamic Society (jihadist groups in Pakistan, Indonesia and Egypt)
jihad	struggle, effort against wrongdoing in oneself and in the world (greater and lesser jihad)
kafir (kuffar)	unbeliever(s), referring to those who reject God
khalifah	steward/ spiritual leader of the caliphate, literally a successor to the Prophet Muhammad (anglicized as caliph)
khilafah	stewardship. Historically, the term came to refer to a territory defined by Islamic governance over multinational populations based on belief rather than ethnicity. (anglicized as caliphate)

mujahid(een)	one who pursues jihad
mujtahid(een)	highly skilled interpreter of hadiths, authorized to use ijtihad in legal rulings
OIC	Organization of Islamic Cooperation (1969)
Salaf(i)	earliest generation of Muslims, and those who claim to emulate them today
salat	prayer
sharia	laws based on the Quran and hadiths
shura	advice, consultation
Sirah	the Prophet's life experience
Sufi	literally wool, referring to asceticism. Sufis emphasize revelation and immanence over reason
Sunnah	traditions of the Prophet derived from hadiths
surah	chapter of the Quran
tajdid	renewal, referring to rereading 'the text' (Quran)
takfir	charge of unbelief, entailing denial of basic tenets of the faith, which would mean condoning evil and lead to chaos
takfiri	those charging others with unbelief
taqlid	the unquestioning acceptance of the legal decisions of an Islamic religious authority without knowing the basis of those decisions
TTP	Tehrik-e-Taliban Pakistan
ulama (sing.alim)	elite of scholars
ummah	community of Muslims

ACKNOWLEDGMENTS

Many thanks to my editor Diana Collier at Clarity Press, and to Zafar Bangash, Imam and Director of the Institute of Contemporary Islamic Thought (ICIT),[2] and president of the Islamic Society of York Region. Also my supportive family and the Bruce County Library workers.

PREFACE

Capitalism's resilience in the face of repeated crises over the past two centuries is impressive, its corrosive power to dissolve pre-capitalist cultures and harness disparate peoples around the world to its vision for humanity—formidable. Capitalism still prevails because personal material rewards are a powerful incentive in a world where most hover on the edge of starvation, and the market is the highest form of harnessing self-interest.

Capitalism in its corporate form motivates the amoral, egotistical, the clever to prevail and—most important—puts infinite wealth in the hands of those few who actually succeed at it. Godly society attracts a very different mindset, more unworldly idealist than Mr Moneybags—often ineffectual in resisting/ countering capitalism's lure.

At the same time, devout Muslims are a hard nut for capitalism to crack, fearless Davids in the face of the powerful Goliath. Whatever I might think of the Taliban's version of Islam, their selfless resistance to the US occupiers in Afghanistan leaves me in awe. It is almost impossible to recruit Muslims as spies. Post-9/11 CIA counterterrorism head Robert Dannenberg admitted: "It was much easier to convince a Soviet that your way of life was better. You could take them to Kmart in the US or to Wal-Mart, because they were driven by many of the same things that we're driven by." US officials continue to be stymied by

ISIS/IS. General Nagata's Strategic Multilayer Assessment Committee at the Pentagon called on academics to help out, including "business professors examining the Islamic State's marketing and branding strategies. We have not defeated the idea. We do not even understand the idea."

The CIA report "Ramzi Ahmed Yousef: A New Generation of Sunni Islamic Terrorists" (1995), reflecting on the 1993 World Trade Center (WTC) bombing, which came seemingly out of the blue, stated, "Unlike traditional forms of terrorism, such as state-sponsored or the Iran/ Hizbullah model, Sunni extremists are neither surrogates of nor strongly influenced by one nation. They are autonomous and indigenous." Ex-CIA director George Tenet notes in his memoirs, "Al-Qaeda boasts that while we fear death, they embrace it."

Non-Muslim European terrorist acts have a venerable tradition. The Gunpowder Plot of 1605 is celebrated each November in Britain as Guy Fawkes Day. Anti-capitalist acts date to the 19th century anarchists, who inspired latter-day groups such as Baader Meinhof (Germany), Red Brigades (Italy) and Students for a Democratic Society (US) in the 1970s. And the striving for martyrdom is fundamental to all religions, including Christianity and Judaism, whose fundamentalists stoutly deny the 'separation of church and state' and anticipate an apocalyptic end to this life in favor of paradise/ hell. But Tenet recognizes there is something profoundly different about Islam, with implications that continue to reverberate. Robert Kaplan writes admiringly of this in the account of his travels with the mujahideen in the 1980s:

> The ability to endure, year after harrowing year... [is] the most lethal weapon the Pathans had in their battle against the Soviets. Pathans

> represent the primitive, vestigial lone warrior from past but also future where the only people willing and able to fight a superpower will be poverty-stricken peasant guerrillas who have no motive to surrender because they have no material possessions at risk.

At the same time, Kaplan (and no doubted Tenet) despises Islam. "To me, the monologue of the Koran had always symbolized the sterile authoritarianism of the East, where all public debate was drowned out. I was cynical toward the culture of Islam, and the more Islamic countries I visited and the more I listened to the relativist thinking of the region's experts in the media and the State Department, the more cynical I became."

The mainstream literature is littered with ad hominems aimed at the various actors: Osama Bin Laden is "notoriously cheap", Afghan Mullah Omar is a "dim-witted fanatic with significant delusions of grandeur", 9/11 architect Khalid Sheikh Mohammed is "the short, fat man ... with his fat fingers". The language of the American pursuers of the bad guys is often scatological (to Tenet, Khalid Sheikh Mohammed is "the fat f***"), and laced with self-congratulatory "slam-dunks", "God bless America" and the implicit approval of "enhanced interrogation techniques". Even western 'human rights' defenders—humanists and leftists—do virtually nothing to fight the victimization of Muslims, if they are labeled 'al-Qaeda' or 'Taliban'. This even applies to the Muslim Brotherhood (MB) in Egypt, now vindicated by the Egyptian population's boycott of the May 2014 post-coup election and continued resistance. The daily murder and ongoing torture of Islamic activists, sanctioned—indeed perpetrated—by the US government and its allies, is silently condoned. 'Better safe than sorry.'

The name-calling is of course counterproductive. Notes Nagata, "When I watch Americans use words like cowardly, barbaric, murder, outrageous, shocking, etc., to describe a violent extremist organization's actions, we are playing right into the enemy's hands. They want us to become emotional. They revel in being called murderers when the words are coming from an apostate." To say nothing about putting western hypocrisy on display for the world to see. Even the term "terrorist" is loaded (see Introduction and Chapter 5).

As I was reading the nth 9/11 self-proclaimed bestseller, I realized it is necessary to directly address the al-Qaeda phenomenon and 9/11 in the context of the resistance to the western secular order and the ongoing re-emerging Islamic civilization, whose modern history predates al-Qaeda, and has historic roots in the jihad of the Prophet Muhammad (saw). The startling successes of ISIS/IS in Syria and Iraq in 2014 further call for a less dismissive approach to the al-Qaeda phenomenon.

The failure of past (secular) resistance movements must be confronted, and the nature of the more resilient Islamic resistance movements understood. Effective resistance to imperialism requires clear understanding of the forces at work, and the cooperation of anti-imperialist forces. With this in mind, I have written this work, based on my recent work, *From Postmodernism to Postsecularism: Re-emerging Islamic Civilization*, assessing terrorism before and after 9/11, looking seriously at the draw of al-Qaeda-type insurgencies, and focusing on the reform elements and movements which are essential to the successful re-emergence of the genuine Islamic alternative. Then asking:

- What is left of the historic 1979 upheavals—the Islamic revolution in Iran and the Islamic resistance movement in Afghanistan?

- Are new forces such as Hizbullah and Hamas evolving political mechanisms capable of more effectively resisting imperialism?
- How does 9/11 fit into the equation of Islamic resistance? Is al-Qaeda's long term project still on track?
- Are its offshoots and likeminded jihadists such as ISIS/IS dupes of imperialism or legitimate resistance movements?
- What conclusions can we draw from the Arab Spring?

Originally, this analysis sought to ascertain which groups were following a truly Islamic path, and to establish a basis for distinguishing between them as 'good' and 'bad', justifying this categorization. Accordingly, those with a balance of faith and reason, immune to the wiles of the imperialists, were viewed favorably, as opposed to those who allow themselves to be manipulated into helping empire, wittingly or unwittingly, or worse, were willing to use the methods of empire, especially terrorism, to further their goal. But I came to realize that a prohibited action can become an acceptable one in certain contexts. "Men make their own history, but they do not make it as they please ... in such epochs of revolutionary crisis they anxiously conjure up the spirits of the past to their service." Whether or not we approve of some of the actions of the Taliban or ISIS/IS, we must acknowledge their right to resist the US occupation, and see that increased terrorism, say in Sinai, is a direct result of the July 2013 US-backed coup in Egypt, not something that we can blame on Islam.

I am often asked: "What about beheadings and hand-chopping?" I counter: "Would you prefer to die as a result of beheading, or as a result of a drone?" The drone attacks kill dozens of others; the culpability of the target may not even be certain. At least beheading is 'targeted', carried out after a trial, and in any case the number of beheadings are a handful. Hyping these non-western punishments and using them as an excuse to bomb and kill is like a murderer pointing his finger at a distraction, at the very moment he robs and kills you.

The real tragedy is the West's killing thousands of people as a routine part of the criminal occupations of Afghanistan, Iraq and who-knows-where next. In an important sense, the responsibility for every death today in these and other similar tragedies around the world (including the beheadings) lies with the US. The West can't expect to wipe out Islamic activism. It is urgent to reverse this horrendous cycle of violence. And ending violence means changing the context, ending the policies that generate the violence.

| Introduction |

THE LOGIC OF RESISTANCE

The main threat—and stimulus—to a renewed Islamic civilization continues to come, perniciously, from outside. The geopolitical 'games' that were played out in the Middle East have meant that both the imperialist West and the communist East were hostile towards Islam and either dismissed it as a reactionary force or tried to tame it and manipulate Muslims to further their own ends. Satirist magazine *Charlie Hebdo* editor Charbonnier stated in 2011, "We have to carry on until Islam has been rendered as banal as Catholicism."[1]

Geopolitics: Great Games I & II

The original Great Game—Great Game I[2]—is the classical imperialism of the West starting in the fifteenth century and reaching its peak in the 19th–20th centuries. Muslims were directly affected by the upheavals it caused, which reached their peak in the nineteenth and twentieth centuries, as the imperial powers chipped away at the Ottoman Caliphate,[3] seized Muslim lands, fought each other in horrendous world wars, bankrupting all but the final victor—the US. The colonialists had marched into Asia and Africa on their Great Game I "civilizing mission", carrying the so-called white man's burden. After WWI, they seized the entire Muslim world. But by the end of WWII, stirrings of revolt were evident everywhere; nationalist movements were demanding independence, forcing the occupiers to abandon their colonies.

WWII marked the culmination of Great Game I, ending in defeat for all but the US and the Soviet Union, who became the chief protagonists in Great Game II. Millions of colonized peoples perished in the independence struggles—buying into and preserving the imperialist-established nation-state system, giving the imperial strategists time to transfer power into the hands of assimilationist neocolonial elites, and thereby prevent communist or Islamic revolutions. The Dutch and British were driven out of the East Indies after a vicious war of liberation, leaving behind states fashioned out of their colonies. The British abandoned the Indian subcontinent after an even worse bloodbath, leading to the creation of India and Pakistan. Other neo-colonies were created in Africa, the Levant and Asia, including of course Israel, carved out of Britain's Palestine Mandate.

The Europeans did not go into Africa or Asia to help those societies develop by making use of modern technology for the benefit of the local peoples. Their mission and purpose was altogether different: first, to take control of the resources of those societies and shape their economies to meet imperial needs. Then, to leave control in 'safe hands'—if leave they must.

The textile factories of Britain were built with wealth stolen from India as was its railway system with money stolen from Argentina, a former Spanish colony. Even the diamonds in the Queen's crown are stolen property. By WWI, Britain had 'exported' much of its manufacturing and was essentially living off the rents reaped from its colonies.[4] Other European colonial powers—France, Germany, Belgium, the Netherlands, Spain, Portugal and others—

acted no differently. Western economies for nearly 100 years have been sustained and built on cheap fossil fuel from the Middle East and the Persian Gulf. While the vast majority of people in the Muslim world remain impoverished, their tiny ruling elites, sequestered into statelets, have enriched themselves by aligning with western powers and allowing them to exploit the energy and mineral resources of Muslim lands.

The colonial enterprise transformed the Third World, tying it to the imperial centers in many ways. In the new Great Game II, to stabilize the post-colonial world order under US hegemony, the major capitalist powers created a number of coercive instruments, such as the United Nations, NATO, the International Monetary Fund, the World Bank, the International Atomic Energy Agency, and 'free trade' agreements culminating in the World Trade Organization in 1995.[5] Within the UN, the Security Council has five permanent members who act like supervisors or arbiters of global affairs. In recent years, organizations like the G-8[6] and G-20 have also emerged, a club of countries that have unilaterally assumed the authority to determine how the rest of the world should conduct its affairs. Washington decides who is invited or barred from the club.

All these organizations pursue essentially the same agenda: to maintain the West's hegemony in global affairs. Any country that refuses to follow the imperialist agenda is immediately faced with severe problems imposed through or sanctioned by one or the other of these organizations. The IMF and WB are used to undermine the economies of countries that try to act independent of US wishes. Thus, currently, Islamic Iran is subjected to severe trade and financial sanctions through a series of Security Council resolutions as well as unilateral US sanctions. Other countries—postmodern nations—go along with Washington not because they believe in US policy but because it is expedient for them to do so.

But global political and economic structures for the exercise of domination were not the only legacy: colonial educational systems, supplanting local languages with colonial languages, distorted patterns of production, and changed the tastes, habits, cultures and even the diets of the colonized societies. This produced whole sectors of people that were brown in color but behaved and acted like the white colonial masters. They were, in the words of Lord Macaulay, perfect "Brown Englishmen". Independence was a myth, a cruel hoax perpetrated on the impoverished peoples of Africa, Asia and the Middle East.

Despite (and because of) this heavy legacy, if the imperialists had simply abandoned their colonies after WWII, there would have been communist or Islamic revolutions. China, North Korea and Cuba were the only liberated countries where the imperialists failed to prevent a sustained communist revolution following WWII, and they developed unique, if flawed, independent paths of development. Islamic activists were part of the liberation struggles in their territories, though ironically the only state specifically created with a Muslim identity, Pakistan, was created by the British, where power was passed to a British-educated secular elite which became dependent on the former colonial master and the now-dominant US for survival.

There were independent Islamic activists in Egypt poised to take power—the Muslim Brotherhood—but there was no room in the international order, dominated by the US and the Soviet Union, for them to forge an alternative Islamic social order. The MB was pre-empted by a secular socialist regime under Gamal Abdel-Nasser which stopped short of Cuba's communism, accepting a place in the post-WWII international order dominated by the US.

There were other attempts in the Muslim world to emulate Egypt, including in Iran under Prime Minister Mossadeq (r. 1951–1953) and in Algeria under the National Liberation Front (r.1962) but because secular anti-imperialists and Islamic activists were at loggerheads, all failed—including in Egypt, where Major Gamal Abdel-Nasser's socialism is unlikely to be emulated by General Abdel Fattah el-Sisi, his 21st century military-secularist parody.

Eerily, those nominally Muslim ruling elites turned out to be even more oppressive than the colonial masters, resulting in a perverse nostalgia by those who served the colonial masters.

The Soviet Union was an outsider to the new world order (and thus 'the enemy'). The communists faced constant subversion, were excluded from the IMF and WB, and played a spoiler role in the UN with regards imperialist plans. As such, they gave support to the liberation struggle of Third World nations, in particular, the Palestinians in their struggle to regain their occupied lands. In Muslim regions, they also supported socialists such as Nasser and regimes in Iraq and South Yemen. But the Soviet Union's militant atheism made it hostile to the Islamic project. Politically astute Muslims see both systems—capitalist and socialist—as problematic, as encapsulated in the MB slogan "Neither capitalism nor socialism, rather Islam" or Khomeini's "Neither East nor West".

In the post-WWII period, in contrast to Nasser's Egypt, Iran under Reza Shah complied fully with the western-imposed set-up, emulating the staunchly secularist Turkish dictator, Mustafa Kemal of Great Game I, who abolished the Ottoman Caliphate in 1924, ending all pretences of a united ummah. Reza Shah's successor, Mohammad Reza Shah, was installed by the British to replace his pro-Nazi father in 1941 and continued to follow the capitalist model and established close relations with Israel.

Egypt, following the successful coup by Nasser and the Free Officers movement in 1952, was less compliant with the US-led empire, but continued along the secularist path as an ally of the Soviet Union, returning to 'the fold' after the death of Nasser in 1970.

Saudi Arabia from its founding as a nation state in 1932 professed to be Islamic, but it is an absolute monarchy under US hegemony. Islamists in Sudan were part of the government under military dictators in the 1980s, but Sudan has been torn by civil wars among dozens of tribes and between the Muslim north and Christian south since its 'independence' in 1956. Thus, the first genuine Islamic revolution came in 1979 in Iran, recapitulating Cuba's anti-imperialist revolution, motivated not by communism but by Islam.

The Shia revolution in Iran had echoes in the Sunni world. It inspired a young Egyptian Muslim Brother, Essam el-Erian (now imprisoned Freedom and Justice Party vice-chairman and MP), to say at that time, "Young people believe Islam is the solution to the ills in society after the failure of western democracy, socialism and communism to address the political and socio-economic difficulties." It prompted Saudi rebels to occupy the Kaaba that same year in an attempt to spark revolution, Syrian Muslims to rise against their secular dictator Hafez al-Assad in 1980, and future al-Qaeda leader Ayman Zawahiri to conspire to assassinate Egyptian president Sadat in 1981.

Great Game III: Resistance and Reform

The imperialists had a strong influence on the development of political Islam during Great Game II (empire against communism), encouraging Muslims opposed to atheism/secularism and their nationalist and/or socialist offshoots to resist leaders such as the Syrian and Iraqi Baathists and Egypt's Gamal Abdel-Nasser (1950s–1970s). This resistance caught fire in the 1980s as Afghans were catalyzed to oppose the Soviet occupation of Afghanistan.

When the Soviet Union was destroyed in 1991, the imperialists simply abandoned their new Islamic allies, and sought (whether through 'soft power' or merely ridicule) to 'reform' Islam and subsume it *a la* Christianity into the West's secular, democratic order—even as they were promising support to the Shia uprising against Saddam in Iraq. Coincidentally, it was also necessary to extend the empire's reach along the Silk Road—the Eurasian region of the Caucasus through to Afghanistan and China—newly opened for business, and populated by Muslim peoples. But the battle-hardened fighters who had brought down the Soviet Union had only accomplished half the goals for which they had fought.

From the empire's point of view, this new Great Game was a more sophisticated version of what the Portuguese, British, Dutch, etc. did in days of yore—sailing around Africa and Eurasia, attacking peaceful primarily Muslim traders in West Africa, Zanzibar, Madras, Aceh, etc., killing them, sinking their ships, and burning their trading posts, introducing new, more lethal arms and large-scale plantation slavery,[7] monopolizing trading routes and actual trade.

As the West invaded the Muslim world in the 19th–20th centuries, it was only natural that local Muslims resisted the occupation—both physical and cultural—of their world. Marx and Lenin's predictions of exploitation, war and resistance was starkly demonstrated and couldn't help but prompt resistance (though the 'how' and 'what will replace the colonial order' was not clear). In sixteenth century Aceh (present-day Indonesia), Muslims resisted the Portuguese, and in nineteenth century Algeria, Abd al-Qadir's guerrilla movement fought the French while in Nigeria and Sudan, dan Fodio and Ahmad (the Mahdi) fought the British. The resistance movements were localized (in the face of the powerful empires, which, while rivals, worked together to contain the Islamic opposition everywhere. For them, Islam was the structuring principle for their societies, and the bond that held them together to fight the enemy.

Meanwhile, traditional Islamic scholars, the ulama, were not much help. Confronted by the invaders, and faced at home with movements which sought to emulate the West, including nationalists and secularists, they retreated, shutting down debate about how to extricate the Muslim world from the grip of empire.

In defiance of the traditional ulama, and reacting to the radical challenge of the emerging secular imperialist order, there arose a political movement of Islamic renewal, appealing to all Muslims, beginning with Sunni Muhammad ibn Abd al-Wahhab (1703–1791) in the Arab Peninsula calling for strict emulation of the Prophetic way of life and thought (Salafism). Wahhab revived the spirit of jihad of Ibn Taymiya (1263–1328), who had exhorted Muslims to fight the Mongol conquerors in the fourteenth century, to defy the decadent Ottomans, leading to the first successful establishment of a political order inspired by Islam.

In contrast, at the same time, a very different reformer, Shah Wali Allah (1703–1762) in India, decided that open accommodation with the newly arrived British colonial masters was necessary, given the backwardness and rigidity of the Islamic establishment. He stressed literacy and using new technology to promote economic development.

These two movements came together in the person of the Persian Jamal al-Din al-Afghani (1838–1897), who attempted to combine the concerns of both Wahhab and Wali Alla—the impulses for resistance and reform. He gave the term Salafism a new meaning in an era of imperialism, when occupation of Muslim lands by empire and migration was accelerating, projecting it as a return to the essence of Islam, as a means to resist imperialism. He travelled throughout Europe, the Middle East and Central Asia, encouraging Muslim thinkers and leaders to resist the imperial onslaught, reasserting the international, cosmopolitan nature of Islam and reaffirming its political nature. His likely Shia roots did not prevent him from working with both Sunni and Shia; he recognized that overcoming sectarianism was the key to re-establishing Islam in the face of the powerful secular society of the West.

These very different figures, intent on renewing Islamic civilization in their own way, highlight the dilemma: whether to accept the current order and work within it, or reject it, insisting that secular industrial civilization—whether capitalist or socialist—is inconsistent with Islam. The former can be called accommodationists and assimilationists, to varying degrees accommodating empire and promoting absorption into the world market system.

This dilemma was not clear in the early years of imperialist expansion. The first definitive critiques of capitalism/ imperialism did not appear until the late nineteenth century in the works of Karl Marx and Vladimir Lenin. When Afghani began his political movement, the stage was set for Islamic resistance to join the secular movements based on Marx and Lenin.

The new economic order, embedded in the legal systems being fashioned by the occupiers, was resisted by both secularists and Islamists. Marx et al clarified the underlying problem: 'the law' in each land was being refashioned to meet the needs of the economic order, where all economic activity was condoned as long as it is carried out in conformity with 'the law'.

But what is 'the law'? The driving force behind this 'law' is exploitation in pursuit of unlimited profit, leading to world wars which leave humanity and nature in peril. The 'law', for instance, includes condoning gambling (both explicit and metaphorical in the form of the 'stock market'), and regulating various forms of moral degeneration (prostitution, drunkenness). All the while, legal recourse against crimes committed by the most powerful in this world order is virtually impossible, given their control of the economic and hence political processes, and indeed, the intergovernmental institutions.

It is this enforced ascendancy of economic power over the popular political will that makes 'political Islam' necessary today, after the defeat of the communist resistance to capitalism. Nothing short of a new 'law' will do, where a code of ethics is embedded. The communist revolutions for the most part failed to achieve this and Islamists became the main force of resistance to imperialism by default.

Saudi/ Pakistani 'Islamic states' – Terrorism as Blowback

Even as the reform movements got underway, empire's strategies remain devoted to manipulating local forces everywhere to promote its ends, and what better way to neutralize Islam than using 'Islamic states'?. The first modern Islamic state, Saudi Arabia, was set up with the helping hand of Britain in 1932, and another one, Pakistan, in 1947. The logic being, if the local Muslims accepted their new post-colonial rulers, the rulers could keep their countries in compliance with empire, following the Islamic principle that you should obey even unjust rulers "so long as they uphold prayer among you".[8]

This ambitious imperial program became the logic for Great Game III imperial rule, but it came with a price for the chief collaborators, Pakistan and Saudi Arabia. Pakistan from the start has been mired in civil strife, at war with India over Kashmir, and beholden to the US for its very survival. The Saud tribal leaders had an easier time of it as the central figures in the preservation of the faith, "guardians of the holy places" (Medina and Mecca) in the bleak desert of Arabia. They turned to their inward-looking Wahhabi establishment for legitimacy in the eyes of both Saudi citizens and the broader Muslim ummah, creating a sterile, intolerant culture, and working hand-in-glove with the imperialists, leaving anti-imperialists to create their own movements.

Most of the terrorists (those implicated in the 9/11 hijackings, the foreign fighters in Afghanistan in the 1980s and now in Syria/ Iraq) were/are understandably disaffected Saudis, rich on oil wealth, educated at western universities (or unemployed), yet disgusted by the Saudi alliance with imperialism (and by implication, with Israel) that was blessed by the Wahhabi establishment—so-called neo-Wahhabis.[9] They found allies in their Pakistani brothers, betrayed at 'independence' when the British handed Muslim Kashmir over to India. There is little room in their thinking for the hard part of reconciling means and ends, determining what a post-imperialist Islamic world order would actually look like in the modern age and making sure the move towards it is consistent with Islam. To a large extent, their aim "is simply to destroy Babylon,"[10] leaving it to a revived sharia to provide a clear civilizational outline for the future.

CIA analysts coined a term for this type of counterproductive outcome resulting from attempts to manipulate political developments—"blowback"—in its internal analysis of its own orchestration of the 1953 coup in Iran, warning of future anti-Americanism as a result of the coup.[11] The neo-Wahhabis provide another, even more serious instance of blowback, where the Islamists, angry with Muslim official complicity with imperialism, started using strategies of revolution and the arms of the imperialists against both the US and their own leaders and peoples.

They are the bitter fruits (for us all, Muslim and non-Muslim) now being reaped in the so-called Global War on Terror, which targets all Muslims, lumping together genuine terrorists, teenage Palestinian rock-throwers, Hizbullah resistance fighters, and elected Hamas, Iranian and Egyptian politicians.

The very word "terrorism" is misleading, with no legally binding definition—in the West it is almost a synonym for "Islamism" or "jihadism", used by officials and the media to delegitimize the state's political opponents. To supporters, these "terrorists" are "freedom fighters". (Criminal protection rackets are not labeled terrorists because they are no ideological threat to the state system.)

Common definitions refer to violent acts that are intended to create fear (terror); are perpetrated for a religious, political, or ideological goal; and deliberately target or disregard the safety of non-combatants (e.g., neutral military personnel or civilians), effectively lumping together occupier and occupied, putting the state's own (terrorist) use of armed force on the same footing as the much weaker insurgency. ANC leader Nelson Mandela was branded a terrorist by the South African state and western officials and media.[12]

Even Hamas, which fought a deadly battle with ISIS/IS supporters in Jerusalem in 2009, and has been dismissed by ISIS/IS as a distraction from its caliphate project, refuses to condemn ISIS/IS as terrorist, "a term used by many countries for political purposes," according to Hamas spokesman Sami Abu Zuhri. "We are all Islamists, and it is ideologically difficult for us to condemn them as terrorists. We are accused of the same by the West and some Arab countries," he said, stressing that Hamas will never join the US alliance against ISIS/IS. [13]

Hamas leader Ahmed Youssef explains: If the insurgency in Syria and Iraq is seen as terror, based on the killings taking place there, then the United States and Israel, which have killed thousands of innocent people, ought to be condemned as well. "Nevertheless, we condemn all acts that fall outside the context of the international law and Islamic teachings." [14]

Here I will use the term "terrorism" circumspectly and focus on "terrorist acts", carried out by both a handful of jihadists, and on a regular basis by western states which claim to be fighting a "Global War on Terror". Which is not 'war' at all, when one side is amorphous or so weak, it can only hide or lose. The 'war' is really invasion, occupation, obliteration. That sort-of worked for Afghanistan and Iraq because they are distinct geographical entities, but it is impossible to occupy or obliterate resistance, including al-Qaeda type resistance, where there are no boundaries. You can't stop all resistance to injustice.

On the contrary, blowback by jihadists (terrorist acts) feeds on the violence of imperial reaction in a vicious circle, the "intervention trap".[15] To emerge from this vicious circle, it is necessary to return to the principles of Islam for defense of self and religion, where the means do not contradict the end. Destroying a US warship and its crew in a Muslim port, as part of the resistance to the ongoing subjugation of the ummah, is not necessarily to be condemned. But killing innocent non-Muslims and/or Muslims who are not attacking or subverting the ummah is. This simple rule of thumb has been violated over the past three decades by those Muslims who have (wittingly or unwittingly) consented to a dubious and unholy alliance with imperialism, or unwittingly facilitated its objectives, and are ignorant of the rules of war prescribed by the very religion in whose name they fight.

Endnotes

1   *Charlie Hebdo* specializes in defamation of the Prophet Muhammad. The magazine was unsuccessfully sued in 2006 by Islamic organizations for publishing the *Jyllands-Posten* Muhammad cartoons. The cover of a 2011 issue, dubbed "Charia Hebdo" (a pun on Sharia law), depicted a cartoon of the Islamic prophet Muhammad. Nine Charlie Hebdo employees were shot in a revenge killing in January 2014.
2   See Walberg, *Postmodern Imperialism*.
3   Five million European Muslims were driven from their homes, 1821–1922, as a result of Europe's policy of promoting ethnic nationalism and undermining the Ottoman Caliphate. Alastair Crooke, *Resistance: The Essence of the Islamist Revolution*, Pluto Press, 2009, 44.
4   Walberg, *Postmodern Imperialism*, 37–38.
5   There are also important regional trade agreements such as the North American Free Trade Agreement (1994) and the Trans-Pacific Partnership (2005) which operate within the remit of the WTO.
6   Or G-7, now that Russia has been excluded over Ukraine.
7   Very different from the largely domestic slavery which predominated under Islam. Slavery was discouraged by the Prophet Muhammad, and freeing slaves was repeatedly advocated in the Quran as a means of demonstrating repentance for wrongdoing. Gradually, primarily by manumission, slavery was abolished in early Islam, though with the wars and the decay of Islamic civilization it returned. However, it was always domestic slavery; the horrendous plantation slavery under capitalism would never have been possible. See Eric Walberg, *From Postmodernism to Postsecularism: Re-emerging Islamic Civilization*, Clarity Press, 2013.
8   Hadith of al-Muslim.
9   See Seyyed Hossein Nasr, *Islam in the Modern World: Challenged by the West, Threatened by fundamentalism, Keeping faith with Tradition*, USA: Harper One, 2010.
10   Ibid., 56.
11   *Clandestine Service History—Overthrow of Premier Mossadeq of Iran—November 1952–August 1953*, CIA, 1954.
12   See definition of terror at Wikipedia.
13   Asmaa al-Ghoul, "Why won't Hamas label Islamic State as terrorists?", *Almonitor*, December 2014. http://www.al-monitor.com/

	pulse/originals/2014/12/hamas-islamic-state-gaza-terrorist-attacks.html
14	Asmaa al-Ghoul, "Why won't Hamas label Islamic State as terrorists?", *Almonitor*, December 2014. http://www.al-monitor.com/pulse/originals/2014/12/hamas-islamic-state-gaza-terrorist-attacks.html
15	Olivier Roy, "The Intervention Trap", *New Statesman*, 7 February 2013.

PART I

TOWARDS A THEORY OF POLITICAL ISLAM

| CHAPTER ONE |

POLITICAL SPIRITUALITY AND JIHAD

The Iranian revolution in 1979 marked the first substantive break with the secular world order, heralding the new Great Game III, where the protagonist for the empire was the Muslim world. On a visit to revolutionary Tehran in 1979, Michel Foucault called the revolution "the first great insurrection" against the "global systems" of the West—in which he clearly included communism and its secular socialist variants. "Islam has a good chance to become a gigantic powder keg, at the level of hundreds of millions of men."[1]

Foucault, Jurgen Habermas, and others in the so-called Frankfurt School of critical theory, were actually mirroring Islam in challenging the western mainstream assumption that the materialist approach to social theory was the only valid one. The Frankfurt School critiqued consumerism, the shaping of a de-politicized culture by corporations, the vicarious pseudo-experience of happiness through popular identification with film idols, the desensitization and isolation of individuals pursuing "lifestyle aspirations". "Culture survived, but privatized—as a way of life, not as a public network of norms and rules."[2] What has emerged with the end of communism and the triumph of neoliberal capitalism is a "false state of reconciliation" as epitomized by Francis Fukuyama's breezy claim of the end of politics/history with the collapse of communism.

For the most part, the Frankfurt School's critique of modernism led to a dead end in postmodernism, feminism and identity politics, but Foucault's identification with the seemingly out-of-place Islamic revolution was an important wake-up call coming from a prominent western intellectual, a demand for political authenticity, one which was for the most part overlooked.[3] A prominent French communist intellectual, Roger Garaudy, took Foucault's call to its logical conclusion, converting to Islam in 1982.

Religion and Social Thinking Embedded in Human Nature

Habermas and Foucault looked for some form of autonomy that might lead to the creation of truly democratic institutions capable of withstanding the onslaught of neoliberalism and corporate media. This secular western critical theory, focused on the individual, ironically mirrors (in a distorted way) the Islamic vision constraining the power of money and denying the centrality of economics, asserting Allah as all powerful and the Quran as the guide to social values based on justice, equity and respect, whether as the guiding force of resistance or of ultimate social and spiritual reward.

The West keeps misreading events in the region because it interprets Islamism as a simple struggle over power and sovereignty. It is not. It is a distinct view of human behavior that posits an alternative method of thinking about the human being; his or her place in natural order; his or her conduct towards others; his or her place in society; the ordering of his or her material needs, and the management of politics.[4]

The western view of the human focuses on the rational individual as the organizing principle around which society should be shaped. The Islamic vision sees spiritual life and Allah's guidance as integral to a humane, just society, with man as more than just the sum of his appetites.

Western psychologists have confirmed the Islamic view, showing that our brains are wired to make us instinctively social beings. Our joys are primarily social. The Apostle Paul was right: We get more pleasure from *giving* (oxytocin, for bonding especially in mothers) than *receiving* (opioid-based pleasure processes in brain). Moral truths have a physiological basis. Empathy is hardwired. Alain de Botton puts this whimsically: living for others is such a relief from the impossible task of trying to satisfy oneself.[5]

Scientists have also shown that we are hardwired for religious experience.[6] Why would this ability of the brain 'evolve' if there was no underlying truth to it? The most sensible explanation is that indeed religion is the living embodiment of moral truth which helps people align themselves with the moral axis of the universe (and thereby survive). This is possible without religion, but requires a highly developed moral sense.

We need to recognize these fundamental—evolutionary—truths and revise our social system accordingly. We are social, spiritual animals, and secularism undermines our very being. The very concepts of freedom and tolerance, so often touted by supporters of secularism, but with little regard for what they actually entail, must be redefined. Living in submission to the laws of God liberates the mind, soul and body from the evil influences of the world. This is the very opposite of the meaning of freedom as understood by the secular world, which means dismissing the laws of God and giving free rein to worldly desires.

Materialism is (dangerously) pushing us away from what evolution made us. For instance, there has been a sharp decline in social capital in recent years: in 1965 45% of freshmen listed "very well-off financially" as a life goal, less important than "helping others/ raising a family". In 1989, being well-off financially is the goal of 75%, far eclipsing social goals.

Jihad

Foucault was no doubt familiar with Sheikh Abdullah Yusuf Azzam's fatwa of 1980, calling on Muslims from around the world to go to Afghanistan to fight the Soviet occupation, and saw the coming together of Sunni and Shia as the basis of the new challenge to imperialism, organized around a different concept from previous revolutions—"political spirituality".[7] As such, this proposed a fundamental cultural, social and political break with the modern western order as well as with the Soviet Union and China. The affinity between this European critic of modernity and the anti-modernist Islamic radicals on the streets of Iran is startling, but makes sense. Both were searching for "a new politics as a counter discourse to a thoroughly materialistic world"; both were disdainful of modern liberal judicial systems as tools of the elites; both "admired individuals who risked death in attempts to reach a more authentic existence".[8]

Foucault's "powder keg" was not an allusion to indiscriminate violence—some kind of 9/11—but to the latent energy of the masses that fusing politics and man's spiritual life would release, as he witnessed in Iran. Though not one of the 'five pillars' of Islam, jihad is the distillation of this fusion. Jihad is in the first place a spiritual struggle inspired by and devoted to Allah, and jihad as war is strictly circumscribed in the Quran. According to a hadith, Prophet Muhammad surprised his warriors on returning from the bloody Hunayn expedition, declaring: "We are back from the lesser jihad to the greater jihad." The transcendent, allegorical "greater jihad", he explained to them, is "fighting the self [ego]", the inner struggle "that takes people from the natural tension of passions to the peace of spiritual education".[9]

The only clear call to armed jihad in the Quran is when you are directly attacked: it then is an 'individual duty' (*fard ayn*) to fight to defend yourself and your community. "To those against whom war is made, permission is given to fight, and ... [to] those who have been expelled from their homes in defiance of right for no cause except that they say: 'Our Lord is Allah!'" (22:39–40) It is wrong to *start* a war: "Fight in the cause of God those who fight you, but do not commit aggression." (2:195) Jihad as war is only for defense of freedom of religion, for the defense and liberty of one's community (22:39–40, 2:190). A corollary of this (via *ijtihad*, i.e., independent reasoning based on Islam), is that only the leader of the ummah (caliph) can declare war.

There is no basis in the Quran to support insurrection against a Muslim leader who allows the practice of faith and the use of sharia law. Even an unjust Muslim ruler should not be overthrown violently, in the interests of preserving the unity of the umma, "so long as they uphold prayer among you". This indicates clear recognition not only of the horrors of war and the chaos that ensues, but also of the possibility of moral suasion, if the premises upon which it is based, the Quranic teachings, are still acknowledged. In such instance, Muslims should openly criticize misrule, according to the hadith "The best Jihad is a speech of truth in the presence of a tyrant ruler."[10]

Wherever possible, Prophet Muhammad achieved victory over his enemies by negotiations. Muslims finally entered Mecca in 630 peacefully, leading to the upsurge of faith that his dawa and indeed praxis[11] inspired. The Quran opposes force and coercion in religious matters. Violent jihad is wrong when peaceful dawa and reconciliation are possible.

This clear call for openness and struggle to defend the faith and lands of Muslims has been distorted into something quite the opposite, the imperialists charging Islam with being a (violent) 'conspiracy', inspired by the Prophet, and acted out by secretive terrorists bent on subverting the West's 'natural order', the same charge formerly made against communism, Marx and his followers.

But neither communism nor Islam were/are conspiracies; rather both openly declared their goals of resistance to an unjust social order and offered their alternatives. Communism was flawed in its repression of religion as vital to life, and was unable to prevail, entrenched in and ultimately succumbing to the desires of the material world. Islam has the goal of a spiritually-centered world, governed by the laws of God. Foucault recognized this, shocking his secular followers, who did their best to bury his truly radical insight. Events since then have not followed the path that Foucault was hoping for, though he would not have been surprised—he died in 1984—by the ruthless resistance of the imperialists to the new, evolving dispensation, including the unremitting hostility of the West to Iran, the anti-Islamic coup in Algeria in 1992, the invasions of Afghanistan and Iraq, and the violent reaction they inspired

Endnotes

1 "A Powder Keg Called Islam", Corriere della sera, 13, February 1979. Quoted in Janet Afary and Kevin Anderson, *Foucault and the Iranian Revolution: Gender and the Seductions of Islamism*, USA: University of Chicago Press, 2005, 4.

2 Alastair Crooke, *Resistance: The Essence of the Islamist Revolution*,

	Pluto Press, 2009, 20.
3	The shallow identity politics and continued demonization of Iran is a degenerate form of politics which Foucault would surely attack today.
4	Ibid., 29.
5	Encephalization (deviation of brain size from body size) in humans is four times greater than, say, for chimpanzees. The large energy-burning brain in humans (2% of body weight, 20% of energy usage) is not just for reasoning and social learning, but more for ensuring social harmony in larger groups (150 is the optimal size for the cohesive group) to allow processing of complex relations. Matthew Lieberman, *Social: Why Our Brains Are Wired to Connect,* Crown, 2013.
6	The existence of higher levels of consciousness has been 'proved' by science at least indirectly, by registering sensory-motor effects of EEG brain patterns during meditation. The *soul level* "meditation with form" is characterized subjectively by love, compassion and altruism, and objectively by brain hemispheric synchronization. The *spiritual level* is characterized subjectively by an expanded sense of self, compassion, love, care, and responsibility. and objectively the cessation of alpha, beta, theta brainwaves and an increase in delta waves associated with deep, dreamless sleep. The 'highest' level of "formless meditation" is experienced subjectively as infinite freedom, and objectively the cessation of all mental activity. See Ken Wilber, *A Brief History of Everything*, USA: Shambhala 2000.
7	Janet Afary and Kevin Anderson, *Foucault and the Iranian Revolution: Gender and the Seductions of Islamism,* USA: University of Chicago Press, 2005, 13.
8	Ibid., 13.
9	Hadith reported by Bayhaqi, though its authenticity is disputed.
10	Hadith of Abu Dawud and Tirmidhi.
11	Unity of theory and practice.

| CHAPTER TWO |

SUNNI FAILURE IN EGYPT

The dilemmas facing Muslim activists graphically witnessed in Egypt in the twentieth century in the experience of the Muslim Brotherhood (MB). A peaceful, evolutionary approach to renewing Islamic civilization can, under extreme persecution of Islamic activists, descend into violence, despite the best efforts and intentions of the Islamic leaders. Muslims who reject random violence and violence against civilians can be pushed onto the same 'side' as those who have turned to violence, when the powers-that-be persecute them both as if they were one united movement.

As the traditional heart of Islam for centuries, home of Al-Azhar University, founded in 970 as a center of Islamic learning, Egypt was ruled from the nineteenth century until 1952 by descendants of Muhammad Ali, an Ottoman officer who established a dynasty which acquiesced to the British occupiers. It experienced a strong movement seeking to return to its Islamic roots rather than just to join and be subservient to the new imperial order.

As the liberals were increasingly discredited over time, the Muslim Brotherhood (MB), like the Wahhabis in the Arabian Peninsula, began as an insurgent movement independent of the traditional ulama against what were viewed as illegitimate rulers—in the case of the MB, the British occupiers, in the case of the Wahhabis, the Turkish Ottomans. But unlike the case in what would become Saudi Arabia, Muslims in Egypt did not have the luxury of overthrowing a distant caliph, and establishing a state in what was then the nonstrategic, sparsely populated desert of Arabia, home to Islam's holy cities, Mecca and Medina. The British nurtured a weak, westernized monarchy in Egypt, which had a patina of legality and prevented this new breed of Islamist from repeating the Wahhabis' success in attaining power in the desert wastelands next door.

Unwilling to remain passive in the face of social decline and disintegration of the umma, Egyptian Islamic activists established a movement, focusing on moral/ social reform, educational/ social welfare projects, hospitals, mosques, schools, cottage industries and social clubs, in preparation for a future post-colonial Islamic state. This remarkable exercise in *ijtihad*, in reaction to both the continued occupation *and* the new western-style nationalism, gave rise to a movement of revolutionary Islamic activism across the Muslim world, combining religion with social activism in a revivalist ideology through mass organizations.

Egypt's long transition—from (capitalist) 'independence' (1922) to (socialist) 'independence' (1952) and later back to capitalist 'independence' in 1972—during which the MB played a vital insurgent role, makes Egypt unique. The various forces of change contending with each other—liberalism, nationalism, socialism, Islamism—have been battling it out for more than a century now. As the MB rapidly grew during the 1930s, it—rather than the liberals and socialists—became the focus of anti-colonial resistance.

Banna and Political Spirituality

MB founder Hassan al-Banna (1906–1949) sought to infuse his grassroots organization "with some of the spiritual values of Sufism without its devotional excesses". When he was twelve years old, he became involved in a Sufi order, and became a fully initiated member in 1922. At the age of thirteen, he participated in demonstrations during the revolution of 1919 against British rule. As leader of the MB, he called himself murshid (guide), a title usually reserved for the leaders of Sufi orders. "His favorite reading, Ghazali's *Revitalization of the Religious Sciences*, is strongly informed by Sufi mysticism."[1]

Banna clearly took inspiration from Ibn Taymiya's *ijtihad* allowing jihad against non-Muslim rulers, though he was faithful to the original meaning of jihad as, before all else, a struggle to enlighten via the Quran. The basic theory and strategy of Banna's organization is deceptively simple: to work within and beyond the secular framework of the nation through grassroots organizations to gradually create a new society based on Islamic principles, transforming a secular nation-state into an Islamic social order: social activism, using the pen, tongue and heart rather than sword.

The Brotherhood's English language website *ikhwanweb.com* describes the principles of the Muslim Brotherhood as including firstly the introduction of sharia as "the basis controlling the affairs of state and society", and secondly, working to unify "Islamic countries and states, mainly among the Arab states, and liberating them from foreign imperialism". "We believe that political reform is the true and natural gateway for all other kinds of reform."

Banna proved to be a master organizer, establishing an array of administrative structures in the 1930s which mobilized peasants, workers and professionals. Outreach was both local and abroad, relying on the revolutionary new telegraph and telephone. British state-of-the-art financial and administrative methods were turned against the occupiers. Banna relied on pre-existing social networks, in particular those built around mosques, Islamic welfare associations, and neighborhood groups. This weaving of traditional ties into a distinctively modern structure was at the root of his success. Directly attached to the Brotherhood, and feeding its expansion, were numerous businesses, clinics, and schools. Members were affiliated to the movement through a series of cells called *usra* (family). The money nexus had eroded traditional allegiances, leaving Muslims humiliated and alienated, and the MB quickly became a new grassroots family, based on the powerful ties of Islam.[2]

Rooted in Islam, Banna's message tackled issues including colonialism, public health, educational policy, natural resource management, social inequalities, Arab nationalism, the weakness of the Islamic world on the international scene, and the conflict in Palestine. By emphasizing concerns that appealed to a variety of constituencies, Banna was able to recruit from among a cross-section of Egyptian society, though modern-educated civil servants, office employees, and professionals remained dominant among the organization's activists and decision-makers. Incipient nationalists found an articulate and principled foe of imperialism, but without the chauvinism that characterized European nationalism in the 1930s–1940s.

Charity work and dawa (preaching) included social welfare activism, which substituted for ineffective or nonexistent government services. All this required creative *ijtihad* by what were layman scholar-activists, reinforcing the Muslim duty to create balance (*mizan*) and justice (*adl, qist*), in sharp contrast to the occupiers' racism, cruelty, injustice, and their Christian missionaries, advocating apostasy and accommodation with imperialism.

Banna is accused by critics of secretly planning to overthrow the monarchy by using the MB's Special Organization, which had been set up in the late 1930s to provide military assistance to the Palestinians. Like any organization intending to replace the existing order—whether by evolution or revolution—as the MB became more powerful, it was increasingly impossible to control. In an atmosphere of anti-colonial unrest and violence in Egypt and Palestine in the 1930s–1940s, government officials were killed—the most famous being Prime Minister Ahmed Maher whom the British installed in 1945 to ensure that Egypt finally declared war against Germany. In November 1948 the government arrested 32 MB leaders, and in December the British-installed Prime Minister Mahmud Nokrashi ordered the dissolution of the MB, only to be assassinated by one of its members, veterinary student Abdel Meguid Ahmed Hassan. A month and a half later Banna himself was murdered by government agents.

Banna tried over his lifetime to achieve a peaceful transition to Islamic rule. He accepted the principle of peaceful elections, in keeping with the above-quoted hadith about obeying an unjust ruler.[3] Banna announced he would run in the 1941 elections in Alexandria, but King Farouq pressured him to withdraw, promising to ease restrictions on the MB, an empty promise as it turned out. Banna ran in blatantly rigged elections in 1945, thereby demonstrating that trying to move forward within the system of electoral democracy imposed by empire was problematic at best.

The pattern of rigged elections and suppression continued under the dictatorship of Nasser, but despite this, the organization never advanced a strategy of violent revenge or overthrow of the regime. An assassination attempt on Nasser by a devout hot-headed veterinary student in 1954, which may have been staged (Nasser was never in real danger), was the pretext for an attempt by the new socialist dictator to eradicate the organization, something that the British and monarchy had never contemplated. Whether or not this was Egypt's very own false flag act, Nasser's manipulation and sidelining of the MB was bound to result in blowback in the post-colonial world, where Islamists, nationalists, socialists etc. were competing for 'hearts and minds', where no one had a monopoly on what should constitute the new world order.

MB leaders have consistently disowned violence, as seen in the grassroots social justice focus of the organization from the start.

> In Islam, it is forbidden to slay women, children, and old people, to kill the wounded, or to disturb monks, hermits, and the peaceful who offer no resistance. Contrast this mercy with the murderous blanket warfare of the 'civilized' people and their terrible atrocities! Compare their international law alongside this all-embracing, divinely ordained justice![4]

The MB follows traditional Muslim discourse. Consultation and community consensus are important, but insofar as the will of the people may err, it remains subordinate to the Divine Will (the goal being the realization of God's realm on earth). In the context of electoral democracy this means creating a top-down hierarchy much like the democratic centralism of communist parties (where the will of party members was subordinated to the Central Committee's guidance towards achieving the goal of revolution). This intensely collectivist ideology, with the

MB hierarchy submitting to God, perhaps accounts for the lack of charismatic leaders within the movement, at the same time that followers are fearless when faced by the army's guns. It is the antithesis of western-style electoral contests characterized by personal charisma, messy campaigns and hyped upheavals, where alternative parties take power to basically tweak a system which is off-bounds to any genuine reformers.

Qutb Emphasizes the Cultural Divide

After Banna, the best-known MB theorist (or rather, ex-MB, as he and his writings were publicly disowned when he was hanged for treason in 1966) was Sayyid Qutb (1906–1966), credited with inspiring today's militant Islam in the Muslim world, both Sunni and Shia. He studied in the US in 1948, and intensely disapproved of what he saw as a society obsessed with materialism, violence and sex. He wrote *Social Justice in Islam* (1949), rejecting western capitalism and calling Islam a global civilization based on a law that "consists of mercy, love, help and mutual responsibility between Muslims in particular and all human beings in general".[5] Parliamentary government and democracy were manipulated by modern elites in cooperation with landlords to control the masses, allowing a concentration of political power, wealth and resources, economic exploitation, corruption and social injustice under a veil of democratic legitimacy. The cult of materialism was undermining religion, morality and the family.

Given their common opposition to imperialism and the injustices of capitalism, initially, the MB and Nasser's Free Officers' movement had worked together. They had struck a friendship during the first war between the Arab armies and Zionist Israel in 1947–1948. Many MB volunteers shared trenches with Egyptian soldiers and officers. After the 1952 coup, as a Muslim Brother and proponent of Islamic socialism, Qutb supported Nasser's coup, espousing a "just dictatorship" that would "grant political liberties to the virtuous alone."[6] He acted for a time as Cultural Advisor to the ruling Revolutionary Council set up by the Free Officers.[7] When it became clear to the MB, however, that the officers were not interested in establishing an Islamic State as they had vowed earlier, rather a state based on Arab nationalism, they parted ways. In January 1954, the Revolutionary Council dissolved the Muslim Brotherhood and Qutb was among the thousands of Islamists sent to prison.

While in prison under Nasser from 1954–1964, he wrote *Milestones* (1964), borrowing from Maududi[8] and the Ibn Taymiya doctrine of offensive jihad. The success of the Wahhabis in overthrowing their Ottoman rulers, and Afghani's frustration with both the Ottoman/ Qajar monarchs and the imperialist occupiers, inspired both Qutb and Maududi. This trend towards revolution in Islamic renewal had finally found an articulate, even charismatic, spokesman in Qutb.

Milestones prompted his re-arrest and execution in 1966. Here he rejected both capitalist and socialist systems. The problem with socialism was that it asserted that society was fundamentally based on class, and that the working class was the repository of truth. However, truth lies not with a class but in the Quran, which would overcome class differences without violent revolution of one class against another, by promoting their mutual regard through non-exploitative economic relations and engendering a sense of responsibility for the ummah's well being. Islam in the seventh century had provided answers to the sectarian strife and rising economic disparities without resorting to class.[9]

Qutb emphasizes the importance of instituting sharia, a complete system extending into all aspects of life, which when instituted would, as was the communist or anarchist promise, require no government at all, allowing the 'withering away of the state', true freedom. "Assemblies of men which have absolute power to legislate laws"[10] or even a 'just dictatorship' is un-Islamic, where the laws are not based on Islam. Secular regimes such as Nasser's were illegitimate as they were based on human (and thus corrupt) authority, rather than divine authority, submitting to secular laws which revolved around the market, ignoring moral laws which demand political, economic and social restraint.

The way to bring about this freedom was for a revolutionary vanguard to fight *jahiliya* (the state of ignorance) with a twofold approach: dawa, and undermining the organizations and authorities of the *jahili* system by "physical power and jihad". The vanguard movement would grow through preaching and jihad until it formed a truly Islamic community, then spread throughout the Islamic homeland and finally throughout the entire world, attaining leadership of humanity. "Jihad against the polytheists by fighting, and against the hypocrites by preaching and argument."[11]

Qutb's writings and death at the hands of the secular state prepared the way for a new movement of renewal and reaction to imperialism—and its weapons—inspiring Ayatollah Khomeini in Iran as well as Egypt's Islamic Society and Egyptian Islamic Jihad in the 1970s, and al-Qaeda in the 1980s–2010s.

Reformist Muslims questioned his understanding of sharia, and his increasing dismissal, in line with the Wahhabis, of not only all non-Muslim culture, but much of Muslim culture that developed following the period of the first four caliphs.[12] Fundamentalist critics condemned Qutb's reformist ideas such as social justice and redistributive economics as western *bid'a* (innovation). They condemned him for using *ijtihad* and for redefining *ijma* (consensus) so that it takes in the entire umma, rather than just the ulama (his stateless society would run on consensus, without exploitative representative government).[13]

Shortly after his death, the ulama of Al-Azhar University took the unusual step of putting Qutb on their index of heresy, declaring him a deviant (*munharif*). MB Murshid Hassan al-Hodeibi, under house arrest in 1969, disowned Qutb and wrote *Preachers Not Judges*, arguing it was not the state of ignorance (*jahiliya*) but ignorance (*juhl*) that needed to be fought—via dawa. A transformed people, having built Islamic institutions, would eventually transform the state. This evolutionary path would bring about an Islamic society, not violent civil war. The MB was biding its time until the Nasserites and revolutionary Islamists like Qutb burned themselves out—or were taken out.

Qutb is one of the most influential Muslim thinker-activists of the modern reform era, not only for his ideas, but his life work and how he died. *Milestones* fuses "together the core elements of modern Islamism: the Kharijites'[14] takfir (charge of unbelief), Ibn Taymiya's fatwas and policy prescriptions, Rashid Rida's Salafism, Maududi's concept of the contemporary *jahiliya* and Banna's political activism",[15] and like Vladimir Lenin's pamphlet *What Is To Be Done?*, remains a snapshot of its times, hinting at the revolutionary energy that social changes and the struggle against imperialism had unleashed. Qutb's journey from the MB's evolutionary social Islam to revolutionary offensive jihad aiming at a stateless Islamic society, governed only by sharia, must be put in its context—the era of world communist revolution against capitalism—which had just planted a Jewish colony in the heart of Islam.

Qutb's execution pre-empted any final judgment on whether he meant *jahiliya* to justify war against fellow Muslims he chose to label as unbelievers. Ironically, the

Kemalists, by disestablishing Islam and trying to eradicate it, boosted the likes of Banna, Qutb and Khomeini, opening up Islamic thought to the level of popular street and mosque culture, severing links to its superstructure that had provided stability for 1400 yrs, even while creating conditions for revolutionary movements. Bin Laden further fragmented authority in Sunni Islam (leaving collegiate Shia leadership as the only body remaining institutionally intact).

From the late 1970s on, Islamism eclipsed secular ideologies as the primary source of political activism in Egypt.[16] 'Islam is the solution—not capitalism or socialism' captures the supra-class nature of the MB's appeal, attracting youth much like western youth were attracted to communism in the secular West, but more so. At a time when Vaclav Havel was feted in the West as Czechoslovakia's great dissident who was "living within the truth" (conveniently confronting the West's current enemy), thousands of MBers in Egypt were actually doing this under much worse conditions, without any western support. Their "project of moral and social renewal is a constructive and life-affirming one ... not just against the status quo but for a better alternative."[17]

The MB's patience seemed to have paid off by 2011. The Arab Spring was/is an Islamic Awakening, as confirmed in five elections/ referenda in Egypt, where Islamists consistently won two-thirds of the vote in the freest elections in any country in recent times. Money was not a significant factor thanks to limits on candidates' financing (no corporate or Super PACs a la US, or foreign donations), the brainwashing of the old order no longer worked, and the ballot-box-stuffers of the past were not present.

Foreign relations were shifting towards a more confrontational stance with Israel, defying Israel on Gaza, and moving towards more cooperation with other Islamic governments and movements, in particular Iran, but also throughout the Muslim world, while avoiding any open challenge to the Saudi monarchy. President Mohamed Morsi's first stop was Saudi Arabia, which initially promised support. Qatar's Sheikh Hamad sent $8b in aid ($2b of which was since returned by the coupmakers). The Morsi government delayed and delayed on the 'generous' IMF loan, finally proposing a compromise that included a demand to cancel part of what it termed the 'odious debt' from Mubarak years—which it was. The Islamists' constitution—accepted by a popular vote, but post-coup replaced by another authorized by the military—put the family squarely at its heart, confirming both individual rights regardless of belief, status or ethnicity, and responsibilities.

These tantalizing developments confirm the validity of the MB strategy of confronting imperialism. But the military's July 2013 coup put an end to this experiment in Islamic democracy, with the secularists in open collusion with the still powerful Mubarakite establishment, who collectively had boycotted the MB government and fomented discontent by sabotaging the economy. We will return to this discussion in later chapters.

Endnotes

1   Malise Ruthven, *Fundamentalism: The Search for Meaning*, UK: Oxford University Press, 2003, 174.
2   This is in line with scientific finding about brain evolution, which suggests that the optimal size of a social network is 150. See Lieberman, *Social*.
3   "We have announced our acceptance of democracy that acknowledges political pluralism, the peaceful rotation of power, the fact that the nation is the source of all powers, the freedom of the press, freedom of criticism and thought, freedom of peaceful demonstrations, freedom of assembly, and the independence of the judiciary." http://ikhwanweb.com/

4 Hassan al-Banna, "Kitab al-jihad", 239.
5 Quoted in John Calvert, *Sayyid Qutb and the Origins of Radical Islamism*, USA: Columbia University Press, 2010.
6 Qutb wrote this is in an article in *Al-Akhbar*, 8 August 1952.
7 According to Hamid Algar in his introduction to the translation of Qutb's *Social Justice in Islam*, Islamic Publications International, 2000.
8 Abdul Ala Maududi (1903–1979) founded Jamaat i-Islami (Islamic society) in 1941 in British India as a religious political movement to promote Islamic values and practices. Maududi was against the creation of Pakistan, but presented with a fait accompli after the partition of India, he was forced to redefine Jamaat i-Islami in 1947 to support an Islamic state in Pakistan, and headed the organization until 1972. In *The Islamic Law and Constitution* (1941) he coined and popularized the terms 'Islamic state' and 'Islamic revolution'. He was admired in the Shia world as well. Ayatollah Khomeini met him in 1963, and Maududi welcomed the Iranian revolution and hosted a delegation of Iranians at his home in Lahore in 1979. He interpreted Islam as "a worldly ideology capable of mobilizing Muslims to submit themselves actively to God. Only an Islamic society and polity could guarantee the believer's piety and salvation." (quoted in Jalal, *Partisans of Allah*, 258.)
9 But then, that was before capitalism, with its corporations and assembly lines.
10 Qutb, *Milestones*, 93.
11 Ibid., 64.
12 Abou el-Fadl, *The Great Theft*, Canada: Harper Collins, 2005, and Abdelwahab Meddeb, *Malady of Islam*, USA: Basic Books, 2003, 104.
13 "Reformer Sayyid Qutb exposes his socialistic ideals" <http://www.hizmetbooks.org/Religion_Reformers_in_Islam/ref-51.htm>, Ahmad S. Moussalli, *Radical Islamic Fundamentalism: the Ideological and Political Discourse of Sayyid Qutb*, Lebanon: American University of Beirut, 1992, 223.
14 The Kharijites were an extremist sect who murdered the fourth caliph Ali in 661. As a movement they died out early, though the Ibadi sect in Oman still traces their origins to the Kharijites.
15 Daniel Benjamin and Steven Simon, *The Age of Sacred Terror*, USA: Random House, 2002, 62.
16 Carrie Wickham, *Mobilizing Islam: Religion, Activism and Political Change in Egypt*, USA: Columbia UP, 2003, 1.
17 Ibid., xi–xii.

| CHAPTER THREE |

SHIA SUCCESS IN IRAN

The major twentieth century reform thinkers (Banna, Qutb, Maududi, Khomeini, among others) all were motivated by a deep anger at the ravages of colonialism, the apparent success of the Zionist colonial project, and the suppression of Islam by Kemalist client governments. In one way or another, they advocated the revival of sharia law and creation of an Islamic state to replace the modern secular laws and nation states imposed on them. Like the earlier notion of the caliphate, the modern Islamic state is modeled after the example of Prophet Muhammad and rooted in Islamic law.

Saudi Arabia (1932), Pakistan (1956), Mauritania (1958), Iran (1979), Afghanistan (1992, 1996, 2004)[1] and Sudan (1993) all bill themselves officially as Islamic governments/ states/ republics—but are not necessarily regarded by Muslims themselves as genuine. The twentieth century experience of 'Islamic states' and attempts to return to the sharia traditions prior to imperialism have produced mixed returns. The Saudis actively conspire with the imperialists to undermine both Iran and Egypt's Islamic revolutions. Pakistan, Mauritania, Afghanistan and Sudan are all weak states plagued by ethnic violence, using the claim of 'Islamic state' more as a means to consolidate power and win unmerited approval.

Even as Egyptians mourn their martyrs killed by military dictator Sisi, and Saudis fume under their 90-year-old pro-US/ Israeli monarch Abdullah, Iran continues to gain admiration—among both Shia and Sunni Muslims and non-Muslims—for its principled defiance of empire, confirmed in a smooth transition to a reformist government under President Hassan Rouhani in 2013. It stared down the US and Saudis in Syria, and looks poised to end the 34-year US-Israeli campaign of subversion against its revolution without having compromised on principles.

Ayatollah Khomeini

The Iranian revolution was seen in the West as a product of a confluence of circumstances: the collapse of a westernizing, illegitimate monarchy which had propped itself up by using an oppressive police state. But the revolution is also rooted in Islam and Iranian history, and like Russia's communist revolution in 1917, this revolution too challenges the very foundations of the western imperialist system.

Like most other Muslim societies, Iran suffered at the hands of colonialism. But unlike other societies that were predominantly Sunni, Iran was a Shia majority country. The Safavid rulers adopted Shiism during the sixteenth century in order to distinguish themselves from the Turkish sultans and Central Asian Uzbeks.

Shia insist that Islamic civilization was flawed after the early period of the Rightly Guided Caliphs (632–661). The subsequent Sunni ulama were guilty of accepting the subversion of the khilafah (the system of government established after the Prophet) into hereditary monarchy, allowing the corruption of Islamic governance. (Sunni Salafis too criticize the decline of Islamic governance after the rule of the four Rightly Guided Caliphs as due to hereditary monarchy, but they also criticize the Shia for still promoting hereditary transmission via the descendants of the Prophet, starting with Ali, even though he was not the Prophet's son, but rather his cousin and son-in-law.)

However, in the face of Sunni dominance after 661, the Shia ulama were guilty of implicitly accepting the (flawed) ruling order by reason of their quietism, shunning all worldly authority until the return of the twelfth Imam, Imam Mahdi, their last accepted leader, who disappeared in 941. They allowed corrupt rulers to usurp power and pass it on to their children. Over time, some Shia ulama felt the need to change this approach; hence, the *ijtihad* of Persian Usuli ulama beginning in the seventeenth century. Their call for a supervisory role for the ulama in political affairs was taken a step further by Ayatollah Khomeini (1902–1989), who formulated a new theory in the 1960s and then went on to lead the revolution against the Shah.

Like Banna, Ayatollah Khomeini came from an intellectual and religious tradition. From very early age, he was immersed in the study of *irfan* (gnosis) and mysticism, and later *fiqh* (law). He began to raise and discuss issues of injustice from a young age, and at the same time rose to a high rank as a religious scholar. In one of his lectures delivered after the Shah signed the Status of Forces Agreement with the US in autumn 1964 (granting immunity from prosecution for American personnel and their dependants), Ayatollah Khomeini pointed out that under the new agreement, even if an American were to run over a government minister or a *marja* (leading religious figure), they would have no recourse for restitution in an Iranian court. He condemned those members of the Majlis (parliament) that had voted for this agreement and denounced the Shah's regime as illegitimate, calling for his overthrow. As a result he was exiled first to Turkey and then Iraq (Najaf). Unlike Nasser's treatment of Qutb at the same time in Egypt, the Shah did not dare to prosecute Khomeini.

He continued to denounce the Shah as an American puppet, and Iran as an American and Zionist colony, and demanded not only freedom for the Iranian people but also the liberation of Palestine and al-Quds (Jerusalem), linking the struggle of the Iranian people with that of the Palestinians, and leaving aside Shia-Sunni differences. He argued that the Muslim world was still effectively colonized and that imperialists and Zionists continued to dominate these societies, preventing their natural development.

His religious lectures attracted large audiences because he applied a religious dimension to the plight of Muslims in the contemporary world, and called upon people to rise up against the illegitimate rulers as well as their imperial and Zionist masters. Interestingly, during the Ayatollah's exile in Iraq, Iraqi dictator Saddam Hussein tolerated his anti-Shah statements, though many Iraqi Shia scholars avoided him. They felt that he was pushing Shiism too much towards politics and that if this trend continued, it would dilute the traditional message of Shiism that was based on the idea of waiting for the arrival of Imam Mahdi to set things right. They also were reluctant to attract the attention of the Iraqi dictator, who had murdered thousands of Iraqi intellectuals and had the great Shia thinker Mohammad Baqir al-Sadr murdered in 1980. The masses, however, found in Khomeini a leader who was courageous, knowledgeable and charismatic.

Vilayat-e faqih

In *Hukumat-e Islami* (*Islamic Government*, 1971) Khomeini outlined the concept of *vilayat-e faqih* (guardianship by jurists). This laid the foundation for the struggle against the Shah's regime leading to the establishment of the Islamic government in Iran. In *Islamic Government* Ayatollah Khomeini asks: Because the Imam is absent, should sharia no longer be enforced? In other words, "Is political authority firmly based upon authority of sharia not necessary?" The answer being yes, sharia is necessary. Ayatollah Khomeini "always believed that the leadership of political activities should be in the hands of the foremost religious scholars."[2] After the revolution, power should be decentralized. There should be local self-government with the mosque as its center, allowing genuine mass participation.[3]

Also in the 1970s, Shia scholar Baqir Sadr was developing his program for Islamic governance in Iraq, rejecting the primacy of private property derived solely from individual rights. The rights and obligations of both private individuals and rulers are subordinated to God's demand that human society should be conducted with justice, compassion and equity. "Trusteeship" and direct popular elections would regulate day-to-day life, while guardianship of the whole project would be overseen by Islamic scholars *a la* US Supreme Court acting as guardian of the values of US constitution.

Muslim identity focused on the struggle for just and effective governance and set of ethics to underpin social change. This flowering of political Shiism relied on mobilization and an

> activist revolutionary ideology mooted by Sayyid Qutb; ... translated into popular mobilization by Shariati; and taken to a revolutionary conclusion by Khomeini. It has then evolved under the direction of Sayyed Hassan Nasrallah into a more incrementalist form of moblization.[4]

Peaceful revolution

Khomeini reinterpreted governance within the nation-state, not as executing the interests of a powerful elite but as "a catalyst and tool for igniting and promoting massive behavioral change, in order to bring about a just community ... to recover government for human interests."[5] This corresponds to such leftist thinkers as the Algerian Franz Fanon, whose *Wretched of the Earth* (1961) was translated into Persian in the 1960s by Ali Shariati, an ally of Khomeini, and coins the distinction between the "colonized" and "independent" brain.

Although some Shia ulama opposed his *ijtihad* on Islamic government and direct involvement in politics, and continue to do so even today, Khomeini's authority overshadowed all such objections as the movement against the Shah gained momentum. His *ijtihad* on Islamic government brought Shia political thought into line with the most resolute of Sunni thinkers since the days of Ibn Taymiya.[6] Khomeini was able to mobilize both young and old, both men and women, to get involved in the affairs of the people so that oppression and exploitation would be brought to an end. They confronted the Shah's heavily armed military in the streets of Tehran and other major cities, not by taking up arms, but through unarmed nonviolent resistance.[7] Note the adulation in the West of Mahatma Gandhi as the great proponent of nonviolence while Khomeini, despite his emphasis on nonviolence, is dismissed as a terrorist. But then, Hinduism posed no real threat to the empire, and could not counter the presumptuous British claim to ownership of 'civilization', while Islam poses a real threat to empire and its claims of superiority to non-western cultures.

One can immediately see the effectiveness of this approach. Had the Muslims of Iran in the 1960s–1970s taken up arms and pursued assassination and terrorist attacks as did the Sunni Egyptians and Algerians later with disastrous consequences, the movement to overthrow the Shah's regime would almost certainly have failed. The state has far greater capacity for violence; when people take up arms, they provide the state with the pretext to unleash its massive firepower against them (not to mention instigating false-flag terror itself), and justify it under the rubric of maintaining "law and order".

The Islamic movement in Iran led by Ayatollah Khomeini, instead of answering the soldiers' bullets with their own, appealed to the soldiers not to shoot and kill unarmed civilians. It was at this level that the very serious threat posed by the Shah's military was neutralized. The world witnessed how the Shah's soldiers ultimately turned against their officers, first by disobeying orders to shoot civilians and then arresting senior officers for the crimes they had perpetrated against innocent people and handing them over to the revolutionaries.

Ayatollah Khomeini understood the West's nature well. Though the product of a traditional Islamic education, he was clear about what imperialism and Zionism stood for. He understood that imperialism is a system based on *kufr* (denial of God's authority); hence, he urged its completed overthrow.

> Let us overthrow tyrannical governments by: severing all relations with governmental institutions; refusing to cooperate with them; refraining from any action that might be construed as aiding them; creating new judicial, financial, economic, cultural, and political institutions. It is the duty of all of us to overthrow the *taghut* [illegitimate political power and authority] that now rule the entire

> Islamic world. Such governments must be replaced by institutions serving the public good, administered according to Islamic law. In this way, an Islamic government will gradually come into existence."[8]

He did not resort to western vocabulary or mode of operations. He did not call for setting up political parties within the *taghuti* system, nor did he tell people to approach the Shah's illegitimate courts to seek redress for injustices inflicted on them. He was clear: all these institutions were illegitimate and they had to be dismantled. In their place new institutions "administered according to Islamic law" that would serve the interests of the people based on fairness and justice should be created.

Given the inherently violent nature of the neocolonial state, this meant providing a safeguard to protect the new Islamic order. Immediately following the revolution in May 1979, the Army of the Guardians of the Islamic Revolution, known as the Revolutionary Guards, was founded as a branch of Iran's military to function as a counter to the regular military, initially seen as a source of opposition and loyalty to the Shah. They still assist the ruling clerics in the day-to-day enforcement of the government's Islamic codes, protect the Islamic system, and prevent foreign interference as well as coups by the military or "deviant movements". The Basij Forces (Mobilization Resistance Force) were founded in November 1979, a network of up to a million active individuals who could be called upon in times of need. Related to it is the Qods Force to provide assistance and training to various militant organizations around the world.[9]

Other movements since the Iranian revolution (Egypt 1981–1997, Algeria 1992–1997) failed precisely because they were repressed by the army despite overwhelming popular support, and pushed towards violent means to overthrow the regime and/or effectively resist the neocolonial state forces confronted by ascendant Islamic forces. In the process, the Islamists lost support, as people were successfully manipulated by regime propaganda and provocations. The 1992 coup in Algeria and 2013 coup in Egypt are chilling reminders of the ruthlessness of the neocolonial state faced with dismantling by a popular Islamist movement unable to establish adequate institutions to defend its gains.

Rejecting the political party approach to win an election and take power, Ayatollah Khomeini utilized two other platforms effectively since he was not in direct contact with the people because of his exile: the network of mosques in Iran, and ordinary cassette tape. Unlike in much of the Sunni world, the environment in Iran enabled the Shia ulama to keep mosques outside government control. Mosques in most Sunni countries are controlled by the regimes through their co-opted Sunni ulama. In countries like Saudi Arabia, Egypt, Kuwait, Jordan and the UAE, for instance, the content of *jumah khutbahs* (Friday sermons) is strictly controlled by the regime through the Ministry of Religious Affairs or Awqaf (religious endowments). In Iran too, the Shah's regime attempted to control messages emanating from the mosques, but since the Shia considered all worldly authority to be illegitimate, they found ways to circumvent these restrictions—and there was consensus on doing so.

Khomeini insisted that the Islamic movement in Iran would be a movement open to all people. All kinds of people joined the movement including opportunists who thought once the Shah's regime was overthrown, they would be able to grab power. Such opportunists had also assumed—as did the ulama in 1953—that Ayatollah Khomeini would retreat to his madrassah after ridding Iran of the Shah, leaving the affairs of state to them. Their assumption was not wrong; after the success of the revolution, Ayatollah Khomeini actually did retire to Qum, but when he saw the manner in which the western-educated elites compromised the principles of the revolution, he returned to Tehran to supervise the affairs of state more directly.

Khomeini addressed every issue from the Islamic perspective and used Islamic means to deliver his message. While he fully supported the rights of the Palestinian people, he never endorsed or supported their hijacking of planes. For him, the end did not justify the means. Both means and ends had to be based on Islamic values.

So why did he support the taking of hostages at the US embassy in Tehran in November 1979? That was because of the colonial legacy of the CIA/MI6-engineered coup that brought the Shah back to power in 1953, deposing the elected government. After that, the US embassy in Tehran became the control center for CIA spying in the entire Middle East. The revolutionaries feared that through the US embassy, the CIA was again plotting to overthrow the new revolutionary government. Documents—many shredded by the American embassy staff and painstakingly pieced together by Iranian students—confirmed their worst fears. The Americans were indeed plotting to overthrow the Islamic government. A number of Iranians were on their payroll. The revolution was saved from another CIA-inspired coup by exposing this plot. When Americans denounce the siege of the embassy, they talk about "diplomatic immunity", that the revolutionaries should merely have declared them *persona non grata* and expelled them from Iran—allowing them to dispose of the evidence of their plot against the revolutionary government, absolving them *ex ante* of their crimes.[10]

Other avenues used by Ayatollah Khomeini included the Hajj. He was keenly aware of its importance as a pillar of Islam and how much it means to ordinary Muslims. Like many other aspects of Islam, he saw the Hajj too as reduced to a set of rituals empty of its true content and meaning. He called for rallies at the time of the Hajj, despite loud objections by the Saudi rulers. Khomeini used the occasion of Hajj to highlight the plight of Muslims rather than turn to such western-created institutions as the United Nations. He fully understood that imperialist-created and imposed institutions were not there to solve the problems of Muslims or any oppressed people; they were created to safeguard the interests of the western powers.

One of the revolution's first acts, in February 1979, was to shut down the Israeli embassy in Tehran, transferring the building to representatives of the Palestinian people. One of the first foreign visitors to Tehran after the victory of the Islamic revolution was PLO leader Yasir Arafat. There was no Sunni-Shia split when it came to support for the Palestinians, and Iran from then on became the most reliable ally of the Palestinians.

Khomeini's strategy of resistance to imperialism overcame the stagnation in Shia political thought, outwitting both the Shah's regime and its western backers. He was able to mobilize the people of Iran, keeping them focused on removing the remaining traces of the Shah's regime completely, and at the same time, to appeal to the broader Muslim ummah and indeed other oppressed peoples worldwide.[11]

The success of the Islamic revolution in Iran shook the foundations of the imperialist order. In its attempt to bring Iran back under the hegemony of the existing western-imposed world order, the US has used various tactics—punitive sanctions, internal sabotage in Iran, assassination of leading figures of the revolution (including a president, prime minister, chief justice, members of parliament and religious scholars), as well as a brutal eight-year war waged against it via Iraq, which included the Iraqi use of chemical weapons, to which the Iranians never responded in kind. The US has invaded Iranian neighbors Afghanistan and Iraq, and currently threatens Iran's ally, Syria. And in later years, it has killed Iranian nuclear scientists, conducted cyberwarfare by introducing the Stuxnet virus into Iran's Bushehr and Natanz nuclear facilities, incited uprisings by internal groups such as Jundallah, while further tightening sanctions targeting banks outside Iran for doing business with Iranian banks and prohibiting Iran's use of the international banking SWIFT system for money transfers. All this has failed to bring down the Islamic government.

Comparing the Iran-Egypt Experience in Context

Nasser's nemesis—and Khomeini's inspiration—was the Muslim Brotherhood, which quickly became the main opposition to both the British occupiers before 1952 (who by dawdling, discredited the liberal Wafd Party) and to Nasser after his coup and ouster of the British. Though rejecting secular socialism as an alternative social order to capitalism, the MB's emphasis on social justice from its founding in 1928, and its credibility as a truly national movement, unbeholden to either the imperialists or the Soviet Union, gave Nasser the opening to pursue a socialist program dressed up as Arab nationalism, more-or-less consistent with Islam, even as he ruthlessly suppressed the Islamists.

It was only the collapse of this secularist vision, with the invasion of Egypt by Israel in 1967 and the obliteration of the Egyptian forces, that put paid to this program. Once again, the field was left open to the MB as the only credible force remaining in Egyptian politics.

Iran's 1953 western-backed coup had the same effect on Iran as Sadat's pro-US-Israel 'coup' had on Egypt two decades later. Both resulted in the discrediting of secular nationalist regimes, spurring a return to Islam, though in both cases the movement was persecuted. Egypt's greater integration into the western economy as a result of its direct occupation, its two decades of Nasserist socialism, and the 1973 'victory' against Israel delayed its Islamic revolutionary moment till 2011, while giving the MB the chance to proceed with Islamization from below.

The discrediting of the neoliberal model, especially in Egypt after Nasser and more so since 2008, has buttressed Iran's Islamic regime, which has been able to defy the West and continue to increase its prestige among all those who oppose the US empire. The so-called Green Revolution of 2009 by the pro-western forces failed, despite intense pressure from outside and the permanent economic crisis which Iran suffers.

By 2012, Egypt and Iran had 'caught up' with each other: the political see-saw that these countries experienced in the past half century was finally coming into sync. Both were following an Islamic path in defiance of the US, though the MB had only taken the first tentative steps in exercising actual power. This synchronization of Egyptian and Iranian politics represented a potential coming together of Sunni and Shia political dynamics, which was the wish of Islamic reformists Afghani and Abduh more than a century ago, and has been happening gradually since the Iranian revolution, despite the opposition of the Saudi and Gulf monarchies. Hints of this lie in the fact that:

- From the start Ayatollah Khomeini notably played down Shia-Sunni differences,
- Sunni Islamists such as Qutb and Maududi are widely read in Iran,

- Shia resistance to Israel is respected in the Sunni world. Saudi King Abdullah recognized this by establishing a center for dialogue among Islamic sects at the Organization of Islamic Cooperation summit in Mecca in 2012.
- The Egyptian MB's professed #1 foreign policy priority is Palestine, putting it in sync with Iran.

The steady increase in pro-Palestinian support around the world is the catalyst now uniting anti-imperialist forces in the Arab world with Iran's principled support of the Sunni Palestinians, and sympathy with the nonviolent Sunni path for the re-emerging Islamic order spearheaded by the Egyptian MB. Sadly, the current impasse in Egypt has put on hold this reordering of Middle East politics.

Endnotes

1. From 1992–1995, Afghanistan was an "Islamic state", and from 1996–2001, it was an Islamic emirate. In 2004, President Karzai announced that Afghanistan was an "Islamic republic"—under the watchful eye of his US patrons.
2. Hamid Algar, "A short Biography", in Abdar ar-Rahman Koya (ed.), *Imam Khomeini: Life, Thought and Legacy*, Islamic Book Trust, Kuala Lumpur 2009, 26-27; also Hamid Algar, *The Roots of the Islamic Revolution*, Open Press, 1983.
3. Hamid Algar, *The Roots of the Islamic Revolution*, Open Press, 1983.
4. Crooke, *Resistance*, 108.
5. Ibid., 135.
6. Kalim Siddiqui, *Processes of error, deviation, correction and convergence in Muslim political thought*, Crescent Publications (UK), for the Institute of Contemporary Islamic Thought. 2001.
7. The nonviolent nature of the Iranian revolution is well documented. See for instance Stephen Zunes, The Iranian revolution (1977–1979), *http://www.nonviolent-conflict.org*, 2009, and http://repositories.lib.utexas.edu/handle/2152/21097

8   Ghada M. Ramahi, "Tradition of Reform", in Abdar ar-Rahman Koya (ed.), *Imam Khomeini: Life, Thought and Legacy*, 2009, 100.
9   Morris M Mottale. "The birth of a new class - Focus", *Al Jazeera*, 22 April 2010.
10 The Iranians released all the women and African-Americans among the embassy personnel and no one died, was tortured or 'rendered'. Leaving aside the murky Iran-Contra scandal, no ransom payment was made.
11 For instance, Khomeini told a Cuban delegation to Tehran in April 1979, "Government should focus on being in the service of the nations. The nations will then support them." <http://en.imam-khomeini.ir> Fidel Castro supported the Iranian revolution, stating at the time, "We do not think there is a contradiction between religion and revolution." http://ctp.iccas.miami.edu Of course, Mahmoud Ahmedinejad (r. 2005–2013) is the Iranian leader who gained popularity in the West as an advocate of nonviolence, despite being pilloried and ridiculed for writing to leaders such as Mikhail Gorbachev and Bush II, calling on them to accept Islam.

| Chapter Four |

UNITING THE UMMAH

While most Sunni ulama and indeed many traditional Shia ulama are critical of Ayatollah Khomeini's political thought, Hamid Algar, Professor of Near Eastern and Persian Studies at the University of California at Berkeley, embraced it, and predicted in 1971 that an Islamic revolution headed by Khomeini could occur in Iran in less than a decade. The other Sunni political analyst to recognize the significance of the Iranian experience was Pakistani émigré to Britain, Kalim Siddiqui (1931–1996), who hailed the Islamic revolution in Iran as the embodiment of the way forward for a renewal of Islamic civilization. "Progress towards the goal is certain to be uneven in time and space. It may well be that a model society will have to be created and developed in one geographical area before the pace of change can be accelerated in other areas."[1] Siddqui embraced the Iranian revolution as the harbinger of this Islamic resurgence.

Prior to the 1979 Iranian revolution, Muslims had suffered repeated setbacks: the June 1967 defeat of Arab armies by Israel and the dismemberment of Pakistan by the invading Indian army in 1971. In this atmosphere of near total despondency, while the Palestinians hijacked planes in the desperate belief that this would enable them to gain freedom from Zionist occupation, Muslim academics and student activists in London were looking for ways to address the West's domination of Muslim societies. They rejected the colonial-imposed systems in Muslim societies but were not certain what would replace them and more critically, how this would be achieved.

They found little freedom of thought in the centers of 'Oriental Studies' which had begun to appear in the West after WWII, partly sponsored by governments, as vehicles for molding Islam to the needs of the postcolonial world. (The University of London School of Oriental and African Studies was the earliest, founded in 1916.) Orientalism, already a British project due to its earlier imperial efforts in the region, had entailed serious academic study of languages, anthropology, etc., in the service of empire. In America, Oriental Studies came later and was less academic, soon metamorphosing into Islamophobia in Great Game III. The first Near East Center in the US was set up in 1947 at Princeton University. At the time, Hollywood was providing a less sophisticated version of what was happening in the ivory towers, creating a romanticized fantasy of Arabs, at the same time disdaining the Muslims' primitive and exotic ways.

Living and working in the West while trying to avoid compromising his thought, Siddiqui emulated the nineteenth century reformer Afghani in stimulating debate among Muslim intellectuals about the renewal of Islamic civilization, by establishing the Muslim Institute in London in 1974,[2] and embarking on worldwide tours to engage Muslim intellectuals, businessmen, academics and others to solicit their support. He refused to be co-opted by either western academia or Saudi and other state funding, criticizing the Muslim Brotherhood and the Jamaat-e Islami (Islamic

Society) of Pakistan for their failures on that count. While advocating revolution in Muslim countries to overthrow imperialism, he was not swept up in the violent resistance movement in Egypt in the 1980s which morphed into Bin Laden's neo-Wahhabi movement in Afghanistan.

Siddiqui also established the Muslim Parliament in London in 1991 to "transforms the disparaged Muslim minority in Britain into a political community with a will and purpose of its own," relying on power "defined more broadly, including moral authority and ability to persuade, facilitate, co-operate, and, if necessary, obstruct." He sought to create a non-state forum for Muslims in Britain to address Muslim concerns and provide a platform for the views and needs of their separate and distinctly Islamic institutions, which, to survive in a largely non-Muslim environment, required being acknowledged by the British government. He felt that the political system merely co-opted various groups to serve its own interests, so the Parliament discouraged Muslims from entering mainstream politics or even voting in elections. Muslims needed to develop Muslim political power from outside the mainstream political system by raising their consciousness and exerting pressure on the formal political process, much like the women's suffrage movement in the early 1900s and the labor movement. The Muslim Parliament successfully pressured the British government to consider providing funding to Muslim schools that it had hitherto ignored.

It would, like the original state founded by the Prophet, pursue the Quranic injunction "to enjoin good and forbid evil" (31:17), ensuring the community maintained its own standards and acted as an example to "draw deviant mankind back to its spiritual roots ... in this increasingly oppressive climate of moral anarchy."[3]

The concept of the "non-territorial Islamic State" is recognized in Muslim political thought, tracing its origins all the way to the Prophet's life in Mecca where he was in effect the head of a non-territorial Islamic state. Such Islamic thinkers as Shah Wali Allah talked about it, but Siddiqui developed this argument further. A non-territorial state is possible insofar as obedience is exacted by personal willing compliance, much the way Islamic family law is practiced, or indeed sharia now (there are many such sharia courts in the UK), but the limits of what these can do, as opposed to the institutional options of actual government, is clear: acceptance of, say, penalties, would have to be voluntary and non-institutional (no coercion, no jail). Other practices are possible, e.g., providing local access to funding to local Muslim communities so they may avoid riba, etc. Of course, such practices would depend on their acceptance by the state exercising actual jurisdiction.

Siddiqui also discussed setting up a Muslim Parliament of Europe, North America and Africa. The UK Parliament is not active now, but it represents an important precedent for the émigré Muslim ummah—the creation of peaceful, constructive non-state institutions to reflect the views and advocate on behalf of Muslims locally and around the world, a democratic alternative to the seriously compromised OIC-type official international organizations sponsored by existing largely dictatorial Muslim states.[4]

As a Sunni, the major challenge for Siddiqui was to convince the rather hesitant Sunni ulama that while the Iranian revolution was impacted by Shia theology, it was genuinely Islamic because it viewed as a model and precedent the first Islamic State established by the Prophet in Medina. Siddiqui too emphasized the misdirection of Islamic civilization, beginning with the Sunni Umayyad/ Abbasid dynastic rule, which contradicted the rule of a khalifah (steward) through consensus of the ummah (community of Muslims). Historically, the Shia also had succumbed to dynastic rule, and further, they had rejected any possibility of establishing genuine Islam rule until the return of the Hidden Imam. Thus both Sunni and Shia history showed the degeneration of Islamic rule over time.

Siddiqui hailed Ayatollah Khomeini's *vilayat-e faqih* political theory in the absence of the Imam Mahdi as the culmination of a renewal within Shia scholarship. This corrected the quietist Shia political tradition, confirming the possibility of genuine Islamic rule through the establishment of an Islamic state, implying political rule by *mujtahideen* (Islamic jurists).

The apparent coming-together of Sunni and Shia thought based on opposition to imperialism led Siddiqui to urge the convergence of Sunni and Shia into a single global Islamic movement. He argued there is no 'Shia' or 'Sunni' state; the two facets of Islam would overcome their differences by establishing Islamic states guided by Islamic scholar-activists versed in sharia, headed by a khalifah or naib (deputy) of the Prophet. It was the task of both Sunni and Shia scholars and activists to reject the imposed neocolonial and monarchical political systems by overthrowing them. He argued that after 1979, a "global Islamic movement" was already in place and would lead to further revolutions, which would triumph through armed struggle, taking his cue as much from the course of events in Afghanistan as Iran.

Siddiqui's colleague and co-founder of the Muslim Institute, Zafar Bangash, moved to Toronto, Canada in 1974, and transformed a community paper, *Crescent*, into a mouthpiece to reflect Siddiqui's concern with Islamic reform and unity. At the time it was the only Islamic news magazine with global readership, with support groups in Africa and Asia. Now it is joined by many internet Islamic sites, including *islamonline.com* and *muslimvillage.com*, reflecting the innovative use of modern communications to inform and unite the ummah around peaceful reform. Retitled *Crescent International*, it continues to play an important role in promoting Sunni-Shia solidarity and as the most respected news source reflecting an Islamic political outlook.

Reflecting on the state of political Islam in the post-1979 world in *Stages of Islamic Revolution* (1996), Siddiqui looked for guidance to Prophet Muhammad's political legacy, noting that:

- Islam[5] does not shrink from military engagement. However, war is a last resort, and must have a higher moral purpose. It cannot be justified for territorial or economic gain, but only in defense of the ummah. When the Muslims emigrated to Medina, the Quraish sought to attack Medina to prevent it from becoming established as an Islamic state, but their efforts to discredit and militarily defeat the Prophet actually helped consolidate the political and military power of Islam there and subsequently over the Arabian Peninsula. Similarly, the Iraqi invasion of Iran and ongoing threats by US-Israel to invade Iran strengthened the Iranian revolution.

- Establishing Islamic rule requires an open movement approach which gathers all on board, as Prophet Muhammad established in setting up Medina as the first Islamic state. The political party approach is divisive, and gets bogged down by early compromises and deals with existing political forces. (This happened in Iran immediately after the revolution when liberal Prime Minister Mehdi Bazargan and President Abolhassan Banisadr objected to the anti-imperialist course of the revolution, the former resigning in November 1979, the latter plotting a new uprising and forced to flee abroad in 1981. Also, in 2013 in Tunisia and Egypt, liberals similarly split and then worked to sabotage the revolution.)

- In an Islamic state the leadership must be *muttaqi* (pious, upright) and the citizens must pledge allegiance based on *taqwa* (piety) for the system to dispense justice. The state structures of the previous exploitative state must be replaced. Khomeini's *velayat e-faqih*, and the establishment of the Revolutionary Guards and the Baseej security forces prevented the paralysis that has occurred in post-revolutionary Tunisia and Egypt under the unreconstructed security forces of the old regime.)

Siddiqui's works hark back to Sayyid Qutb in their militancy. "All modern Muslim societies are living examples of societies that have undergone mindless, uncontrolled, unguided and imposed change ... developed in the West in the name of progress." He shared the enthusiasm among western Muslims for the collapse of the Soviet Union and the eclipse of secular communism as an ideology, and saw the uprisings from 1979 on in Iran, Afghanistan, Chechnya, Bosnia and Kashmir as part of an anti-imperialist continuum, which would result in the overthrow of existing neocolonial governments.

Siddiqui approved of Qutb's rejection of nationalism in *Milestones* and his call for broad-based revolution, leading to the overthrow of the imperialist order. But the revolution in Iran was not Qutbian. In line with Qutb, Siddiqui criticized the Muslim Brotherhood and Maududi's Jamaat-e Islami in Pakistan for being captive to nationalism, and as superficial attempts to oppose the secular order.

Dismissing nationalism wholesale is problematic. As Marx noted, men do not make history as they please. While nationalism was not a major force in overthrowing the Shah (who, as his popularity continued to wane, had tried to whip up Persian chauvinism to counter Islam), the unity of the post-revolutionary state in the face of invasion certainly relied on a gut patriotism. After the revolution, even dissident secular Iranians, including Tudeh (the banned communist party), have rejected western calls for invading Iran and overthrowing the Islamic government.

The MB in Egypt indeed faced pressures to adopt a political platform more favorable to nationalism, but refused. One of the charges against deposed President Morsi was excessive sympathy for the Palestinian cause, to the extent that he was called a traitor, part of a conspiracy against the Egyptian people, more interested in liberating al-Quds (Jerusalem) than in helping Egyptians. Ironically, the coup united people outside Egypt in condemning it, while it split Egyptians largely based on the appeal of a chauvinistic nationalism.

Siddiqui also criticized MB members for having gone to Saudi Arabia and implicitly conforming to Saudi Wahhabism, after taking employment in the Saudi state in the professions, especially teaching, engineering and medicine. Indeed, many MBers had found refuge in Saudi Arabia when persecuted by Nasser. Released from Egyptian prison in 1972, Qutb's brother Muhammad (1906–2014) moved to Mecca and was a professor of Islamic Studies at Umm al-Qura University, editing his brother's books and writing works which tried to reconcile MB thought and Saudi Salafism.

One could ask, what option did they have? Siddiqui's claim that they became "partners" in a "Saudi-American conspiracy"[6] is certainly belied by both the Saudi persecution of pro-MB Saudis and Saudi approval of the Egyptian post-coup outlawing of the MB as a terrorist organization. As the MB gained strength, attempts by both the West and the Saudis to co-opt them were inevitable. Whatever interaction there is between Islamists and imperialists and their clients is a two-way street.

Though Siddiqui comes down strongly in advocating Khomeini-type revolutions, the Egyptian MB's strategy—building grassroots mass structures in parallel to the 'soft state' and pursuing legitimacy through elections—is a valid response given the narrow room for maneuver in today's geopolitical world. A categorical refusal to openly participate in electoral politics would reinforce the accusation of excessive secrecy leveled at the MB. On the contrary, even where the dice are loaded in elections by media bias, and financial and legal impediments, the opportunities provided for advancing the message of political Islam during electoral campaigns is an essential short term strategy/ tactic for Islamists.

Under pressure from the US to institute a democratic electoral facade, Egyptian President Hosni Mubarak loosened the reins in the 2005 elections, permitting MB candidates to run as independents and win 88 seats (20% of the total, the legal opposition winning only 14 seats), despite ballot rigging and the arrest of hundreds of its supporters. The Brotherhood became "in effect, the first opposition party of Egypt's modern era",[7] outshining the historic Wafd and the threadbare Nasserists. The MB was praised for an "unmatched record of attendance", attempting to transform "the Egyptian parliament into a real legislative body, as well as an institution that represents citizens and a mechanism that keeps government accountable".[8]

Those who support the MB approach would argue that devout Muslims must use every opportunity to promote a program based on Islam, as ultimately that is the only way out of the inevitable crises and degeneration that imperialism produces. The goal is to establish democracy based on Islam, and all tactics and strategies, short term and long term, must be built on that verity. That is why astute US politicians from 2011–2013 were forced to work with

Egypt's Islamist government, forced to acknowledge the overwhelming popularity of the uprising, and hope that the Islamists could be managed. That is also why Egypt's military dictator-president Sisi announced in his presidential election campaign in May 2014 that if he won, "the MB will not exist," an arrogant claim that foreshadowed his dictatorial intent and reveals his determination to maintain Egypt as part of the US-Saudi-Pakistani(-Israeli) alliance.

Is Siddiqui vindicated by the 2013 coup in Egypt, which overthrew the democratically-elected MB government? Is Iranian-style non-violent revolution the only way out? Or will Iran's Islamic revolution remain unique—the exception that proves the rule? Iranian leaders have not spoken out strongly about recent events in Egypt. Iran supported the Egyptian Islamists' struggle after 2011 and criticized the coup in 2013, but is now faced with the dilemma of *realpolitik*, the need to balance correct relations with other Muslim states, while continuing to strive for unity of the ummah with a long-term strategy which reflects the goal of Islamic renewal.

Siddiqui's militant analysis, like Qutb's earlier one, was appropriated by the al-Qaeda types, whom he dismissed in 1996 as "pockets of obscurantist conservatism", who also denounce nationalism (though they are noted for their Saudi/Arab chauvinism), dismiss western-style elections, and spurn a broad alliance with leftists/ liberals. Conflicts of the 1990s involving Islamists (Bosnia, Kashmir, Afghanistan, Egypt) were hailed by both Siddiqui and the neo-Wahhabis as harbingers of a growing tide of Islamic revolution following the path of Iran and Afghanistan, but have not led to any clear victories.

On the contrary, as these struggles were co-opted by al-Qaeda, they became hostage to imperialist intrigue. Afghanistan's trauma following the Soviet retreat in 1989 and the ongoing travails of the Arab Spring, where neo-Wahhabis have been active, contrast with Iran's largely peaceful revolution, which was able to extricate Iran from the machinations of the imperialists. The conflicts in Bosnia and Kosovo were more ethnic/nationalist than religious, and the Muslims in Bosnia and Kosovo ended up welcoming the imperialists as their 'saviors'; Kashmir is a hostage to Indian-Pakistani state rivalry; and the fundamentalists free of the nationalist bug, the "pockets of obscurantist conservatism", took control in Afghanistan and continue to insinuate themselves into legitimate struggles in such places as Algeria and Mali, and now in Syria and Iraq, with little positive outcome.

These instances of conflict are inspired not so much by the intent of the Quran, but by the insurgents' hatred of their mortal enemies, the imperialists, who themselves made terrorism against civilian populations the bedrock of twentieth century totalitarian rule, making it routine. In a sense, the Bin Ladens are the dying gasp of the imperialist order, sharing the stage with their American and Saudi nemeses. The al-Qaeda types took Qutb's nineteenth century anarchist-like revolutionary strategy to a fatal extreme, and have compromised more thoughtful efforts at Islamic renewal.

In retrospect, it was premature for Siddiqui to assert that a "global Islamic movement" was already in place following the victory of the Islamic revolution in Iran and the mujahideen in Afghanistan, hailing the "emergence of political consensus amongst Muslims all over the world." Eager to move forward, he argued that, "the globalization process is now complete ... new ideas based on hard political facts and the setting of goals attainable by defined and tried methods are now setting [its] agenda."

Events since then show that Islamists are far from united:

- Most western Muslims, faced with Islamophobia, are assimilationist;
- Secularist or Muslim client rulers are able to manipulate nationalism to create a kind of Islamophobia even among the ummah;
- Neo-Wahhabi "obscurantist conservatives" working at times with the imperialists (Libya, Egypt, Syria) have served as excellent tools to block any genuine Islamic alternative;
- Stark sectarianism, however engineered, now plagues the ummah, confirmed by the ongoing mass sectarian killings of both Shia and Sunni civilians in Iraq, the persecution of Shia in Saudi Arabia and Bahrain, and the civil war in Syria. Iran's example engenders more envy than a desire to emulate it among Sunni leaders, while their fear of its influence sadly translates into suspicion of Iran and Shia.[9]

Jihadists, battle-hardened and martyred in Afghanistan, have been the unwitting tools of the Saudis and/or Americans. The same goes for Egypt's liberals, *not* the MBers languishing in Egyptian jails or teaching in Saudi universities and now demanding the restoration of the elected government. The Taliban, protégés of the Wahhabis, did more to undermine genuine Islamic renewal than to promote it through their tribalism and Salafist *taqlid*,[10] though the US invasion of Afghanistan to overthrow them only made matters worse for everyone.

As Siddiqui argued, the Iranian revolution alone was able to stop imperialism in its tracks. Thus, Iranian experience is indeed germane to the Sunni world, which will only move towards genuine independence through mass support for local Islamists across the ummah. Twentieth century experience confirms that the strategies of Egyptian and Iranian Islamic revolutionaries to

Re-assessing Strategy based on Islamic Principles

Near the end of his life, Siddiqui emphasized the study of the Sirah (life of the Prophet) and the Sunnah literature (traditions of the Prophet derived from the hadiths) as a "storehouse" of data which must be used as a basis for strategy to defeat imperialism.[11] Instead of past Sirah commentaries which are largely descriptive, he called for an analytical approach to the study of the Sirah, laying emphasis on the power dimension, exploring how the Prophet acquired power, how he used it and what the consequences of his approach were in establishing a just socio-economic political order in society.

An understanding and acceptance of the centrality of the role of political power and the need to exercise it is central to Islam; you can't relieve oppression/ injustice if you are weak. Prophet Muhammad was a brilliant political strategist, and his progress from simple trader to head of a powerful new socio-political and religious formation deserves careful consideration by his followers today. For while earlier prophets acknowledged by Judaism, Christianity and Islam also became rulers (Joseph, David, Solomon), they inherited rule from previous sovereigns. Prophet Muhammad was the first to build a political formation from scratch, providing a template for any future Islamic society.

What is the Prophet's understanding of 'power'? How did he acquire and use power? What role did military campaigns play in generating more power? How did the Prophet share power with others?

These are the questions that Siddiqui raised and that Zafar Bangash addresses in *Power Manifestations of the Sirah* (2011), where he analyzes in detail Prophet Muhammad's political writings—the *hijra* (migration), the Constitution of Medina, treaties with various tribes, letters inviting world leaders to Islam, and the Prophet's final sermon—and reflects on their relevance in today's world.

There are 250+ letters, treaties of the Prophet. The prophetic mission lasted 23 years, and the next 10 years saw the rapid triumph of Islam throughout the Arabian Peninsula, the result of careful planning, strategic alliances, and judicious use of force to neutralize the power of enemies without wholesale destruction or massacres.

Lessons from these documents include:

- A wise leader pursues not war, but 'soft power'—making treaties honoring the legitimate needs of participating constituencies. Meccan Muslims moved to Medina by invitation, not invasion, and later returned to Mecca after the Meccan chiefs violated the terms of a treaty to maintain peace and not indulge in killings. (Europeans were not invited to the New World, nor were Jews invited to colonize the Holy Land.)

- The *hijras* (to Abyssinia, Medina) were necessary both for personal safety and to propagate the message of Islam as well as, in the latter, to provide a secure base for establishing Islamic governance. In sending some of his followers to Abyssinia, Prophet Muhammad boldly wrote directly to the Negus, king of Abyssinia, asking him to provide asylum to the Muslims. The king's response indicated recognition of the germ of an Islamic state whose leader held temporal power on the level of a king even though Muhammad was at that time in Medina in exile.

- The Constitution of Medina is arguably the world's first

constitution as it established rights and rules agreed to by, and encompassing, Muslims, Jews, Christians and pagans, binding them into a society conforming to Islamic belief. It established principles such as: any believer in need is the responsibility of all other believers; Jews have equal status with Muslims; mercy is better than punishment, but punishment is also a form of mercy to 'rebalance accounts' and protect the ummah; no individual/ group can enter into separate arrangements with enemies of the state.

- The latter allowed Prophet Muhammad to make formal treaties with nearby tribes, preventing them from allying with the Quraish of Mecca, and thereby consolidating Muslim power. This culminated in the Treaty of Hudaybiya with the Quraish, where the Prophet made significant compromises to achieve his political goals, foregoing the Hajj that year but agreeing a peace treaty intended to last for 10 years. This achieved implicit recognition by the Quraish of the Muslim state in Medina, allowing the rapid expansion of Islam, temporarily forestalling further Quraishi attacks.

- Prophet Muhammad's political testament came in his final sermon during his last Hajj to Mecca, where he emphasized the cultivation of an Islamic personality, the necessity of both economic and social justice, and stressed the danger of *riba* (usury, based on greed) as opposed to *sadaqa* (charity, based on compassion).

- A revolution requires a strong, tenacious leadership, motivated by a compelling belief and compassion. Already aware of his power and authority through his divine inspiration, Prophet Muhammad told Quraishi leaders who were persecuting him early on that they would conquer the Byzantine and Persian empires if they accepted Islam. They laughed at him and drove him out of Mecca, but he returned 10 years later peacefully—though he smashed their idols—and they willingly converted en masse to Islam. And together, the Muslims conquered the Byzantine and Persian empires.

- Power must be consolidated in the hands of a just executive authority (state) to represent all factions in the body politic. Institutional injustice cannot be corrected by laws alone but by moral suasion and belief. Whereas corrupt politicians seek to amass rights and wealth for themselves and minimize their responsibilities to society, Muslims even where they are a minority have an extra responsibility to society, based on the belief that this life is a prelude to the afterlife, a journey in which a test of their faith, deeds and good works takes place. Without the fearless self-assurance that comes with submission to divine guidance, the individual as well as societies soon succumb to the corrosive influence of power and wealth. 'Power corrupts; absolute power corrupts absolutely', unless the leadership holds to the moral laws that are effectively good guidance from God. Islam regulates use of power to avoid the rich (powerful) using their advantage to exploit the weak (poor).

Looking back on the fateful period in Egypt that marked the brief rule of the Morsi government, there are many lessons to be learned by both Muslims and non-Muslims. Not cynical Machiavellian ones, but ones grounded in the Quran, which, along with the life experience of the Prophet (Sirah, Sunnah), is the basis for Muslims formulating a response to today's crises:

- The Prophet Muhammad's struggle against the Quraish

suggests that when you conduct your struggle with an intent and in a manner approved by God (as Muslims believe), a new order can be ushered in relatively peacefully. The Islamic revolution in Iran confirmed this, even in the age of empire, as did the Arab Spring in Egypt.

- Alliances with non-Muslims are necessary, but beware traitors.

- Yes, nationalism is dangerous, but it is wrong to ignore the real forces shaping people's actions, which must be harnessed.

- Sharia is essential, tied to the core principles in the Quran, interpreted in evolving circumstances, involving careful input from both scholars and the ummah. Whether this can be done without the coordinating management of an Islamic government/ state is questionable. But how such a government can be achieved remains a thorny issue for Islamists.

Endnotes

1   Hamid Algar, *The Roots of the Islamic Revolution*, UK: Open Press, 1983, 314.

2   After Siddiqui's death in 1996, Zafar Bangash succeeded him as head of the Institute of Contemporary Islamic Thought (ICIT) that replaced the Muslim Institute. The Institute was relaunched in 2009 as a more mainstream organization of intellectuals. Iqbal Siddiqui. Siddiqui's son, has launched a website to make Kalim Siddiqui's works available. <http://kalimsiddiqui.com/>

3   Kalim Siddiqui, "The Muslim Parliament of Great Britain: political innovation and adaptation", <http://kalimsiddiqui.com>, 1992.

4   Organization of Islamic Conference, set up in 1969 by Saudi Arabia. Another organization aiming at uniting the ummah is Hizb ut-Tahrir, which is considered below.

5	Salam (peace) derives from the same root as Islam (meaning submission to Allah who alone guarantees peace).
6	Siddiqui, Kalim, *Stages of Islamic Revolution*, UK: Open Press, 1996, 23.
7	James Traub, "Islamic Democrats?", *New York Times*, 29 April 2007.
8	Joshua Stacher and Samer Shehata, "The Brotherhood Goes to Parliament", *Middle East Report*, 2007.
9	Sectarianism is basically a political rather than a theological phenomenon that is deliberately stoked by certain vested interests—Saudis, Qataris, Emirates, etc., to create confusion and disunity among Muslims, especially against the Shia. It is also used by the US to keep Muslims divided and weak. A survey by Worldpublicopinion.org found that 67% of Muslims worldwide want unity, not division in their ranks.
10	Unquestioning acceptance of the legal decisions of an Islamic religious authority without knowing the basis of those decisions.
11	Kalim Siddiqui, *Political Dimensions of the Seerah*, Institute of Contemporary Islamic Thought (ICIT), 1998.

PART II

THE EXPANDING PARAMETERS OF POLITICAL ISLAM

| CHAPTER FIVE |

FROM SALAFI TO KHARIJITE

Where did Bin Laden and his followers come from, and just how representative of Muslims are they? Are they a natural development within Islam, or merely a result of blowback from the Saudi-Pakistani alliance with empire? Al-Qaeda sympathizers would say "both". Most Muslims dismiss them as unIslamic, a result of blowback, but this smacks of the same takfirism that these neo-Wahhabis indulge in—a kind of takfirism in reverse.

Both the Wahhabis and their neo-Wahhabi al-Qaeda offshoots are literalists, fundamentalists, similar to Christian and Jewish literalists, who take their sacred texts as the actual Word of God. The term Salafi is used to refer broadly to all Muslims intent on returning in some fashion to the original *ibada* (form of religious practice broadly speaking) of the Prophet Muhammad and the early Muslims, though the term now is generally reserved specifically to refer to the fundamentalists, who insist this requires emulating the dress and behavior of the Prophet as closely as possible. As with Christian fundamentalists, this literalism is also manifested in the more apocalyptic character of their belief, in al-Qaeda's desire to implode the western system *a la* USSR, to wipe out the colonial legacy (vs the gradualist mainstream Islamists).

While literalists in their reading of the Quran and in their rejection of western attire in favor of traditional dress, they nonetheless are proficient in their use of secular science and technology, and unthinkingly practice politics and economics which are far removed from the *maqasid* (goals) of the Quran, except for the formal banning of interest and a rigid adherence to their version of sharia.[1]

In his memoirs *Knights Under the Prophet's Banner: Meditations of the Jihadist Movement* (2001), Zawahiri welcomes his critics' identification of al-Qaeda with the seventh century Kharijites, citing Abdel-Rahman's[2] assertion at his trial that "Power is for Allah," and that "If these words were said in the first age [of Islam] those who said them were Khawarij. If they were said in this age, those who said them are Mujahideen."[3] Abdel-Rahman, Zawahiri and their followers see themselves as the true heirs to the Rightly Guided caliphs and the later Ibn Taymiya, fighting to preserve the purity of Islam in the face of backsliders.

They have a point, as when the Prophet died in 632, some Bedouin tribes stopped following the pillars of Islam, disputing in particular the requirement to pay zakat, and false prophets arose. Though the purity of Islam was reasserted in the Wars of Apostasy under the first Caliph, Abu Bakr,[4] the puritanical streak continued, leading to the fourth Caliph Ali's assassination. The subsequent monarchical system inaugurated after the Rightly Guided caliphs, flying in the face of tradition, was also cause for dissent, resulting in the founding of Shiism.

The 13th–14th century Mongol and Timurid invasions marked the nadir of Islamic civilization. Mongol rule again strayed far from traditional Islamic rule. Ahmad ibn Taymiya (1263–1328) challenged the Mongol hegemony, using *ijtihad* (reasoning based on the Quran), and urged Muslims to rise against the Mongols as illegitimate rulers, despite their claim to have converted to Islam. Mongol hegemony finally ended and Ibn Taymiya remains today a revered figure in Islam.

Centuries later, Abdul al-Wahhab used Taymiya to justify his nineteenth century jihad against the Ottoman rulers, in alliance with the Saud tribe. But the gates of *ijtihad* closed for the Wahhabis after the Sauds conquered the Arab Peninsula in alliance with the British, and after the decline of the British, the new ruler of the world, America, was befriended and accommodated.

However, the spirit of Wahhab/ Ibn Taymiya/ the Kharijites lived on. The Saud tribal leader, Ibn Saud (King Abdulaziz, 1876–1953), had to quell his own Salafi Ikhwan rebels, who wanted no truck with the imperialists and considered the Saud monarchy, now in league with the imperialists, illegitimate.[5] The Ikhwan were bombed out of existence by the British, and Saudi rule was able to dominate the Arabian peninsula for the next half century.

Sayyid Qutb used *ijtihad* to refashion elements of 1960s secular anti-imperialist revolutionary thought in strictly religious terms, dismissing the neo-colonial Arab regimes as un-Islamic. This neo-Wahhabi movement became popular throughout the Middle East, attracting Muslim youth disillusioned with their secular accommodationist leaders, including Nasser, especially after the 1967 defeat, as Qutb correctly identified the real enemy of Islam as the imperialists, and by association, their Wahhabi allies in Saudi Arabia and the Gulf.

Just as no one talks about "Catholic terrorism" in reference to the IRA, some feel it would be more accurate to call the terrorism emanating from the Muslim world "Qutbian terrorism",[6] and the suicide bombers as Islamo-anarchists, followers of "a western tradition of individual and pessimistic revolt for an elusive ideal world" rather than imbued with the true Quranic concept of martyrdom.[7]

Salafis' Personal Integrity

What is overlooked by critics is that even as they adopted many of the imperialists' arms and strategies (compromising the goal of renewing Islamic civilization), the personal morality of Salafis and their neo-Wahhabi offshoots is very different from that of the imperialists. In fact, that is what the rich civilizational religion is reduced to for them—imitating the Prophet's behavior as it specifically related to worship, while ignoring the societal implications of the guidance from Allah, and the wisdom of the strategies by which the Prophet spread the faith peacefully.

When serving alongside imperialism, as Bin Laden did in Afghanistan, or inadvertently furthering its objectives, like Zawahiri (by sowing confusion, promoting chaos and death primarily in the Muslim world, and blackening Islam), these leaders still build their own following through their personal moral rectitude and incorruptibility.

Bin Laden fasted (the full-day dry fast) two days a week throughout his adult life and lived with no luxuries, giving away his wealth to support individuals in need and the causes he believed in. According to Michael Scheuer, former CIA Chief of the Bin Laden Issue Station (1996–1999), Bin Laden was "pious, brave, generous, intelligent, charismatic, patient, visionary, stubborn, egalitarian, and, most of all, realistic ... wars are only won by killing."[8] He always stressed that it was the Afghans who won the war, that Arab volunteers were there to learn from the Afghans, and was grateful for Afghans' heroism and for allowing Arabs and other Muslims to play a part in their epic saga. His program was to use sharia to regulate relations and provide services, without any need for a rich lifestyle. At least initially he avoided sectarianism against Shia and Arab Christians. His personal example soon created a legend: Islam's great personalities were Muhammad, Saladin, and ... Bin Laden. As such, he became a role model for disaffected Muslims.

Most respondents in a World Public Opinion poll[9] reflect this admiration of al-Qaeda types among many Muslims, despite their overwhelming condemnation in the media. Three in ten viewed Bin Laden positively. Large majorities approve of many of al-Qaeda's principal goals (average 70%) such as: "stand up to Americans and affirm the dignity of the Islamic people," "push the US to remove its bases and its military forces from all Islamic countries," and "pressure the United States to not favor Israel." But large majorities in all countries—Indonesia 84%, Pakistan 81%, and Egypt 77%—say violence against civilians cannot be justified at all.

The personal probity and integrity of Muslim leaders who become enemies of the empire is ignored, dismissed or worse. To discredit such jihadists, the secular Algerian leaders, as an instance, were willing to resort to creating a state of terror by infiltrating the so-called Armed Islamic Groups in the 1990s and perpetrating mass false flag terror[10] both to turn the locals against the Islamists and to frighten the West into unconditionally supporting the coup makers. A similar scenario is taking shape in Egypt following the 2011 uprising and 2013 coup overthrowing the elected Islamic government, where most of the violence has been perpetrated by the security forces.

There is politico-military logic behind al-Qaeda martyrs blowing up the Khobar Towers in Riyadh in 1996 (killing 19 US military personnel), or the attack on the *USS Cole* in Aden in 2000 (killing 17 US military personnel), or other 'successful' targeting of foreign troops in Iraq and

Afghanistan, however tragic for the victims.[11] Occupation of Muslim lands by the non-Muslim imperialists calls for resistance, the exercise of the right of self-defense—as international law recognizes. There is little doubt that the Muslim world (and western anti-imperialists) respects this resistance.

The western media sensationalizes and condemns the handful of medieval beheadings by al-Qaeda types in a crude implementation of sharia, but this symbolic punishment of a handful of westerners and Muslim collaborators is a red herring. Can it truly be regarded as worse than the kind of weapons used in Vietnam or Fallujah or elsewhere, where thousands of innocent victims suffer chemical-induced incineration? Beheading is shocking, underlining the cruelty of death, a graphic example for citizens to encourage them to obey the law. It is traditional in virtually all cultures, including capitalism (France only stopped the use of the guillotine in 1977). It would be much easier just to shoot those fated to execution (and better public relations). In none of the cases of revenge justice or hostage-taking involving beheading is there systemic use of *torture* by the 'terrorists' (compare this to the Catholic inquisition and western practice both in the past and today).

The Canadian diplomat Robert Fowler,[12] for example, condemned his kidnappers, but at the same time admires them, is even at times awed by their selflessness and courage. In Fowler's 'season in hell' as a hostage in the Sahara, the hostages were treated the same as the captors treat each other. Fowler understands why they became terrorists and why simple Muslims support them: their personal asceticism, disdain for western consumerism, personal commitment to Quranic principles, desire to emulate the great leaders/followers of the past, and their bravery in contrast to the venality of the Muslim establishment. Fowler's treatment by his captors contrasts with official Saudi treatment of westerners such as William Sampson, who was arrested by Saudi police, held in solitary confinement, repeatedly tortured, and forced to sign a false confession of involvement in a bombing in Saudi Arabia.[13]

In his analysis of Yemen, Gregory Johnsen shows how al-Qaeda groups sprang from local reaction to the injustices of Yemen's corrupt dictatorship supported by the Saudis and US. In the Zanjubar 'emirate' declared in May 2011, there were a few instances of *huddud* penalties being enacted (the right hands of two teenage thieves were amputated with a sword though they were later compensated 'to start a new life'), but at the same time the rebels distributed water to families, returned stolen property, strung up electrical lines, addressing problems that the government was incapable of dealing with.[14]

Kharijite Revival

The catalysts that turned a conservative movement to revive Islam as the guiding force in society into a no-holds-barred revolutionary jihad modeled on the Kharijites came together in the 1970s:

- Anwar Sadat's open accommodation with Israel in 1979. The clause in the 1981 treaty promising a Palestinian state within five years was mere window-dressing, with the treaty seen by Muslims as Egypt abandoning the struggle to free Palestine in exchange for the return of Sinai (which was not really returned to Egyptian control, being policed by the US in consultation with Israel), and billions of dollars of 'aid' from the US.
- The early application in Egypt of Reaganomics and

Thatcherism. The empire's new neoliberal ideology promoting privatization, deregulation and the dismantling of social welfare ignored any role for Islamic entrepreneurship balanced by social protection. No longer would the Muslim states promise to fulfill even minimally the Quranic obligations to provide for social welfare, as the local elites became super-wealthy through corruption and accommodation with the West, while their economies stagnated.

- Nasser and Sadat's persecution of the MB. This drove hundreds of articulate, well-educated, activist Islamists to seek refuge in Saudi Arabia, where they taught in schools and universities, educating a generation of Saudis into Hassan Banna and Qutb's world of anti-imperialist, anti-communist jihad. They included Banna's son-in-law, Said Ramadan, Abdullah Azzam, Omar Abdel-Rahman[15] and Qutb's brother Muhammad, who wrote several textbooks for the Saudi school curriculum.[16]

- The Islamic revolution in Iran in 1979, suggesting that politicization of Muslims on the basis of Islamic ideology could lead to the overthrow of their pro-western leaders.

- The Soviet Union's occupation of Afghanistan in support of a secular socialist revolution in 1979. Communism's militant atheism made it a more egregious foe to Muslims than capitalism, and suddenly the 'lesser of the two evils' was providing a blank cheque to fund the destruction of the 'greater evil'.

Though most western analysts continue to scapegoat the neo-Wahhabis as psychopaths, Michael Scheuer, CIA Special Advisor to the Chief of the bin Laden unit from

September 2001 to November 2004, recognized the above catalysts in his book, *Imperial Hubris* (2004), noting "how easy it is for Muslims to see, hear, experience, and hate the six US policies bin Laden repeatedly refers to as anti-Muslim":[17]

- support for apostate, corrupt, and tyrannical Muslim governments.
- stationing US and other western troops on the Arabian Peninsula.
- support for Israel that keeps Palestinians in the Israelis' thrall.
- pressure on Arab energy producers to keep oil prices low.
- occupation of Iraq and Afghanistan.
- support for Russia, India, and China against their Muslim militants.

Scheuer contends that al-Qaeda is following a rational military strategy (more so than the original Kharijites, who imploded as a movement by assassinating the caliph and were oblivious to 'public opinion'), citing Clausewitz that one must strike the enemy's "center of gravity", which translates in this case into the US dollar and global empire, best symbolized by the WTC.

He argues it is not terrorism but (Ibn Taymiya-style) Islamist insurgency that is the core of the conflict in places such as Kashmir, Xinjiang, and Chechnya, which are "struggling not just for independence but against institutionalized barbarism."[18] Osama bin Laden commended Scheuer's *Imperial Hubris* in a 2007 statement, suggesting that it revealed "the reasons for your losing the war against us".

It is not reasonable to conclude that Bin Laden was a psychopath (though that is possible, just as are, many assert, many western leaders). His thinking, though extreme, was strategic and logical, recognizing that small 'terrorist' acts were like pinpricks, capable of inciting the US to invade Muslim countries (some governed by secularists such as Saddam Hussein), and encouraging Muslims to commit collectively to jihad (*fard kifaya*) for world liberation (not conquest), led by a committed core of believers willing to sacrifice their lives.

Internationalizing Jihad

If a Muslim is living in *dar al-harb* where it is impossible to follow sharia law, Ibn Taymiya affirms, then they must emigrate, emulating the early Muslims' hijra. In the early 1970s, the Egyptian *Takfir wa al-hijra* (unbelief and emigration) was organized, advocating that religious persons withdraw from the world because so many sinful Muslims had abandoned their faith. But this smacked of Christian monasticism, which was explicitly forbidden in the Quran. In any case, genuine *hijra* was no longer possible under imperialism, where the entire Muslim world was under the rule of kuffar. Sadat's Egypt was at peace with Israel, even as Israel was killing and dispossessing Palestinians, in violation of sharia, making Egyptian politicians the enemy as well. Where was a good Muslim to go?

The Wahhabi argument for armed jihad against kuffar leaders, updated by Qutb, attracted those fed up with their worsening situation.[19] Distant Iran responded at the time to the Iranian version of these problems (the Shah had long been a tacit supporter of Israel, and US economic policy was the order of the day) with a full-fledged Islamic revolution. However, the Arab world was much more deeply incorporated into the neocolonial order than Iran, though jihad was in the air. The officially atheist Soviets became a target that everyone could agree on, bringing all into a common effort—Wahhabis, Salafis, neo-Wahhabis, accommodationists, traditionalists, backed initially by the US, Saudi Arabia and Egypt, and soon joined by China and Israel. The newly Islamic Iran was fighting for its own survival in the 1980s against the US-backed Iraqi invasion, and was not a significant player in the Afghanistan resistance.[20]

The US thus managed to 'kill two birds with one stone' in the 1980s: encouraging both Saddam Hussein's war against Iran (keeping the ummah divided), and the mujahideen's jihad against the Soviet Union (keeping Iran out of the process of resolution of the conflict).

The neo-Wahhabi mujahideen/ terrorists/ what-have-you were suddenly the heroes of the day, feted by Reagan in the White House as "freedom fighters",[21] and found their follow-up to the charismatic Qutb in the guise of Saudi millionaire ex-business administration student, Osama Bin Laden, who established al-Qaeda in 1988,[22] threw scholarly caution to the winds and began to issue fatwas, using videos and later the internet.

Young idealistic Saudis flocked to his call for jihad. Saudi intelligence guessed 15,000 Saudi youths trained in Afghanistan (probably fewer). What to do with these battle-hardened jihadists after the 'liberation' of Afghanistan then became a serious problem. Referring to ISIS/IS, Hamas leader Ahmed Youssef explains: "The US used to call the Afghans who fought the Soviet Union mujahideen, but when they started fighting against America, they became terrorists."[23]

There was no easy way out. Saudi counter-terrorism differed sharply from that of the West—the terrorists were allowed to return to Saudi Arabia, where they were interrogated and for the most part were released, with efforts made to "rehabilitate" them through employment and other compensations. Other countries did not let the fighters return, so they became a stateless, vagrant group of religious mercenaries, experienced in the ways of air travel, fighting both for cause and pay, with many staying in Pakistan and integrating, some going to fight in Kashmir, Kosovo, Bosnia, Chechnya and other centers of unrest.

What looked like a clever two-pronged strategy to shape the region had unforeseen blowback by opening the path for thousands of committed Islamists to fly hither and yon in the pursuit of their goals (which continued to evolve in response to circumstances). Even as the hoped-for re-emergence of Islamic civilization via this road of terror failed to materialize and imperialist oppression continued, indeed worsened, the now legendary organization continued to attract disaffected youth.

Retail Terrorism:[24] Suicide Bombers, Hijackers, Kidnappers

In the eighteenth century, Britain considered US rebels to be terrorists. The American colonists considered Britain to be the imperial oppressor carrying out terrorist acts. Not all armed resistance is to be condemned, as international law admits. And as noted above, there is nothing peculiarly Islamic about armed resistance against invaders and martyrdom in the cause of religion.

The most sensational terrorist act now associated with the Muslim world is suicide bombing. The first Muslim suicide bombing (the Hindu Tamils in Sri Lanka first 'popularized' the tactic) was during the Lebanese civil war. The Shia bombing in Beirut that killed 299 US marines and French forces in 1983 was motivated by US-French support for Israel's invasion of Lebanon. It succeeded in prompting the US to evacuate, but by no means in ending the civil war or Israeli occupation. Palestinian suicide bombings in Israel in the 1990s–2000s shocked the world, bringing the reality of the occupation into western homes, though again their actions did not end the occupation, or succeed in engaging the sympathies of the broad western publics for their cause. Today, Afghan martyrs kill occupation troops almost daily. While they do not succeed in ending the occupation, they do succeed in forcing the occupiers to abandon their long term plans to subdue the country. These tragic acts are justified by the right of self-defense against attacks on Islam and threats to life, as confirmed by Islamic scholars such as Yusuf al-Qaradawi, though he condones them only within the Occupied Territories.[25]

Al-Qaeda and then Taliban and Iraqi Sunnis took this martyrdom to a new level from 1998 on with suicide bombings (the US embassy bombings in Tanzania and Kenya) killing largely civilians in large numbers, with no clear goal beyond creating chaos and fear among the occupiers and those cooperating with the occupiers, acts which were universally condemned in the Muslim world.

Such suicide bombings should not be confused with politically-motivated hostage-taking where the intent is to force officials to comply with justifiable demands, though at considerable risk to the lives of innocent civilians as well as to the lives and cause of the perpetrators. Like suicide bombings, hostage-taking must be considered in context. There have been very few after the spate of airplanes successfully hijacked by Palestinians as hostage-taking operations up to the early 1970s. The best known hijackings prior to 9/11 were by Palestinian Leila Khaled in 1969 and 1970 which did not result in any deaths.[26] Was she a terrorist? In a *Guardian* interview shortly after 9/11, she said: "Whenever I hear this word I ask another question.

Who planted terrorism in our area? Some came and took our land, forced us to leave, forced us to live in camps. I think this is terrorism. Using means to resist this terrorism and stop its effects—this is called struggle."[27]

Consider the hostage-takings by Palestinians at the 1972 Munich Olympics, by the Chechens at a Moscow theater in 2002, the Gilad Shalit affair in Gaza in 2006, and the Algerian In Amenas gas plant incident in 2013. Only the Shalit affair entailed a successful negotiation (due to the overriding Israeli concern for the safety of Shalit) resulting in the freeing of at least 450 Palestinian political prisoners. The others ended in the 'rescuers' massacring both perpetrators and hostages, with the death toll then sensationalized in the media, doing great harm to the cause of the hostage-takers, even though the rescuers were the perpetrators of the slaughter. Hostage-taking is in fact a common occurrence around the world for purely monetary motives by run-of-the-mill criminals, so the few high-profile instances perpetrated by 'terrorists' must be judged in context and according to the likelihood of their 'success'—and their results.

Whether or not 19 al-Qaeda members (15 Saudis) hijacked the planes on 9/11 (with every intent to kill civilians, and no intent of exchanging hostages or for ransom), and despite their intention to emulate the Prophet in their personal morality, the tactics of the wannabe Bin Ladens were shaped by their western occupiers in ways that diverged from Islam. Leila Khaled is no follower of Bin Laden.

Endnotes

1 Wahhabis participate in the global economy on the imperialists' terms. Neo-Wahhabis use anarchist-type violence, using modern technology.
2 The Egyptian Islamic Society's 'Blind Sheikh' Omar Abdel-Rahman

(b. 1938), convicted in the 1993 World Trade Center bombing and sentenced to life imprisonment in January 2015.

3   Ayman al-Zawahiri, *Knights Under the Prophet's Banner: Meditations of the Jihadist Movement*, 2001, 50. The followers of Wahhab were from the start identified with the Kharijites (by eighteenth century Hanafi scholar Ibn Abidin).

4   Note ISIS leader Ibrahim Awwad Ibrahim Ali al-Badri al-Samarrai took the name Abu Bakr al-Baghdad.

5   See Chapter 11 below.

6   Karen Armstrong, "The Label of Catholic Terror was never used about the IRA", *Guardian*, 11 July 2005.

7   Olivier Roy *Globalised Islam*, 44.

8   Scheuer, *Bin Laden*, ix.

9   WorldPublicOpinion.org, April 2007. <http://www.worldpublicopinion.org/ pipa/articles/brmiddleeastnafricara/346.php >

10 False flag referring to a sabotage operation supposedly carried out by the resistance forces, but in fact by infiltrated agents of the empire to discredit resistance forces. The CIA's Operation Northwoods and NATO's Operation Gladio are perhaps the most famous. Also Israel's Lavon affair in Egypt in the 1954. See Walberg, *Postmodern Imperialism*, 225.

11 These attacks stand in stark contrast with the US policy of "targeted killing" via drones, which have killed thousands of civilians. This violates the 1907 Hague Convention and the Geneva Conventions of 1949, which call for all feasible precautions to ensure the target is military and that the method used to attack it should not inflict excessive civilian harm. "Violence and the Use of Force" The International Committee of the Red Cross, 2011.

12 Robert Fowler, *A Season in Hell: My 130 Days in the Sahara with al-Qaeda*, HarperCollins, 2011. UN Secretary General Ban Ki-moon appointed Fowler to be his Special Envoy to Niger, with the rank of Under-Secretary-General in the Secretariat of the UN in 2008. In December 2008 he was kidnapped in Niger, after visiting the Canadian-owned Samira Hill Gold Mine. The kidnappers showed them western atrocities, "our side's methodically applied, officially sanctioned, and so casually administered barbarity, parsed into the bureaucratic banalities and legal niceties of officially sanctioned abuse and torture... If we were capable of such outrages, then we had indeed strayed into truly dangerous ethical territory" p57 Fowler criticizes the post 9/11 West for "perverting the law and sullying the reputation of our friends and neighbours—perversions that have done and continue to do the West incalculable harm throughout the world... [We are] guilty by such

association. And Louis (Guay) and I were reaping the consequences." P58

Fowler was impressed by the kidnappers' "absolute commitment to what they perceived to be [Islam's] fundamental principles, including jihad—to which a growing number of Muslims refer as the "Sixth Pillar of Islam". ... their viciousness appeared to be neither arbitrary nor casual. Their every act was considered and needed to be justifiable in terms of their chosen path of jihad." p150. He was intrigued by "the utter irrelevance of time to our captors" which he realized "was a cultural hurdle. Time is the enemy of western societies. We want everything right now... aggressively determined to ignore the imperatives of time-imposed realities (aging, health, education, books, food...) always preferring entertainment to knowledge, appreciation and understanding later. ... [He noted] the profound conviction of our abductors that time was on their side." p154. This was a "no-holds-barred jihad but [they] did not steal cookies" from relief packages sent from Burkina Faso and Mali presidents. It was "at that point that I really appreciated the depth and the single-mindedness of their commitment to jihad and the breadth of the cultural gap between us." p191. "'Democracy' my kidnappers insisted, in part because of their perception of our fickle attachment to it, is 'your religion'. 'You love democracy when it suits you." Fowler agrees that the West misuses its democracy propaganda, supporting the overthrow of democracy in Algeria in 1992, and rejecting the election of Hamas in occupied Palestine in 2006.

Fowler admired and befriended several of his captors. He is convinced al-Qaeda will continue, that many young recruits will continue to commit themselves, not concerned with long life (their options in the Muslim world are bleak), but rather authenticity and martyrdom. Fowler clearly admired the kidnappers' leader Mukhtar Belmokhtar (who lost an eye in Afghanistan), a leader of Al-Qaeda in the Maghreb, and his colleague Al-Jabbar, and had nothing but scorn for the Canadian and American governments. In December 2012, Belmokhtar set up his own organization, Al-Mulathameen ("Masked") Brigade.

13   He and eight other westerns were finally released in 2003 after almost three years. He was so traumatized that he eventually committed suicide. William Sampson, *Confessions of an Innocent Man: Torture and Survival in a Saudi Prison*, McClelland & Stewart, 2005.

14   Gregory Johnsen, *The Last Refuge: Yemen, al-Qaeda, and America's War in Arabia*, Norton, 2013.

15   See endnote 81.

16   Trevor Stanley, "Understanding the Origins of Wahhabism and

	Salafism", *Terrorism Monitor* Volume 3 Issue 14, *jamestown.org*, 15 July 2005.
17	Michael Scheuer, *Imperial Hubris: Why the West is Losing the War on Terror*, USA: Potomac, 2004, 241.
18	Similar to the European resistance movements during WWII. Ibid., 253.
19	This reasoning ironically convinced many Muslims that it was fine to emigrate to the Christian/Jewish West in search of a higher standard of living, as the Muslim world was occupied by the West in any case. As the war against Islam ramped up, this put them on the front line and resulted in some turning to terrorism, others to greater efforts to assimilate under heightened Islamophobia.
20	Iran sponsored the "Tehran Eight", Hazar resistance fighters, which was independent of the main Sunni coalition, the "Peshawar Seven".
21	Walberg, *Postmodern Imperialism*, 89.
22	Peter Bergen, *The Osama bin Laden I Know: An Oral History of al Qaeda's Leader,* New York: Free Press, 2006.
23	Asmaa al-Ghoul, "Why won't Hamas label Islamic State as terrorists?", *Almonitor*, December 2014. http://www.al-monitor.com/pulse/originals/2014/12/hamas-islamic-state-gaza-terrorist-attacks.html
24	"It is widely believed that "terrorism" is the instrument of the weak, who resort to it out of frustration at their perceived mistreatment and inability to obtain relief by peaceful means. This is a serious mistake. Terrorism is mainly an instrument of the strong, who have the resources to terrorize, a frequent interest in using terror to keep opponents of their rule under control, and the cultural power to define terrorism to exclude themselves and pin the label on their enemies and targets. These targets, successfully named "terrorists", are frequently the victims of really serious terrorism, which has induced their own lesser terrorist response... This primary terrorism can also be called "wholesale terrorism", as it is on a large scale, in contrast with the ANC's terrorism, which we may call "retail terrorism" as it was carried out by a small and poorly armed group and on a relatively modest scale, and, in this instance, was induced by the primary and wholesale terrorism." Edward S. Herman, "The Semantics of Terrorism," *Global Dialogue* Volume 2, Number 4, Autumn 2000. http://www.worlddialogue.org/content.php?id=108
25	Magdi Abdelhadi, "Profile of Sheikh Yusuf Qaradawi", *BBC News*, 7 July 2004.
26	She was released in exchange for western hostages of the PFLP (Popular Front for the Liberation of Palestine).
27	'I made the ring from a bullet and the pin of a hand grenade', *Guardian* January 26 2001

| CHAPTER SIX |

AZZAM: VIOLENCE AGAINST INVADERS

The year 1979 transformed the militant Islamic movement, which gained momentum following the 1967 victory of Israel and its 1981 peace treaty with Egypt. The Iranian revolution and the Soviet occupation of Afghanistan electrified the Muslim world. The struggle to liberate Afghanistan became an inspiration for all Muslims, one that could be supported by both sincere Muslims and corrupt Arab governments, both secularists and those who claimed to be Islamic. Even as the Soviet Union faltered, the 1979 Iranian revolution seemed to offer an Islamic equivalent of the Russian revolution—a revolution against the capitalist-imperialist system, refusing both assimilation into the empire and an evolutionary road of resistance within the neocolonial system. At the time, Afghanistan seemed to be a textbook case of a war of liberation, soon to be followed by Chechnya, Bosnia, and Kosovo. For Muslims inured to secular socialism, the simultaneous 'collapse' of socialism and re-emergence of Islam seemed to herald a new revolutionary politics, where there was no need for working within the neocolonial system.

Immediately after the Soviet Union invaded Afghanistan in 1979, the "Father of Global Jihad", the Palestinian Sheikh Abdullah Yusuf Azzam (1941–1989) issued a fatwa, "Defense of the Muslim Lands, the First Obligation after Faith", declaring that both the Afghan and Palestinian struggles were jihads in which killing occupiers of Muslim land (no matter what the occupiers' faith) was *fard ayn* (a personal obligation) for all Muslims, not just *fard kifaya* (a collective religious obligation). Muslims were called to travel to Pakistan-Afghanistan and become active combatants. The edict was supported by Saudi Arabia's Grand Mufti Abd al-Aziz Bin Bazz, Saudi Arabia's highest religious authority.

Azzam criticized Palestinians for accepting support from the Soviet Union, putting the Palestinians' fate in the hands of the great powers. He argued that Afghanistan heralded a new stage in the renewal of Islamic civilization, that the incipient civil war in Afghanistan showed that Afghans had refused help from any disbelievers. Afghanistan also had the advantage of being remote from the center of imperial intrigues in the Middle East, so it was possible to establish a Sunni Islamic state there as the launching pad for further action.

Azzam became a catalyst for Muslims, attracting both the Wahhabi Saudi and Pakistani establishment, the neo-Wahhabi Saudi revolutionaries such as Bin Laden, and traditionalists such as the Muslim Brotherhood who had earlier rejected the Qutbian call to armed revolution. Azzam's ringing message even allowed an uneasy alliance of Wahhabis and Iranians, despite the Sunni fundamentalist tradition of intolerance of Shia. He rejected using the money raised for Afghan resistance to train for terrorism and forbade killing civilians in terror attacks. For a while, for Muslims, things looked starkly black and white: Soviet bad guys, mujahideen good guys.

However Azzam was not being entirely honest in his assessment of the war in Afghanistan, as from the start it was a US-planned, financed and armed counterinsurgency. And his disdain for Soviet support of the Palestinians smacks of 'biting the hand that feeds'—Soviet support came with far fewer strings attached than did that of imperialism, as Soviet socialism had no internal economic actors which pressed to exact tribute. Rather Soviet geopolitical interests lay in the defeat of imperialism, which coincided with the interests of anti-imperialists everywhere.

However, traditionalists could hardly be blamed for rejecting the Soviet secularist path, which had accumulated a nasty legacy by this point for its persecution of religion, and was unacceptable to believers due to its denial of God. Azzam's fatwa was viewed as uncontroversial, acceptable to all sides—from the corrupt Saudi Wahhabis to the revolutionary neo-Wahhabis. Even the US and Israel were onside with the Islamic element, as it not only galvanized Afghani resistance to the Soviet Union, whose defeat would weaken the Palestinians, but also deflected jihadist energies away from the Middle East, reinforcing the status quo there—or so they reasoned. Azzam found himself riding a tidal wave of jihad, which continued to grow after his assassination in 1989, inspired by events of that fateful 1979—the Iranian revolution, the invasion of Afghanistan, the peace treaty between Egypt and Israel, the siege of the Kaaba—that together gave meaning to Azzam's fatwa.

But a US-led anti-Soviet movement in Afghanistan was already underway—the US and its 'Muslim allies', which included the very different governments in Saudi Arabia, Pakistan and Egypt, were already supporting the Afghan opposition in Afghanistan, relishing the prospects of a Soviet 'Vietnam'. And the geopolitical contexts of Palestine and Afghanistan were starkly different—there is no one-size-fits-all answer to the situations Muslims face in the era of imperialism. Azzam's ringing call was refashioned in ways alien to Islam, ways that had much more to do with a gut reaction to imperialism than with Islam.

Azzam was the first prominent Arab to actively support a jihad by the world's Muslims in Afghanistan, issuing his fatwa immediately after the Soviet invasion, going to teach at International Islamic University in Islamabad and then moving to Peshawar, where in 1984 he founded the Maktab al-Khidamat (Office of Services, MAK) along with Bin Laden to channel funds to Afghan jihadists, and also co-founded the Palestinian Hamas at the same time. His "Join the Caravan" tract (1987) was an appeal for Muslims to establish "a solid foundation as a base for Islam" in Afghanistan by expelling the Russian invaders of this Muslim land. From its victory in Afghanistan, jihad would liberate Muslim land (or areas where Muslims formed a majority as in the case of Mindanao in the Philippines, or formerly Muslim lands in the case of Spain) ruled by unbelievers. The first targets, along with Palestine, were the southern Soviet Republics of Central Asia and the Caucasus, Bosnia, the Philippines, Kashmir, Somalia and Eritrea. Azzam planned to train brigades of Hamas fighters in Afghanistan, who would then return to carry on the battle against Israel.

The Afghan resistance leaders were disdainful of the Arab pilgrims, who were ineffectual as fighters, and were in turn disdainful of the Afghans. However, the Arabs were tolerated as they provided funds and arms. Azzam argued against Arab brigades, insisting that Arabs integrate with the Afghan resistance, but he was overruled by Bin Laden. Given the intrigues and discord in the resistance, presided over by Pakistan, his assassination seems foreordained in retrospect. He had become inconvenient to all sides (except the beleaguered Massoud, isolated in the Panshir mountains, whom Azzam saw as the best of the Afghan rebel leaders[1]).

With the assassination of the unifying figure of the jihad in 1989, things really began to go off-track. Saddam Hussein's invasion of Kuwait shattered the fragile coalition of Muslim leaders, revolutionaries, and their US patrons. Bin Laden became the successor to Azzam. [2]

Endnotes

1. See endnote 126 re Massoud. Azzam "flatteringly compared Massoud to Napoleon." Osama bin Laden sided with Hekmatyar, alienating his mentor Azzam. Steve Coll, *Ghost Wars*, 2004.
2. Azzam did not embrace the Kharijite analogy. Zawahiri's identification with the Kharijites underlines the sharp difference in their thinking "The concept of Jihadism espoused by Abdullah Azzam often appears diametrically opposed to the actions mascarading as Jihad under the guise of Global Jihadism today." in Andrew Hoskins et al, *Radicalization and the Media: Connectivity and Terrorism in the New Media*, Routledge, 2011

| Chapter Seven |

BIN LADEN: VIOLENCE AGAINST THE IMPERIAL CENTER

Early Life

The dean of the terrorists, Osama Bin Laden (1957–2011), a Saudi-born Yemeni, studied economics and business administration at King Abdulaziz University and inherited an estimated $300m in 1967.[1] The charismatic 22-year-old Osama bin Laden joined what he may at least initially have been unaware was a US-sponsored jihad, initially following Azzam's agenda to liberate Muslim lands from foreign occupation, and personally recruiting 4,000 volunteers from his own country. While the US channelled funds and arms through Pakistan's Inter-Services Intelligence (ISI) to Azzam and Bin Laden's Office of Services, the CIA insists "they had no direct link to bin Laden," despite Reagan's frequent praise for mujahideen as Afghanistan's "freedom fighters".[2]

Bin Laden returned to his homeland in 1990, hailed in the Saudi media as a hero of jihad, who along with his Arab legion, "had brought down the mighty superpower" of the Soviet Union. But even as it preened itself on its role in the defeat of communism, the Saudi monarchy was suddenly put at risk by Saddam Hussein's Arab nationalism, with his lightening invasion of Kuwait in August 1990. And Bin Laden was no comfort. His proposal to King Fahd that he (Bin Laden) lead another jihad, this time against Saddam Hussein, to 'liberate' Kuwait was met with 'shock and awe'. As Saudis, both Bin Laden and King Fahd loathed and feared Saddam Hussein, as a potential Wahhabi nemesis. But it was also clear that Bin Laden had no intention of ever buckling to the Saudi monarchy. Bin Laden conceivably viewed himself as the new Wahhab or perhaps mahdi, destined to carry the Wahhabi project to its logical conclusion, absent the Saudi monarchy.

In fact, the monarchy was doubly shocked when it tried to mobilize the Arab world against the Iraqi dictator and discovered that—in that particular context—most Arabs supported Saddam Hussein, including the governments of the Palestinians, Sudan, Algeria, Libya, Tunisia, Yemen and Jordan. Secular Syria, the Saudis' enemy (but also Saddam's enemy), Egypt, Pakistan and Bangladesh were their only major Muslim country 'allies'—along with the US and Europe. It required all Saudi efforts to pass a number of Arab League resolutions condemning the invasion and reaffirming Kuwait's sovereignty, but they were unable to mobilize member nations under a pact for its defense. To the shame of devout Muslims everywhere, the Saudis proceeded to invite a half million US and NATO troops onto Saudi soil to launch the invasion.[3] Whether or not it succeeded in defeating Saddam Hussein, the Bin Laden option would have meant the end of the Saudi monarchy. For Bin Laden, that was the next—third—step (after the 'liberation' of Afghanistan and Iraq) in the liberation of the entire Muslim world, inspired by the Saudis' very own Wahhabi fundamentalist Islam.

Fahd realized that further empowering the charismatic Bin Laden and abandoning Saudi Arabia's place in the US empire would mean the end of the (corrupt) monarchy. In any case, the ragtag mujahideen would be no match for what was billed by US advisers as a massive Iraqi army, which supposedly could 'easily' march from Kuwait into Riyadh, where Saddam Hussein would presumably set up a client regime and then control most of the world's best oil resources. Of course, the Saudi fears reflected not a genuine threat of invasion from Iraq, but their own insecurity as less-than-legitimate leaders, who could be overthrown not so much by what was in actuality a ragtag Iraqi army, but by a zealous core of jihadists led by the charismatic Bin Laden. Even if Fahd had wanted to flirt with Bin Laden's fantasy, the US would never have allowed either scenario, and would itself have moved unilaterally to occupy the Saudi oil fields—a plan that was prepared and even hinted at earlier in 1975 by Kissinger.[4]

Bin Laden's offer to King Fahd was probably a necessary maneuver in order to allow him to wash his hands of the monarchy, to show to the ummah that by allowing the presence of foreign troops in the 'land of the two Holy Mosques',[5] the monarchy had forfeited its claim to legitimacy as protector of the Muslim holy places.

From Sudan to Afghanistan

Bin Laden fled into exile in Sudan in 1992, now determined, like his newly energized, battle-hardened comrades across the world, to overthrow all the pseudo-Muslim rulers who were playing along with the imperialists, despite their claims to support the liberation of Palestine. He had founded al-Qaeda (the foundation) in 1988, initially focused on driving the Soviets from Afghanistan, but later saw it as a vehicle to rid all Muslim lands—including Saudi Arabia—of imperialist occupation.

Even as al-Qaeda, with its revolutionary strategy of defeating the empireS (both the US and Soviet Union), gathered steam throughout the 1980s–90s, attempts were already underway at fashioning Islamic states—Iran, Sudan and Pakistan—though only Iran succeeded in its attempt at a clean break with the imperialists politically. Sudan for a short period served as a haven for 'terrorists', including Bin Laden, Egyptian Islamic Society and Egyptian Islamic Jihad, Libyan and Palestinian (Hamas) opposition groups, Abu Nidal,[6] and Carlos the Jackal.[7] The Jamal al-Nimeiri dictatorship styled itself as Islamic, which was reinforced with Omar al-Bashir's coup in 1989.

Islamic scholar (and former graduate student at Sorbonne and University of London) Hasan al-Turabi (b. 1932) was trying to implement sharia in Sudan as minister of justice, but was no Wahhabi or neo-Wahhabi. An advocate of greater women's rights, art/ music, and an end to the Sunni-Shia conflict, he was clearly swept up in the new vision of re-emerging Islamic civilization and was initially receptive to Bin Laden's plans to foment revolution, though Bin Laden was disdainful of him (just as he was disdainful of the fractious Afghan factions and the subsequent Taliban consolidation of power around its rigid fundamentalist interpretation of Islam).

However, Sudan in the 1990s was hardly the place to rebuild Islamic civilization, with its heavy colonial legacy, followed by almost constant civil war between north, south and west ever since. As an 'Islamic state', it was spurned by the global empire, and welcomed Bin Laden less for his plans of world revolution than for his millions of petrodollars as an heir to the Saudi Binladin Group. Initially Bin Laden supported the notorious Armed Islamic Groups in the ongoing civil war in Algeria, an al-Qaeda emissary bringing them $40,000 after the coup, but as the slaughter of civilians grew (much of which was only later to be revealed as false flag acts by the government and blamed on the Islamic resistance), Bin Laden withdrew his support. Notably, Bin Laden also spoke with Shia militants and suggested training his own fighters with Hizbullah, though nothing came of this. He was particularly concerned with using to advantage his ace—expatriate Arabs scattered around the West (France, Spain, US, Lebanese in Kuwait, Yemenis in Saudi), who had experience in the West, no strong nationalism, and might, as potential martyrs, be willing to work towards his pan-Islamic goals. Bin Laden indeed bought land, built up various economic enterprises (and of course training camps), but the $20–150m which he brought were a drop in the bucket.

When he was cut off from his inheritance by the Saudi government and his brothers in 1994, so was his estimated $1m/yr income, leaving Sudan willing to offer him up to the Saudis or Americans in 1996 before finally sending him to the one country which would take him—Afghanistan. Though US sources deny they were ever offered Bin Laden's head, evidence supports the Sudanese claim that they were willing to hand him over. After all, they had allowed French intelligence to kidnap Carlos the Jackal in 1994.

Reaching America

This Enlightenment-like jihad, once lauded and funded by Reagan as a fight for (secular, capitalist) 'freedom', reached the shores of America with the World Trade Center bombing of 1993, for which Pakistani Ramzi Yousef[8] was responsible. The Egyptian Islamic Society's 'Blind Sheikh' Omar Abdel-Rahman was found complicit in the attack, based on an FBI recording of him issuing a fatwa encouraging acts of violence against US civilian targets. Both are now serving life sentences in the US.

Earlier, Abdel-Rahman had issued a fatwa which allegedly inspired the 1981 assassination of Anwar Sadat by Egyptian Islamic Jihad. He was expelled from Egypt following his acquittal on such charges, and made his way to Afghanistan in the mid-1980s where he contacted Azzam and Bin Laden. He built a strong rapport with Bin Laden during the Soviet war in Afghanistan, and following Azzam's murder in 1989, despite his serious physical shortcomings and high profile, was charged in his US trial with having assumed control of the international jihadist arm of Azzam's Office of Services (MAK) and Bin Laden's al-Qaeda. Supposedly with a view to gaining control of MAK's financial and organizational infrastructure in the United States, he relocated to New York (via Saudi Arabia) in 1990 on a tourist visa issued by the US consulate in Khartoum. Despite his name being listed on a US State Department terrorist watch list, he obtained a green card, becoming a permanent resident and later a political refugee from pursuit by Mubarak's Egypt. While in the US, he preached fiery sermons condoning civilian deaths in terrorist acts which were taped and sent to his followers in Egypt.

It is argued that the Egyptian Islamic Society, responsible for the November 1997 Luxor massacre, in which 58 foreign tourists and four Egyptians were killed), is a spin-off of the Muslim Brotherhood.[9] But the truth of the matter is rather the opposite. When Sadat lifted restrictions on Islamic activists in the 1970s and at the same time made peace with Israel, this resulted in the creation of new militant groups (the Islamic Society and Islamic Jihad) intent on undoing this policy of appeasement. Thus, these groups were rather a spin-off of Sadat's peace accord with Israel and the US-sponsored 'jihad' in Afghanistan (just as jihadist groups that have arisen after the Egyptian coup in 2013 are a spin-off of the coup, not the MB). As the MB reconstituted itself in the 1980s–1990s, it especially attracted students from the Islamic Society, but not the more 'revolutionary' tendency reflected in these Islamic groups, who criticized the MB as passé.

From 1993 on, the US turned against all jihadists, but there remained other jihadist mentors (Saudi Arabia, Gulf states and Pakistan) who had their own interests to pursue. Jihadists became pawns in a geopolitical game. The situation in Kashmir led Pakistan to continue to support jihadists as part of its own strategy vis-à-vis India, contrary to US wishes. To Pakistani generals, Kashmir was more an issue of Pakistani nationalism, or what might be regarded as ethnic Muslim nationalism. They were happy to let jihadists remain in the Afghanistan/ Pakistan border region to train and attack Indian forces in Kashmir, despite pressure by the US. The US even considered labelling Pakistan a terrorist supporter.

The Afghans at best tolerated the Arab jihadists for their access to Saudi/ Pakistani funds and arms. When the Taliban consolidated power in the Islamic Emirate of Afghanistan in 1996, Bin Laden promised to continue supporting them. Thus arose the alliance of convenience of Bin Laden-Taliban-Pakistan, capitalizing on Bin Laden's forced exile, and Pakistan's need for camps in Afghanistan to train fighters for the ongoing insurgency in Kashmir. Bin Laden supported the struggle in Kashmir and the Taliban against Massoud, Rabbani and other mujahideen factions,[10] culminating in his 1998 fatwa (Jihad against Jews and Crusaders, issued jointly with Zawahiri) and the Tanzania/ Kenya US embassy bombings, the first 'successful' attack on primarily innocent civilians.[11]

Bin Laden's Fatwas

Bin Laden's developing strategy is embodied in

two fatwas he issued. (Though well-versed in Islamic jurisprudence, he was not qualified as an Islamic scholar and had no right to issue fatwas):

- The **1996 fatwa** entitled "Declaration of War against the Americans Occupying the Land of the Two Holy Places", calling for jihad against US forces to drive them out of Saudi Arabia.[12]
- The **1998 fatwa** entitled "World Islamic Front for Jihad Against Jews and Crusaders"[13], which provided religious authorization for indiscriminate killing of Americans and Jews everywhere, in response to the US-Israeli occupation of the Middle East.

After he was expelled from Saudi Arabia in 1992, Bin Laden was committed to overthrowing the Saudi monarchy, following the argument of Palestinian Abu Muhammad al-Maqdisi (b. 1959, imprisoned in Jordan and released in 2014). In *The Evident Sacrilege of the Saudi State* (c. 1993), Maqdisi used the Wahhabi doctrine that Muslims showing loyalty to polytheists become like them and are thus kuffar, to denounce the Saudi rulers who had invited US troops onto the sacred Arabian lands in 1990 to attack another Muslim nation, Iraq. This reasoning made both Saudi rulers and US troops fair game (though still not innocent civilians, for which there is no justification in Islam).[14]

By taking Azzam's ringing call to expel kuffars from Muslim lands into the kuffar imperial center, and Abdel-Rahman's purported promotion of high-visibility symbolic acts of terrorism in the imperial center, Bin Laden was implicitly acknowledging that all lands in the era of globalization are *dar al-harb*, and that innocent bystanders, non-Muslim and Muslim alike, are fair game. In his "letter to the American people" of November 2002,[15] he states that "whoever has killed our civilians, then we have the right to kill theirs."

Bin Laden was a hot potato and neither the Saudis nor Americans knew what to do with him. Clinton bombed a pharmaceutical factory in 1998 to punish Sudan for its ties with al-Qaeda and lobbed a few (useless but expensive) cruise missiles at Bin Laden's training camp in the Afghan mountains. The US finally demanded his extradition from Afghanistan in 1999 in connection with the US embassy bombings in Tanzania and Kenya in 1998, but the Taliban were fresh from consolidating power as an Islamic Emirate, and said there was not enough evidence against Bin Laden, and in any case, a non-Islamic court couldn't try a Muslim. In October 2001, after a week of US bombing, they offered to give up Bin Laden to a third country if shown evidence of his responsibility for 9/11, but this was too little, too late for Bush.

At the same time as he was developing his new philosophy of jihad, despite reservations about the Taliban, Bin Laden ensured that they stayed onside—he had nowhere else to go—by working with Afghan scholars, who issued a fatwa in May 1998 which also argued that attacks against American civilians could be justified. (Note this was three months before the US embassy bombings.)

Bin Laden also pledged fealty to Taliban leader Mullah Omar shortly after the embassy bombings, abandoning any pretence at neutrality in Afghanistan's civil war, stating "We consider you to be our noble emir. We invite all Muslims to render assistance and cooperation to you." When Saudi intelligence chief, Prince Turki al-Faisal, accompanied by Pakistani General Naseem Rana, head of ISI, came to Afghanistan to demand Bin Laden's extradition, Omar angrily told them that Bin Laden is doing what Saudis should be doing. "You should put your hand in ours and his, and fight against the infidels," he told them, calling Saudi Arabia "an occupied country". Turki abruptly left, warning him that he would be sorry, effectively threatening a US invasion.

Endnotes

1 An heir to the Saudi Binladin Group (SBG) multinational construction conglomerate headquartered in Jeddah, Saudi Arabia, the largest construction firm in the world, Saudi Binladin Group, founded in 1931 by Sheikh Mohammed bin Laden Sayyid, whose relationship with the country's founder, Abdel Aziz al Saud, led to important government contracts such as refurbishing the mosques at Mecca and Medina. Mohammed overall had 22 wives (including ex-wives) and 53 children. After the death of Sheikh Mohammed in 1968 in a plane crash, the group was headed by Mohammed Bahareth, brother of Mohammed's first wife. In 1972, Salem bin Laden (1946–1988), the eldest son of Mohammed bin Laden, took over as his father's successor, with the assistance of several brothers. Upon Salem's death, also in a plane crash, in 1988, the leadership of the group passed to one of Salem's brothers, Bakr ("We have a mayor and all kinds of political heavyweights. But the true ruler of Jeddah is Bakr bin Laden," said a Saudi source in *Der Spiegel*), the current chairman, along with thirteen other brothers who make up the board of the bin Laden group, the most important of these being Hassan, Yeslam and Yehia. By 2002, the company had 35,000 employees worldwide. Today, SBG has over 100,000 employees and is worth tens of billions if not hundreds; the annual revenue of the group exceeds $30 billion.

In Egypt the SBG is headed by Abdul Aziz bin Laden, and represents that country's largest foreign-owned private equity group, with over 40,000 employees. In Lebanon the SBG, represented by Yehia bin Laden, has been holding negotiations with the local authorities for a $50 million share in the project to rebuild the Beirut Central District within the framework of the Solidere Project and in conjunction with the al Baraka Group and the bin Mahfouz Group. In London the SBG set up a representative firm called Binexport in November 1990. In 2005 it signed a $26.6 billion contract to build King Abdullah Economic City. Abraj Al Bait Towers in Mecca, and recently signed a

US$1.23 billion contract to construct the tallest building in the world, Kingdom Tower in Jeddah.

It was no doubt Osama Bin Laden's hope to convert his siblings to his vision of Islamic revolution and to transform the world's largest construction firm into a mainstay of the revolution (Even were he to achieve consensus among his siblings and any other owners of the company, it would then be undermined, boycotted and bankrupted by the forces of world capitalism, with which it is intimately connected). Osama's inheritance was cancelled by his brothers in 1994. Osama had five wives and 24 children.

2 Phil Gasper, "Afghanistan, the CIA, bin Laden, and the Taliban", *International Socialist Review*, November-December 2001.

3 It was in reality the Americans imposing themselves on the Saudis, as US Defense Secretary Dick Cheney and Secretary of State James Baker presented doctored images of Iraqi armor amassed on the Saudi border for an invasion. <www.Hermes-press.com/like_son.htm>

4 See Walberg, *Postmodern Imperialism*, 158.

5 Al-Masjid al-Haram (Mecca) and Al-Masjid al-Nabawi (Medina).

6 Abu Nidal (1937–2002) is credited with an attack on a synagogue in Vienna, the bombing of the British Airways office in Madrid, the hijacking of an EgyptAir flight to Malta, and attacks on the Rome and Vienna airports. He died under mysterious circumstances in Baghdad. In 2008 Robert Fisk obtained a report prepared for Saddam Hussein in 2002 stating that Abu Nidal was suspected of spying for Kuwait and Egypt, and had been asked by the Kuwaitis to find links between Iraq and al-Qaeda. <http://www.wikpedia/Abu_Nidal>

7 Ramirez Sanchez (b. 1949) was a member of Popular Front for the Liberation of Palestine (PFLP), and is credited with kidnapping 11 members of OPEC in Vienna 1975 to Algiers for ransom. He was kidnapped by French security forces in Sudan in 1994.

8 Ramzi Yousef (b. 1967), the Kuwaiti-born Pakistani nephew of Khalid Sheikh Mohammed (see endnote 49), an engineer, who in 1991 went to the Philippines to establish the Abu Sayyaf organization. In 1994 he and Khalid Sheikh Mohammed planned bombings in the Philippines and the Bojinka plan to blow up 11 airliners simultaneously over the Pacific Ocean (the earlier variant of 9/11), but fire forced them to flee and his laptop provided proof of the plot. He was captured in 1995 in Pakistan and sentenced in 1997 to 240 years.

9 Soon after becoming president, Morsi called for Abdel-Rahman's extradition for humanitarian reasons (he is diabetic and blind), causing a panic among Egyptian secularists, though he promised not to overturn his conviction.

10   See endnotes 122–126.

11   213 killed in Nairobi (including 12 Americans) and 4,000 primarily civilians wounded.

12   Clearly after Belief (Imaan) there is no more important duty than pushing the American enemy out of the holy land. No other priority, except Belief, could be considered before it; the people of knowledge, Ibn Taymiyyah, stated: "to fight in defence of religion and Belief is a collective duty; there is no other duty after Belief than fighting the enemy who is corrupting the life and the religion. There is no preconditions for this duty and the enemy should be fought with one best abilities. (ref: supplement of Fatawa). If it is not possible to push back the enemy except by the collective movement of the Muslim people, then there is a duty on the Muslims to ignore the minor differences among themselves; the ill effect of ignoring these differences, at a given period of time, is much less than the ill effect of the occupation of the Muslims' land by the main Kufr. Full text at <http://www.pbs.org/newshour/updates/military-july-dec96-fatwa_1996/>

13   Signed by five people, four of whom represented specific Islamic groups: Osama bin Laden, Ayman al-Zawahiri (Egyptian Islamic Jihad), Ahmed Refai Taha (Egyptian Islamic Society) who later retracted, Sheikh Mir Hamza (Jamiat-ul-ulema-e-Pakistan), and Fazlur Rahman (Bangladesh Jihad Movement).

14   However, Maqdisi denounced the use of suicide attacks by Hamas against Israel in 1994, and more recently ISIS's declared caliphate in Iraq, as un-Islamic, though he could surely have been coerced into the latter as a Jordanian prisoner.

15   Reproduced at 'God knows it did not cross our minds to attack the towers' *Guardian*, October 30 2004.

| Chapter Eight |

ZAWAHIRI: VIOLENCE AGAINST CLIENT REGIMES

Early Life

There are many actors in the transformation of genuine jihad into indiscriminate violence, all of them building on Ibn Taymiya and Wahhab's *ijtihad* concerning illegitimate leaders. By the end of 1989, the Soviets had withdrawn from Afghanistan, and it was time to negotiate an end to the carnage and for the foreign fighters to return home. But as the need for unity against the Soviet occupation waned, fierce fighting among the seven Afghan opposition factions increased, and Azzam's attempts to keep the fractious groups united and focused on building an Islamic order in the face of western efforts to impose a secular regime, failed. Afghanistan became a failed state.

The foreign fighters faced prison or worse upon returning to their repressive nations (Algeria, Egypt, Libya, Yemen). Bin Laden needed a new project, had willing recruits, and was already looking to take the war around the world with his newly formed al-Qaeda, inviting the most hardened veterans to stay in training camps in the mountains.

Egyptian Islamic Jihad leader Ayman al-Zawahiri (b. 1951), who had met Bin Laden in Peshawar in 1985, and became Bin Laden's close adviser and personal doctor, was eager to move on to target all local pseudo-Muslim rulers and foment more upheavals, regardless of the civilian deaths that would result.

Zawahiri came from an eminent religious-intellectual background. His father's uncle, Rabia al-Zawahiri, was the grand imam of Cairo's al-Azhar University. His mother's father was the president of Cairo University and founded King Saud University in Riyadh. He had been active organizing Islamic extremists since he was 15, when he became the leader of a small group of student militants dedicated to overthrowing Gamal Abdel-Nasser's secular Egyptian government, after he, like millions of other students across the Arab world, read Sayyid Qutb.

Assassinations as a Catalyst

Zawahiri emphasized Qutb's dismissal of those Muslims who cooperated with the secularists as unbelievers, and took undermining the organizations and authorities of the *jahili* system by "physical power and jihad" to mean armed revolution, as opposed to the initial and ongoing MB strategy of patiently building alternative structures and waiting for the bankruptcy of the "*jahili* system".

Ironically, though an opponent of the secular-socialist Nasser, Qutb and his followers took a page from Nasser's thinking. Nasser's Free Officers movement within the army had allowed a usurpation of power from within the establishment. Nasser's strategy to liberate Palestine was to first overthrow the quisling Arab monarchies in movements patterned on his own, in order to create a militant, energetic force, united under the banner of Arab nationalism, which would then confront Israel.

Zawahiri was inspired by the former Nasserist armored corps officer, Issam Al-Qamari, who was behind the assassination of Sadat. He argued that a military takeover was the only means of fomenting a revolution. They were imprisoned together in Tura Prison following the assassination and decided to split from the Islamic Society and form the more ultra-militant Islamic Jihad. The only way to counter the regime, in his view, is to form an armed vanguard to wage battles, to control the capital (Cairo) and engage the armed forces before a violent overthrow could be considered. The jihad in Afghanistan was the training ground for this.

However, the one-shot assassination of Sadat hardly constituted a plan to overthrow his regime, and the experience of military coups in search of social justice (Egypt 1952, Peru 1968, Sudan 1969 and 1989) shows the futility of this strategy. The exception is Qaddafi's officers' coup in Libya in 1969, though it too was finally undone by the western invasion of 2011.

Before his assassination, Azzam had opposed both Bin Laden and Zawahiri's plans, which essentially involved committing mass murder in order to instigate revolution, be it world or local. He was more focused on bringing peace to Afghanistan after the Soviet troops left. He sought to mediate among all the Afghan factions (Rabbani,[1] Sayyaf,[2] Hekmatyar,[3] Haqqani,[4] Massoud[5]), keeping peace between them and the Arabs, while helping the Afghans build an alternative social order based on Islam. His strategy was to then refocus the struggle on *fard ayn (*personal obligation for all Muslims*)*—for the liberation of Palestine. This alienated all sides and he was assassinated, though by whom is still a mystery, as his only real ally at this point was the isolated Massoud. Although Bin Laden and/or Zawahiri are often accused of arranging his assassination, it is more likely the work of the Pakistan's ISI, unhappy with his legendary status and his support for Massoud, who was from the Dari minority and opposed to Pakistan's desire to act as the regional hegemon.[6]

From Faraj to 'Anything Goes'

Bin Laden's strategy rapidly became closer to Zawahiri's with the collapse of the Soviet Union and the death of Azzam. They agreed to turn the jihad first against Muslim lands still under non-Muslim rule in the ex-socialist bloc (Chechnya, Bosnia), and then against US targets abroad.

The death of Azzam moved Bin Laden closer to Zawahiri's takfiri ideology that condoned punishing Muslims for deficient worship or disapproved personal habits (say, praying only three times a day or using tea, alcohol etc.), and killing those guilty of more serious violations of the Salafi version of Islam, regarding anyone nearby those targets as jihadi 'collateral damage'.[7] Zawahiri was following the strategy outlined by Abdus Salam Faraj (1954–1982), one of the people involved in the killing of Sadat. Faraj wrote a tract *Jihad: The Neglected Duty*, in which he argued for eliminating the near enemy [Muslim rulers subservient to imperialists/ Zionists] first before taking on the distant (foreign) enemies, though Faraj's concerns were more politically focused, and his major action was the targeted assassination of Sadat, which harmed no innocent bystanders.

Zawahiri was concerned that joining any 'jihad' promoted by the takfiri leaders of existing regimes to liberate Palestine would merely consolidate their power, and would not result in Islamic rule.

> The secular currents that paid lip service to the issue of Palestine competed with the

Islamic movement to lead the nation in this regard are now exposed before the Muslim nation following their recognition of Israel and adoption of negotiations and compliance with international resolutions to liberate what is left or what is permitted by Israel, of Palestine. [They] support the infidels against the Muslims.[8]

Too bad history doesn't allow you to choose the circumstances of your actions. Working with the US and Pakistan to overthrow the Soviet regime in Afghanistan was a fateful compromise, arguably undermining efforts to liberate Palestine in the long run.

Zawahiri picked up the pieces of the struggle after Faraj's execution in 1982, trying to leave behind the compromise with the US in the Afghan jihad, and after the withdrawal of Soviet troops, focusing on the US client regime in Egypt, formulating a defense of expanding the scope of attacks to include virtually anyone standing in the way of what he hoped would be an ongoing revolution. Initially this meant targeting policemen on the street and eventually even tourists in Egypt, but the difficulty of insurgency in Egypt (a desert and a river) also meant moving abroad for more successful actions.

There are pre-9/11 dates that stand out in modern Islam's confrontation with imperialism, which were generally greeted with respect in the Muslim world:

- 1979 Soviet invasion of Afghanistan, Iranian revolution
- 1981 Sadat's assassination
- 1983/1985 Beirut bombings of US marines
- 1989 Afghanistan 'liberation'

- 1993 World Trade Center bombing
- 1994 Somalia "Black Hawk Down"
- 1995 bombings in Riyadh and the Egyptian embassy in Islamabad
- 1996 bombing of Saudi Khobar Towers
- 2000 bombings of the *USS The Sullivans* (January, unsuccessful) and the *USS Cole* (October) in Aden.

However, the 1997 Luxor massacre and the 1998 US embassy bombings in Kenya and Uganda were greeted with universal condemnation by Muslims, as was 9/11.

The shift to spectacular terrorist acts against the West did not happen overnight, and in any case these acts were few, and quickly burned themselves out. In his memoirs, Zawahiri recalls the 1993 assassination attempt against Egyptian Prime Minister Atif Sidqi (who survived with a broken arm) in which a schoolgirl Shayma was killed. "The unintended death of this innocent child pained us all, but we had to fight the government."[9] The jihadists had warned people "to stay away from the pillars of the regime." So any casualties were unfortunate, but, citing Shafii jurisprudence, Zawahiri said that blood money could be paid to any innocent victims.

He further explains that it was a combination of Egyptian persecution of Muslims (the 1990 killing of Egypt's Islamic Group official Muhiya al-Din, despite his calling for dialogue with the government), the US war against Iraq in 1991, and continuing escalation of violence against Muslims in league with US client regimes that made him move towards indiscriminate violence. "The Islamic Group shifted its policy from long-term call activity to violence by fighting and resisting the government's aggression."[10]

In his memoirs, he justifies killing those leaders who bow to Israel and empire, mentioning a conference in 1996 in Sharm al-Shaykh where Arab state leaders joined the US in an agreement to guarantee Israel's security, denouncing them as effectively dead:

> He who holds his own worth too light
> Will find further humiliation easy to bear
> For you cannot make a person feel pain
> From a new wound if he is already dead.[11]

Even as the Islamic followers in Egypt were definitively abandoning indiscriminate violence by the late 1990s, and the MB was achieving moderate electoral success despite ongoing persecution, Zawahiri rejected both developments, identifying proudly with the extremist Khawarij[12] making his differences with Azzam, who never embraced the Khawarij monicker, clear. While sympathetic to the original MB project under Banna, Zawahiri argued that MB compromises from the 1980s onward were haram, effectively putting them in the same boat as Sadat/Mubarak. Bizarrely, in the same breath, he warned the Islamic Group to be "careful not to isolate itself from its nation ... We must win the people's confidence, respect and affection,"[13]—precisely what the MB was doing and Zawahiri's group were not.

At this point, the US and Saudis (though not the Pakistanis) tried to wash their hands of the Arab mujahideen, now out of US control under their new, more radical leaders. US attempts to set up a secularist regime in Afghanistan had understandably failed, and the Saudis and Pakistanis were happy with the Taliban, trained in Saudi-financed madrassahs in Pakistan. The US temporarily abandoned Afghanistan to the Taliban and their Saudi-Pakistani allies, and began to monitor Bin Laden et al as dangerous terrorists. But it was too late.

Bin Laden as 'Moderate'

Bin Laden's 1998 fatwa was in fact more the work of Zawahiri, according to Pakistani journalist Hamid Mir, who interviewed Bin Laden in 1997 and 1998. The fatwa appeared in February and the US embassy bombings—the first attack targeting primarily innocent civilians—followed in August. One of Zawahiri's arguments was that it is justified to kill as many imperialists and their supporters as the millions of Muslims who have been killed by the imperialists. He had Bin Laden onside now, exemplified by Bin Laden's "letter to the American people" ("whoever has killed our civilians, then we have the right to kill theirs"). This was in line with the thinking of Sultan Bashiruddin Mahmood (b. 1940), the Pakistani nuclear scientist whom the US feared would help al-Qaeda with plans for chemical/ nuclear attacks, and who argued that US killings of Muslims legitimized Muslim retaliation ('an arm for an arm') He used the figure of 4 million.[14]

The 1998 fatwa states:

> To kill the Americans and their allies—civilians and military—is an individual duty for every Muslim who can do it in any country in which it is possible, in order to liberate the al-Aqsa Mosque and the holy mosque [Mecca] from their grip, and in order for their armies to move out of all the lands of Islam, defeated and unable to threaten any Muslim.

This stretches the law of equity permitted in the Quran

("An eye for an eye") to: let America "taste some of what we are tasting". But then, the Bush-Obama current practice of assassinating whoever the US government decides is a terrorist, including US citizens and unavoidably involving 'collateral damage', is exactly in the same line of thinking as these fatwas, once again showing how much a product of Enlightenment thinking the current 'war on terror' is *for both sides*. No court indictment is necessary for a US president, since any evidence is 'top secret', giving him *carte blanche* to kill whoever, wherever he pleases.[15] What is this but a kind of neocon takfirism?

Zawahiri was clearly responding to imperialism's own history of violence.

> The mujahid Islamic movement must escalate methods of strikes ... to keep up with the tremendous increase in the number of its enemies, the quality of their weapons, their destructive powers, their disregard for all taboos, and disrespect for the customs of wars.[16]

In his view, it was now necessary to inflict maximum casualties against the opponents, to encourage martyrdom operations (most successful, least costly), to choose targets and weapons to "deter it enough to stop its brutality and disregard for all taboos and customs." No longer just against the "domestic enemy" but against imperialism worldwide.

The Bin Laden/ Zawahiri terrorist strategy is in line with both imperialist strategy as practiced in WWI and WWII and currently by the US in the Muslim world, and with Wahhabi thought, as confirmed by a more recent fatwa by Saudi scholar Nasir bin Hamad al-Fahd (b. 1977). He argued in 2003 in clear reference to 9/11 that it is justified to attack the enemy with "catapults and similar weapons that cause general destruction" when laying siege to cities.

Both Zawahiri and Bin Laden had left Azzam behind, Zawahiri because Azzam wouldn't support terror against takfiri leaders, Bin Laden because Azzam supported Massoud against the Taliban by 1989, and wouldn't support terror against the US after 'victory' in Afghanistan. Azzam wanted the training camps to stay in Afghanistan and to focus on Palestine. Bin Laden wanted to set them up around the world and unleash terror against the US, Russia, etc.

The debate between the three leaders recalls the debate launched by Jamal al-Din al-Afghani as the imperialists moved into the Middle East in the nineteenth century, both by invading and co-opting leaders, though in the case of Afghani, he moved in the opposite direction. At first, Afghani held a more radical position similar to that of Zawahiri, advocating the overthrow of local corrupt Muslim rulers, but later he had tried to work with those leaders to unite Muslims. Afghani never advocated mass terrorism.

The tension between Azzam on the one hand, and on the other, Bin Laden, with his call for jihad against the US (and for Bosnia, Chechnya, etc.) and Zawahiri, with his focus on Egypt, shows that from the start, al-Qaeda was split between gradualists and ultraists.

Zawahiri's strategy in Egypt had collapsed by the end of the 1990s, with the split between the Egyptian Islamic Society and Egyptian Islamic Jihad,[17] and the revulsion of Egyptians at terrorist attacks, especially after Luxor. Apart from a small core of neo-Wahhabis, the Egyptian people showed no move to support this terrorism. By the late 1990s, the entire Islamic movement had become paralyzed. Tarred with the terrorist brush, 20,000 Muslims (only a handful of whom had been involved in any way with violence) were in custody in Egypt and thousands more had been cut down by the security forces. In July 1997, a deal was brokered between the Islamic Society and the Egyptian government, called the Nonviolence Initiative, whereby the movement formally renounced violence. The next year the government released 2,000 members.

Zawahiri led the opposition to this attempt to stop the terror campaign, terming it "surrender" and a rump Egyptian Islamic Jihad (EIJ) proceeded with the Luxor massacre in November 1997, which the 1998 fatwa establishing the World Islamic Front for the Jihad Against Jews and Crusaders effectively blessed.

Zawahiri's EIJ had also carried out the Egyptian embassy bombing in Islamabad in 1995, which Bin Laden opposed, not wanting to alienate Pakistan. But they agreed upon and jointly carried out the bombings of the US embassies in Kenya and Tanzania in 1998—the first large-scale terrorist strike which reflected their new strategy of targeting the 'far' enemy regardless of who died.

The Saudi narrative tries to shift the blame to 'bad' (Egyptian) Zawahiri for corrupting 'nice' (Saudi) Bin Laden, an interpretation that does not hold water. Here are some indications of how their mutual influences played out:

- We can't blame Zawahiri for the *USS Cole* bombing or the WTC bombings (nor was Bin Laden involved in the 1993 WTC bombing, if indeed he was involved in the 2001 attack.)
- While Bin Laden *moderated* Zawahiri after Egypt's nightmare decade of small-scale terrorist operations culminating in the Luxor massacre in 1997, he expanded Zawahiri's focus to the 'far' enemy, arguing that the collapse of the US would precipitate the collapse of its client states—the 'near' enemies. What did 'far' and

'near' mean anymore in the era of global capitalism?

- Bin Laden also opposed the targeting of Shia by Zawahiri's followers (and his own Wahhabis), especially following the US invasion of Iraq.[18]
- He convinced Zawahiri of the importance of using the media.
- He downplayed Zawahiri's hope for a Nasser-like military coup vs insurgent warfare leading to mass mobilization.

Zawahiri's formal alliance of the EIJ with Bin Laden in 1998 was a pragmatic move, driven by financial desperation and the search for a credible mission to replace the failures of his operations in Egypt. In 2001, Zawahiri formally merged the remnants of the Egyptian Islamic Jihad with Bin Laden's al-Qaeda network, which formally became Qaeda al-Jihad.

Zawahiri's takfiri ideology was taken to an even greater extreme by the al-Qaeda leader in Iraq, Abu Musab al-Zarqawi (d. 2006), and his followers, who targeted Shia in suicide bombings, killing innocent people almost daily, in defiance of Bin Laden's orders. It was a strategy which Zawahiri criticized in a letter to Zarqawi (9 July 2005), since it alienated ordinary Sunnis and distracted from the goal of evicting US troops.[19]

Endnotes

1 Burhanuddin Rabbani (1940–2011) was president of the Islamic State of Afghanistan from 1992–1996. He returned to Kabul and served as a temporary president in November–December 2001, when Hamid Karzai was chosen as leader at the Bonn International Conference on Afghanistan. He was leader of Jamiat-e Islami Afghanistan (Islamic Society of Afghanistan), which has close ties to Pakistan's Jamaat-

e-Islami, and was political head of the United Islamic Front for the Salvation of Afghanistan (UIFSA), an alliance of various political groups who fought against the Taliban in Afghanistan. He later became head of Afghanistan National Front, the largest political opposition to Hamid Karzai's government. He was assassinated by a suicide bomber in his home in Kabul and given the title of "Martyr of Peace". His son, Salahuddin Rabbani, was chosen in April 2012 to lead efforts to forge peace in Afghanistan with the Taliban.

2   Abdul Rab Rasul Sayyaf (b. 1946), an Afghan who in 1973 plotted with Burhanuddin Rabbani and Gulbuddin Hekmatyar to overthrow Afghan President Daoud Khan. The coup failed and he was forced to flee to Pakistan but was imprisoned by the Communist People's Democratic Party of Afghanistan (PDPA) in April 1978, and freed by the second PDPA leader, Hafizullah Amin, who was Sayyaf's distant relative. He led the mujahideen Islamic Union for the Liberation of Afghanistan, mobilizing Arab volunteers, and invited Bin Laden to Afghanistan after his 1996 expulsion from Sudan under Saudi, Egyptian, and American pressure. He trained Ramzi Yousef and Khalid Sheikh Mohammed, and served in the Afghan Interior Ministry under Rabbani in 1992, responsible for the slaughter of the Hazara. He disliked Taliban as 'innovators', and was an ally of both Bin Laden and Ahmad Shah Massoud. At the same time he was accused of assisting the two assassins that killed Massoud. The Philippine Moro terrorist group is named after him. He was elected to the 2003 Loya Jirga, and in 2005, Sayyaf's Ittehad-al-Islami (Islamic Union) was converted into the political party, Islamic Dawah Organization of Afghanistan. His ally Fazal Hadi Shinwari was appointed by Hamid Karzai as Chief Justice of the Supreme Court. Shinwari called for Taliban-style punishments and renewed the Taliban's Ministry for the Promotion of Virtue and Prevention of Vice, renamed the Ministry of Hajj and Religious Affairs. He calls for amnesty for mujahideen.

3   Gulbuddin Hekmatyar (b.1947) is the founder and active leader of the Hezb-e Islami Gulbuddin political party. After escaping from prison in Afghanistan in 1973, he moved to Pakistan and became involved with Pakistan's Inter-Services Intelligence (ISI) to carry out terrorist attacks inside Afghanistan. When the Soviet war in Afghanistan began in 1979, the CIA began funding his Hezb-e Islami mujahideen organization through the ISI. Following the overthrow of Afghan President Najibullah in 1992 (killed while under UN protection together with his brother by the Taliban in 1996), Hekmatyar and other warlords began a civil war, which led to the deaths of around 50,000 civilians in Kabul alone. Hekmatyar became prime minister from 1993–1994 and again

briefly in 1996. This was followed by the Taliban takeover of Kabul and Hekmatyar's escape to Tehran. In 2002 all the offices of Hezb-e-Islami were closed in Iran and Hekmatyar was expelled. In May 2006, he released a video to Al-Jazeera in which he accused Iran of backing the US in the Afghan conflict and said he was ready to fight alongside Bin Laden. In 2010, he called for negotiations with President Karzai and outlined a roadmap for political reconciliation. This contrasted with the views of Taliban leader Mullah Omar and allied insurgent chief Sirajuddin Haqqani, who refuse any talks with Kabul as long as foreign troops remain in the country

4   Jallaludin Haqqani (b. 1950), a senior military leader of the Haqqani network in southeastern Afghanistan from the 1980s. The network was nurtured by the CIA and Pakistan's ISI, and financed by wealthy Arab private donors from the Persian Gulf. He commanded the Mujahideen Army from 1980–1992. Abdullah Azzam and Osama bin Laden both began their careers as volunteers for Haqqani's network. Haqqani was the only Afghan leader to request foreign Muslim fighters, and was the only group to welcome non-Afghans into its ranks. When the Taliban were about to occupy Kabul, he joined them, and accepted a cabinet level appointment as minister of tribal affairs. Jalaluddin's son Sirajuddin has taken over the responsibility of military operations. His son Naseeruddin, a fundraiser, was killed in 2013. President Karzai invited the elder Haqqani to serve as prime minister but the offer was refused.

Links between the Haqqani network and Pakistan can be traced back to the mid-1970s, before the 1978 Marxist revolution in Kabul. During the rule of President Daoud Khan in Afghanistan (1973–78), Jalaluddin Haqqani went into exile and based himself in and around Miranshah, Pakistan. From there he began to form a rebellion against the government of Daoud Khan in 1975. While Pakistan has declared the Tehrik-i-Taliban Pakistan (TTP) as an enemy which engages in attacks against civilians and the state, the Haqqani group refrains from attacking the Pakistani state and thus, has traditionally been considered to be in the Pakistani sphere of what some analysts call the "good" Taliban. The murky role of Pakistan in using the Haqqani group is shown by US claims that ISI ordered the Haqqani group to attack the US embassy and NATO headquarters in Kabul on September 13 2014, killing 16.

5   Ahmad Shah Massoud (1953–2001), a Tajik Afghan, ally of Rabbani, fought against the alliance of militias led by Hekmatyar and eventually the Taliban, who started to lay siege to the capital in January 1995. He was nominally minister of defense 1992–2001, and posthumously

6   named "National Hero" by the order of President Karzai. The date of his death, 9 September 2001, is observed as a national holiday known as "Massoud Day" in Afghanistan. He worked with Rabbani and the CIA (though with little funding after 1992) and surely would have abandoned Bin Laden and been promoted in place of Karzai after 9/11 if he had survived, and made a similar pact with the US.

6   Roy, *Globalized Islam*, 297.

7   The first terrorist attack involving bin Laden was the December 1992 bombing of the Gold Mihor Hotel in Aden, Yemen, intended to kill US troops going to Somalia, but killed only a Yemeni hotel employee and an Austrian national. It was after this bombing that al-Qaeda was reported to have developed its justification for the killing of innocent people, such as the two bystanders at the hotel. According to a fatwa issued by Mamdouh Mahmud Salim (aka, Abu Hajer al-Iraqi), the most Islamically knowledgeable of al-Qaeda's members, the killing of people merely standing near the enemy is justified because they will in any case go to Paradise if they are good Muslims and to hell if they are bad or non-believers. The fatwa was issued to al-Qaeda members but not the general public.

8   Ayman al-Zawahiri, *Knights Under the Prophet's Banner: Meditations of the Jihadist Movement*, 2001. translation in *al-Sharq al-Wasat* <https://azelin.files.wordpress.com/2010/11/6759609-knights-under-the-prophet-banner.pdf> 63.

9   Ibid., 29.

10 Ibid., 28.

11 Ibid., 36. poem by tenth century Arab poet al-Mutanabbi.

12 See endnote 54.

13 Ibid., 50, 63.

14 Mahmood believed Pakistan's bomb was "the property of the whole Ummah". "This guy was our ultimate nightmare," an American intelligence official told *The New York Times* in late 2001. But nonetheless, he was widely respected: the US Institute of Historical Biographies presented him a gold medal in 1998. He has also been awarded Gold Medal by the Pakistan Academy of Sciences.

15 It was enough that US citizen Anwar al-Awlaki was claimed to be tied to plots against the US and to have played a key role in al-Qaida in the Arabian Peninsula for Obama to order him killed in Yemen in 2011. Alwaki's father sued US officials over his killing, but a federal judge dismissed the suit, admitting that while Awlaki had a "plausible" case over violations of his right to due process, she could not step into decisions about warmaking, national security and foreign relations. Mary Ellen O'Connell, professor of international law at Notre Dame

University, Indiana, said in 2012 that more than 2,200 people had been killed by drones during the three years of the Obama administration in Pakistan alone. She has compared targeted killings by drones to the "excessive use of military force" for which the US condemns President Bashar al-Assad in Syria. Another comparison would be with Zawahiri and takfiri: Obama can kill anyone who is not sufficiently acquiescent to US imperialism, or any group of three or more young men who can later be labeled as terrorists, raising the question: is the purpose to eliminate terrorists, or simply to terrorize?

16 Ayman al-Zawahiri, *Knights Under the Prophet's Banner,* 66.
17 Though they had cooperated from Sudan in the Mubarak assassination attempt of 1995.
18 Double agent Ali Mohamed brokered a Sunni-Shia alliance in 1993. See Peter Lance, *Triple Cross: How Bin Laden's Master Spy Penetrated the CIA, the Green Berets, and the FBI–and Why Patrick Fitzgerald Failed to Stop Him,* Regan, 2006.
19 Shia joined the new Iraqi security forces in large numbers, eager to cement their control of the new government (where Shia death squads targeting Sunnis operated). At the same time, the continued bombings of primarily Shia are clearly the work of Sunni insurgents (backed by the Saudis and possibly the US). The anti-occupation Iraqi resistance has been Sunni-dominated from the start, determined to end both the occupation (now 'occupation lite') and Shia control. The resistance demands Shia join them, despite the US-orchestrated sectarian divide which now prevents a united resistance to the US-imposed order, ongoing US military presence despite official withdrawal, and at this writing, a return to bombing and likely boots on the ground. The (Wahhabi) Saudis used these bombings targeting Shia both to provoke a Shia backlash leading to outright civil war, and to show the US that violence will continue unless the US abandons its Shia 'partners'. This is also the strategy of (neo-Wahhabi) al-Qaeda, which formed in Iraq after the US occupation and was led by the Jordanian Zarqawi (1966–2006), once again showing how Saudi/ al-Qaeda interests converge (their only difference being over the sanctity of the Saudi royal family). After Zarqawi's death, the attacks on Shia continued. Currently ISIS/IS is the main al-Qaeda presence in Iraq and is active in Syria along with Jabhat al-Nusra. Zawahiri also condemned the killing of hostages as detrimental to the mujahideen's image. (Shmuel Bar and Yair Minsili, "The Zawahiri Letter and the Strategy of Al-Qaeda", Hudson Institute, 2005.)

| CHAPTER NINE |

MANY AL-QAEDAS: THE LEGACY

Both al-Qaeda and the US Miscalculate

Azzam's intent was to triumph in Afghanistan, and for this victory to act as a catalyst for battle-hardened Muslims to overthrow their oppressors everywhere, starting in Palestine, the Caucasus, Central Asia, Bosnia, the Philippines, Kashmir, Somalia and Eritrea. He did not intend to provoke invasions by the US of Afghanistan and Iraq. Bin Laden and Zawahiri did. Bin Laden's intention was to bankrupt the US and accelerating its decline. Zawahiri added the targeting of compromised Muslim leaders and random violence against their civilians to provoke their retaliation which in turn would lead to mass politicization, with a view to accelerating the process of revolution.

Just as the anarchists of yesteryear (not to mention the original Kharijites) burned themselves out on strategies that turned the disaffected against them, the al-Qaeda revolutionaries' project stalled through its misreading of the beliefs and sentiments of the ummah and the dynamics of empire.

- Bin Laden's offer to Saudi leaders to rely on his rag-tag mujahideen to defend the Saudi kingdom and liberate Kuwait in 1991 was wildly naïve (or intended to show to the Saudi public what the leaders should be doing and effectively discredit them). If the Saudis allowed French commandos to invade the Kaaba in 1979, there was no reason to believe that they would deny US troops access to Saudi soil in 1990.

- In precipitating US invasions of Afghanistan and Iraq to spark all-out war, he did not foresee the overwhelming reaction to al-Qaeda by the US government, assuming the US would be unable to mobilize sufficient troops and sustain a long-term occupation of Muslim lands. The official response was indeed all-out war. But Bin Laden's hopes that US troops would expose themselves as cowards and retreat *a la* Somalia 1994 were in vain. The resulting deaths almost exclusively of innocent Muslims and the devastation of Afghanistan and Iraq as a result of the invasions and the US 'war on terror' can hardly be called a 'rational' strategy, as argued by Scheuer, though this strategy certainly weakens the empire.

- The two leaders did not foresee the reaction to al-Qaeda by the people in the West. Bin Laden was criticized by al-Qaeda members such as **Abu Musab** al-Suri (see below) for not appealing to the enemy to convert to Islam as part of his declaration of war embodied in his fatwas, which he corrected in video appeals after 9/11. But it is not hard to see that mass terrorist attacks would find little support in the West, and become instead the cause of unending torment for Muslims there. While it is true that conversions to Islam proceeded apace after 9/11, this occurred despite 9/11 rather than as a result of it.

- Bin Laden did not foresee the reaction of the ummah to the invasions of Afghanistan and Iraq, which did not evoke mass collective jihad elsewhere, let alone personal jihad. On the contrary, the 2007 World Public Opinion quoted above shows that more than four out of five Muslims do not condone killing of civilians.

- Bin Laden recognized in later messages that the attempt for unity in the World Islamic Front against Crusaders and Jews was "premature". The 'Arab Spring', which Bin Laden praised in his final message,[1] was not inspired by him. There were no placards lauding him during the uprising, and Islamic victories were based on platforms of peaceful local change. While a trickle of jihadists came from Europe and north Africa to Syria following the uprising in 2011, the support for Islamic insurgents there came overwhelmingly from Saudi and western leaders, intent on their own *realpolitik* concerns.[2] (The 2013 coup in Egypt and the subsequent success of ISIS/IS in 2014 may, however, mean that the al-Qaeda plan is back on track, pulling MB-types towards all-out jihad as was the case in Afghanistan in the 1980s.)

- Though Bin Laden called for unity of all Muslims, including Shia and other sects, in the face of the West's hostility (echoed grudgingly more recently by Zawahiri), he made no clear statement disassociating himself from the Saudi/ Wahhabi insistence that the Salafi version of Islam embodied in Wahhabism would prevail, come the revolution, and made no attempt to tie his grandiose plans with the ongoing revolution in Iran. This refusal to bridge the Sunni-Shia divide played into the hands of the US, which seemed poised to invade Iran and made use of sectarianism in Iraq following the US invasion.

Though "pious, brave, generous, intelligent, charismatic, etc.", Bin Laden gambled recklessly on his vision of how to renew Islamic civilization. Geopolitics subverted any attempt at consolidating an independent Islamic state in Afghanistan, and produced a short-lived haven for Muslim terrorists there, inspired by Bin Laden. In Egypt, the 1980s–1990s al-Qaeda-type terrorism had reinforced an unpopular government, more pro-imperialist and corrupt than at any time in its history, and provided a pretext for the 2013 coup and the banning of all Islamic activism.

Even as communism faltered, geopolitics subverted attempts by Muslims in Chechnya and Bosnia from achieving Islamic states there. The end of communism came about more from western intrigues (abetted by the Saudis) which clearly aimed at incorporating the liberated areas not into some version of the ummah of yore, but into the global market system.

At the same time, geopolitics subverted efforts by the West to control jihadists elsewhere:

- The Saudis were happy to let Bin Laden alone as long as he promised not to incite terrorism in Saudi Arabia. He was too popular to extradite and imprison in Saudi Arabia, and was only doing what many thought the Wahhabis should have been doing anyway. They were happy to keep funding al-Qaeda or whoever to perpetrate jihad against western targets, as long as they did so elsewhere.

- Ditto Pakistan, intent on regional hegemony using the Taliban as a proxy, where the network of Saudi-funded madrassahs, the recruiting ground for jihadists, was providing education in areas where the literacy rate is 30%.

- Even as the West was turning against its mujahideen allies in Afghanistan, the Algerian secular state was creating chaos as part of its attempt to turn back the Islamic tide. The Algerian junta declared a "counter-Jihad" in the 1990s, seeking to discredit the Islamic Salvation Front (FIS), winners of the 1991 elections and ensure French support in the name of a secular Algerian nation state repelling terrorists. They did this by infiltrating the Armed Islamic Groups (GIA), the radical insurgency seeking to restore to the FIS its rightful electoral victory, and perpetrated massacres attributed to the GIA, to darken the Islamic movement's image among Algerians, especially from 1995 on. The French theoretically should not have taken sides in the Algerian civil war unless terror reached French shores. Relations with the Algerian state were hardly warm, as it had been 'the enemy' 30 years previously as the then insurgency against the French state. The French at that time had surrendered to their enemy of choice, the secularist socialists rather than the Muslims. French law only went after those inciting violence in France and/or against French subjects. However, a potential Islamic state was inimical to the tradition of *laicite*, the French obsession with secularism.
- As was the case in France, the UK had allowed radical Muslims to operate as long as they didn't threaten violence in Britain and/or against British, providing a sort-of haven which allowed al-Qaeda to recruit and eventually carry out bombings.

New theorists on Jihad

Al-Qaeda theorist Abu Musab al-Suri (b. 1958)

articulated the new post-9/11 strategy in his *Call to Global Islamic Resistance* (2004), written in hiding in Iran after 9/11, published on the internet in 2005, shortly before he was arrested in Pakistan. (He is now in jail in Syria.)

He was with Bin Laden in Afghanistan from 1996 on, saw the jihadi movement as seriously weakened by the drying up of financial resources, the killing or capture of many leaders, the loss of safe havens, and the increasing international cooperation among police agencies, and argued against Zawahiri's strategy of targeting compromised Muslim leaders such as the Saudi monarchy. While the Saudi monarchy's alliance with the US was the real problem, he argued it was better to target the US rather than the monarchy per se, forcing the latter to defend their alliance, further discrediting the monarchy. The goal, he writes, is "to bring about the largest number of human and material casualties possible for America and its allies." In line with Quranic orientation, Suri cautions against killing Muslims "by mistake", innocent women and children, and other noncombatants.

In 1999, Suri had sent Bin Laden an e-mail accusing him of endangering the Taliban regime with his highly theatrical attacks on American targets, and sticking to outmoded methods of organization and warfare that made al-Qaeda easy prey for western armies and intelligence services. While he describes 9/11 as a short-term public relations success for al-Qaeda, he saw it as a long-term defeat for the Islamic struggle in terms of losing Afghanistan as a base of operations and the destruction of an entire generation of militants. In a letter to Bin Laden recovered from a hard drive obtained in Kabul in 2001, he wrote, "We are in a ship that you are burning on false and mistaken grounds," and he mocked what he regarded as Bin Laden's love of publicity: "I think our brother has caught the disease of screens, flashes, fans, and applause."

By 2000, Suri had begun predicting the end of al-Qaeda, whose preeminence he portrayed as a stage in the development of the worldwide Islamic uprising. "Al-Qaeda is not an organization, it is not a group, nor do we want it to be. ... It is a call, a reference, a methodology." Al-Qaeda's main goal should be to stimulate other groups around the world to join the jihadi movement. It was necessary to codify the doctrines that animated Islamic jihad, so that Muslim youths of the future could discover the cause and begin their own spontaneous religious war.[3]

A new strategy was required, Suri wrote, where jihadists train and arm themselves in independent, self-generating terror cells operating locally and supporting local resistance to empire, including the targeting of western civilians.[4] Suri's call for independent local groups with little coordination, relying on ransom payments for western hostages, is in fact making the best of a bad situation.

There are five regions, according to Suri, where jihadis should focus their energies: Afghanistan, Central Asia, Yemen, Morocco, and, especially, Iraq. The 2003 American occupation of Iraq, he declares, inaugurated a "historical new period" that almost single-handedly rescued the jihadi movement just when many of its critics thought it was finished. However, the invasion of Iraq posed a dilemma for al-Qaeda. Iraq is a largely Shia nation, and al-Qaeda is composed of Sunni fundamentalists.

Shortly before the invasion, in March 2003, Bin Laden issued his own list of targets, which included Jordan, Morocco, Nigeria, Pakistan, Saudi Arabia, and Yemen—not Afghanistan or Iraq. Presumably, he regarded the chances of a Taliban resurgence as unlikely, and realized that an Iraqi Sunni insurgency could ignite an Islamic civil war and lead to a backlash against the Sunni minority.

Zawahiri outlined the next steps for the Iraqi jihad in his letter to Zarqawi in July 2005:

> The first stage: Expel the Americans from Iraq. The second stage: Establish an Islamic authority or emirate, then develop it and support it until it achieves the level of a caliphate. The third stage: Extend the jihad wave to the secular countries neighboring Iraq. The fourth stage: It may coincide with what came before—the clash with Israel, because Israel was established only to challenge any new Islamic entity.[5]

The crucial 'first stage' is fleshed out by Abu Bakr Naji, considered the theorist for ISIS/IS, in an internet document titled *The Management of Savagery: The Most Critical Stage Through Which the Ummah Will Pass* (2004).[6] The title refers to the fact that imperial overreach leads to the downfall of empires, creating a vacuum requiring the "management or administration of savagery" between the waning of one power and the consolidation of power of another. In this period, ISIS/IS will have limited aims:

- achieving internal security and preserving it
- fixing its geographical frontiers
- feeding the internal population
- establishing sharia and Islamic justice
- establishing a "fighting society" at all levels within the community.

Youth are more likely recruits due to their natural rebelliousness, and fence-sitters in the jihad should be won over. The kuffar forces are limited. The client regimes have to defend not only themselves, but foreign advisers/workers, petroleum and other resources, and western-style entertainment spots.

A military strategy is required that forces the enemy to spread its resources thinly, exhausting it. A media strategy is required targeting both the masses, in order to push a large number of them to join the jihad, and enemy troops, in order to push them to refuse to fight or, better, to join the ranks of the mujahideen.

As for the killing of innocents, "It is permissible to kill a person of unknown status in the *dar al-harb* as long as one is striving for the general good," but care should be taken in *dar al-islam*. Islamic scholars should be consulted where there is any problem of interpretation. Since the masses receive almost no benefit from the extraction and export of petroleum, disruption in this is not a problem.

The second stage in consolidating the new caliphate requires the mastering of the administration of the regions which are liberated, and raising the level of faith, and forgiveness.

> If there are tribal leaders [lit. ."those who are obeyed."] among us or a group of individuals who are among the primary people of unbelief or the people of apostasy and we find that there is no great danger for forgiving them, we think it is likely that this will lead to uniting them and then their joining and following the people of faith or, at the very least, holding back the evil of their followers from us.[7]

The author of *The Management of Savagery* treatise

bluntly states that there is no room for "softness": "Our enemies will not be merciful to us, so it compels us to make them think one thousand times, before they dare attack us." 'Abu Bakr' is clearly reliving the so-called Wars of Apostasy, conducted by first Caliph Abu Bakr against those who refused to pay zakat and otherwise rejected Islam after the death of the Prophet in 632.

This seeks to legitimize the need to use "rough violence" during a period of the breakdown of authority, as happened under the first Caliph, Abu Bakr, and again after the US invasion of Iraq in 2003. Clearly in this view violence against westerners involved in the occupation is legitimate but mass violence against Muslims is not. Given the continued almost daily bombings of (largely Shia) civilians and officials in the run-up to ISIS/IS's June 2014 capture of Sunni Iraq, and the subsequent truce between Shia and Sunni in captured areas, the state of affairs within ISIS/IS regarding sectarianism is unclear. Experience in 'liberated' areas controlled by ISIS/IS in 2014—and in recent Taliban activity (see below)—is contradictory.

In 2005, Jordanian journalist and former fellow prisoner Fouad Hussein produced what is perhaps the most definitive outline of al-Qaeda's master plan: a book titled *Al-Zarqawi: The Second Generation of Al Qaeda*. Al-Qaeda anticipated the West's targeting of Iranian ally Syria, and predicted that the resulting chaos would allow al-Qaeda to infiltrate and to be within reach of Israel.

Al-Qaeda's twenty-year plan began on 9/11, with a stage that Hussein calls "The Awakening". By striking America—"the head of the serpent"—al-Qaeda caused the US to "lose consciousness and act chaotically against those who attacked it. This entitled the party that hit the serpent to lead the Islamic nation." This first stage, says Hussein, ended in 2003, when American troops entered Baghdad.

The second stage, "Eye-Opening", would last until the end of 2006. Iraq would become the recruiting ground for young men eager to attack America. In this phase, al-Qaeda was projected to move from being an organization to "a mushrooming invincible and popular trend", assisted by the electronic jihad on the internet

The third stage, "Arising and Standing Up," would last from 2007 to 2010. In this period, Al-Qaeda's focus would be on Syria and Turkey, but it would also begin to directly confront Israel, in order to gain more credibility among the Muslim population.

In the fourth stage, lasting until 2013, al-Qaeda would bring about the demise of Arab governments. "The creeping loss of the regimes' power will lead to a steady growth in strength within al-Qaeda." Meanwhile, attacks against the Middle East petroleum industry will continue, and America's power will deteriorate through the constant expansion of the circle of confrontation. "By then, al-Qaeda will have completed its electronic capabilities, and it will be time to use them to launch electronic attacks to undermine the US economy." Islamic activists will promote the idea of using gold as the international medium of exchange, leading to the collapse of the dollar.

Then an Islamic caliphate can be declared, inaugurating the fifth stage of Al Qaeda's grand plan, which will last until 2016. "At this stage, the western fist in the Arab region will loosen, and Israel will not be able to carry out preemptive or precautionary strikes. The international balance will change." Al-Qaeda and the Islamic movement will attract powerful new economic allies, such as China, and Europe will fall into disunity.

The sixth phase will be a period of total confrontation. The now established caliphate will form an Islamic Army and will instigate a worldwide fight between the believers and the non-believers. By 2020, definitive victory will be achieved.

Suria, Naji and Fouad's musings were published at the height of the post-invasion terrorist attacks in Iraq, and were followed by the 2007 "surge" and the US financing and arming of the "Awakening" Sunni militias, which managed to arrest the violence as the US prepared to pull out its troops. However, the violence accelerated after the 2012 US withdrawal, and the success of ISIS/IS since then has added a new dimension to this scenario, dealt with below.

What formerly looked like a wildly optimistic long term plan on the part of al-Qaeda remains eerily on-track, prompting a subtle shift on the part of western strategists. Imperialists are now being forced to differentiate between Islamic movements, turning to the more established ones such as the MB and Iran, not so much in hope of co-opting them, but to give them room to try to manage the now uncontrollable extremists, to stabilize Muslim society where the post-colonial neoliberal model has failed.[8]

Islamists Confront Jihadists

These issues were spelled out by the West's embrace of double agent Omar Nasiri in his memoir *Inside the Jihad: My Life with Al Qaeda A Spy's Story* (2006). Nasiri was involved in the 1990s Islamist insurgency in Algeria, but came to realize it had been compromised by Algerian security agents. Despite his open rejection of the goals of the West in the Muslim world, Nasiri agreed to monitor the Islamic movement for the French and British, especially in London, where he saw through the naive infatuation with Abu Hamza,[9] and Abu Qatada,[10] who initially supported the terror in Algeria in the 1990s. He helped the French and British security forces in order to prevent terrorism, though he still wants imperialists out (and told his minders so), and wants a dignified Muslim culture not modelled on the West.

He writes, "the GIA [the Algerian Armed Islamic Groups] was riddled from the start with spies from the Algerian secret service" and "agent provocateurs who by 1995 were deliberately shifting the campaign of violence into France, to try and draw Paris into the conflict in opposition to the Islamists and in support for the Algerian state." He met many of the GIA operatives in Brussels, including Ali Touchent (d. 1997), who along with Djamel Zitouni (d. 1996), was responsible for the wave of attacks committed in France in the summer of 1995. Nasiri claims both worked for the Algerian secret police, that Touchent was the son of an Algerian commissar of police, and evaded arrest on a number of occasions.[11]

"What I want more than anything is to save Islam from these terrible excesses and innovations," Nasiri writes. The insurgents buying Israeli Uzi machine guns was humiliating, but "now something much worse is happening: we're fighting our wars using our enemies' tactics. If we, as Muslims, let ourselves become like them—which is to say, like you—then there will be nothing left to fight for. This is my jihad."[12]

Nasiri's self-justification for becoming a double agent is intriguing. He represents the movement of rejection of both imperialism and the methods of struggle inherited from the imperialist era within political Islam.[13] The question arises: what is the way forward? Nasiri makes no mention of Iran's revolution, and his own jihad seems to have ended, as he quietly lives an anonymous life under official protection in Germany (Omar Nasiri is a pseudonym). And objectively speaking, what role is he playing here? His embrace by the West would indicate they think his contribution advances their ends.[14]

Both the Wahhabi accommodationists and neo-Wahhabi militants treat Islam as an ideology useful for achieving power and regulating society, rather than as a way of life that encompasses both means and ends. How is it possible for Muslims to ignore the primary and iconic example of struggle: the peaceful conquest of Mecca by the Prophet Muhammad following years of the call to Islam, the training and entrenchment of the people of Medina in Islamic practice and a defensive jihad? In this context, the fusion of politics and religion which characaterized the Arab Spring in 2011 and is implicit even in Nasiri's rejectionism shows that an Islamic awakening is possible which is not based on neo-Wahhabi-style mass terror and provoking the imperialists to embark upon their own violent "intervention trap" response.

The Iranian revolution and resurgence of Islamic activists following the Arab Spring show Muslims shaking off their comprador nationalist elites and challenging both their western political masters and timid conservative ulama, putting the question of how to put Islam into action at the top of the agenda. A more literate population, armed with the internet, backed by a growing community of Muslims in the West, has allowed greater discussion and sharing of history and new ideas. That Muslims around the world can expose the corrupt, quietist ulama with a literate popular discussion of how to bring Islam back to the center of political and economic life is now becoming a possibility.[15]

Thus, while in the past, the US, Britain et al had cynically manipulated Muslims to further their imperial ends, al-Qaeda and other Salafis' success in mobilizing a militant faction in the ummah created a new playing field for traditional Islamic movements. The new situation was a threat to both the West and the stability of local elites.

US qualified support for the MB in Egypt against the socialist Nasserist state was part of its anti-communist Great

Game II. As part of its promotion of electoral democracy and in search of stability in the Middle East, the US surprised secularists by supporting (grudgingly) the democratically-elected MB government in Egypt in 2012. Given the new scenario of al-Qaeda-style out-of-control violence, better to have a popular Islamic state which could control the jihadists and undermine their logic, so the US saw it, than a militantly secular state inciting jihadists to both Zawahiri and Bin-Laden style violence.

Endnotes

1   "The winds of change will blow over the entire Muslim world. God willing." See Jason Burke, "Osama bin Laden praises Arab spring in posthumously released tape", *Guardian*, May 19 2014.
2   The Free Syrian Army rejects foreign jihadists, and competing al-Qaeda-related groups Jabhat al-Nusra and ISIS/IS have undermined the purely domestic insurgency.
3   Lawrence Wright, "The Master Plan: For the new theorists of jihad, Al Qaeda is just the beginning", *New Yorker*, 11 September 2006.
4   Suri was accused of complicity in the train bombings in Madrid in 2004 and London in 2005, as well as with helping to shape Abu Musab al-Zarqawi in Iraq.
5   US Office of the Director of National Intelligence <fas.org/irp/news/2005/10/dni101105.html>.
6   Paul Woodward, "ISIS and the strategy of managed savagery", *warincontext.org*, 3 July 2014.
7   <http://azelin.files.wordpress.com/2010/08/abu-bakr-naji-the-management-of-savagery-the-most-critical-stage-through-which-the-umma-will-pass.pdf>
8   Some US political strategists—even Senator John McCain and PNAC notable Robert Kagan—denounced the coup, along with conservatives such as Ron Paul, though the coup was approved by President Obama, See "Robert Kagan: Why the United States shouldn't support Egypt's ruling generals", *Washington Post*, May 1 2014.
9   Abu Hamza al-Masri (b. 1958), an Egyptian sentenced to seven years in the UK in 2004, he was extradited to the US in 2012 and is now on trial facing charges of supporting al-Qaeda, aiding a kidnapping in

Yemen and plotting to open a training camp for militants in the US. In the early 1990s, he lived in Bosnia, where he fought against the Serbs and Croats during the Bosnian war and was granted Bosnian citizenship. He was the imam of Finsbury Park Mosque until 2003, and a leader of "Supporters of Sharia", a group that believed in a strict interpretation of Islamic law. He continued to support the actions of the Armed Islamic Group in Algeria, even after mounting evidence by 1995 that they had been infiltrated by the Algerian secret police, though he eventually distanced himself from them. He lost both hands and an eye in Afghanistan preparing bombs. He was sentenced to life imprisonment in New York in January 2015.

10   Abu Qatada al-Filistin (b. 1959) A Jordanian Palestinian, granted political asylum in the UK in 1994. In 1995 he issued a fatwa justifying the killing of Muslims who renounce their faith, and of their families, and was accused by Spanish prosecutors of being "the spiritual leader" of al-Qaeda in Europe though he denies even having met Bin Laden, and by 1997 had distanced himself from the Algerian Armed Islamic Group. In 1999, Abu Qatada was sentenced in absentia by Jordan to life imprisonment with hard labour for conspiracy to carry out bombings of the Modern American School and a hotel, and subsequently in 2000 to a further 15 years for his involvement in a plot to bomb tourists. According to *The Independent*, videos of Abu Qatada's sermons were found in the Hamburg apartment of Mohamed Atta. He distanced himself from al-Qaeda following his arrest in London in 2001. Despite doubts about the evidence against him, he was deported to Jordan in 2013 and is on trial.

11   In September 1995, French Interior Minister Jean-Louis Debré said, "It cannot be excluded that Algerian intelligence may have been implicated" in the first bombing, which hit the Saint-Michel subway stop in Paris on 25 July 1995 and killed eight. Ali Touchent's father was in the Algerian security forces, and Touchent was said to be the GIA leader organizing the attacks. Zitouni was in prison in 1995, agreed to work with security, and was released. Jacques Chirac and his Socialist PM Lionel Jospin (1997+) and the US nonetheless sided fully with the Algerian junta after the terror attacks, apparently forgiving them for their terrorist acts as part of the need to prevent genuine Islamic activists from coming to power. Zitouni was sentenced in absentia to ten years in prison in France in 1998, even though the Algerian government claims he was killed in 1997.

12   Omar Nasirim, *Inside the Jihad: My Life with Al Qaeda A Spy's Story,* 2006, 319.

13   Another example of this is the traitor in the movie "Traitor: The

Truth is Complicated" (2008), where the hero Samir Horn, a mixed-race Somali-American and former US Special Operations officer in Afghanistan, apparently defected to work with an al-Qaeda-type terrorist group (Nathir). Special Forces operatives are under the Pentagon but the CIA also has its Special Activities Division recruited from these Special Forces, and inter-force rivalry sometimes results in situations where no one is in control, as the film demonstrates. The hero supports the bombings of Nathir, partly out of anti-US conviction, but all the time had been a CIA (double) agent, and when he was forced to undertake a bombing involving mass civilian targeting in the US, decided to betray Nathir to the FBI for Nathir's "betrayal of Islam". The CIA is depicted negatively vs the FBI (shown as concerned not with wild international conspiracies, but with a narrower defense of security within the US). The hero's anti-Americanism is treated sympathetically, as are his 'terrorist' accomplices who are misled by a Machiavellian leader. This scenario follows the Laurence Wright critique of the CIA as willing to involve itself in risky conspiratorial plots. Morten Storm's memoirs as a double agent used by the CIA to assassinate Anwar Awlaki confirms this. See Morten Storm with Paul Cruickshank and Tim Lister, *Agent Storm: My Life Inside al Qaeda and the CIA*, Atlantic Monthly Press, 2014.

14 Nasiri contrasts with the most spectacular double/triple agent in recent times, Egyptian Ali Mohamed (b. 1952), who worked for both the CIA/FBI and Egyptian Islamic Jihad from the 1980s until his arrest in 1998, and is now seen as instrumental in many of the terrorist acts of the 1990s, including the 1993 WTC bombing, the 1996 Khobar Tower bombing and the 1998 US embassy bombings. In 2000, he struck a guilty plea to receive life sentence without parole and has been held incommunicado since then to prevent embarrassment to the CIA/FBI.

15 Al-Azhar University awarded Saudi King Abdullhar an honorary doctorate in 2014 for "his efforts in serving Muslims and the ummah" according to Egypt's official Middle East News Agency. At the same time, more than 120 Muslim scholars from around the world, including Sheikh Shawqi Allam, the grand mufti of Egypt, and Sheikh Muhammad Ahmad Hussein, the mufti of Jerusalem and All Palestine, joined an open letter to the "fighters and followers" of the Islamic State, denouncing them as un-Islamic. <http://lettertobaghdadi.com/index.php> It condemns torture and "to attribute evil acts to God". "It is forbidden in Islam to declare people non-Muslims until he (or she) openly declares disbelief." The words "Islamic State" are in quotes, and the Muslim leaders who released the letter asked people to stop using the term, arguing that it plays into the group's unfounded logic

that it is protecting Muslim lands from non-Muslims and is resurrecting the caliphate.

But on the other hand, it ignores the very un-Islamic occupation of the Middle East which the Muslim scholars are doing nothing to oppose. In his commentary on Surah Al-Hadid, Mawlana Maududi argues that Allah "sent down iron also so that power may be used to establish the Truth and vanquish falsehood. Thus, Allah likes to see as to who from among the people would rise to support and succor His true Religion even at the risk of their lives." What are the 'house scholars' doing to fight imperialism, Israel, etc.?

| CHAPTER TEN |

TERRORISM: 9/11 AND AFTER

Who dunnit?

The western project to forcibly reform the Muslim world to meet the needs of imperialism—Great Game III—received a Godsend in 9/11. It was as if Bin Laden, the supposed perpetrator of the collapse of the World Trade Center, was in cahoots with the US neocon political establishment, and had provided them on demand with the pretext for a war on Islam.

Did a man in a cave in Afghanistan really orchestrate the most spectacular act of terror in the history of mankind, inexplicable in terms of current technology?

Whether or not al-Qaeda and Bin Laden were the real architects of 9/11 remains disputed. In a 2008 World Public Opinion poll, about half the world believe the official version of al-Qaeda carrying out the 9/11 attacks, a quarter don't know, and a quarter believe it was a conspiracy by some combination of the US, Israel and other Arabs.[1]

9/11 opinion poll %	world	Egypt	Jordan	Morocco	Palestine	Nigeria
al-Qaeda	46	16	11	35	43	71
Don't know	25	18	36	28	3	14
US gov't	15	12	13	16	27	7
Israel	7	43	31	15	19	2
other	7	11	1	7	9	6

The only countries with overwhelming majorities citing al-Qaeda as the perpetrator were Kenya (77%) and Nigeria (Muslims 64% vs Christians 79%). In Europe, approximately 60% said al-Qaeda was behind 9/11. Among Arabs, only Palestinians to a large extent believe al-Qaeda was responsible (43%), vs significant doubt among Egyptians and Jordanians (16%, 11%).

People in the Middle East were especially likely to name a perpetrator other than al-Qaeda. Not surprisingly, Israel is seen as a likely perpetrator among Egyptians (43%), Jordanians (31%), and Palestinians (19%). The US government was named by 36% of Turks and 27% of Palestinians. Among Europeans only Germans (23%) and Italians (15%) accuse the US government, and almost no one accuses Israel.

Among Americans, according to a YouGov poll in 2013, 40% believe the official explanation, 38% "have some doubts", 12% are unsure, and 10% "do not believe it at all." In yet another poll,[2] 11% of Americans believe it was actually the US government.

By factoring in the don't knows in the table above, we can say roughly speaking that half the people around the world believe the official story attributing 9/11 solely to al-Qaeda (apart from Egyptians and Jordanians), about a quarter believe it was some complex conspiracy using Arab patsies manipulated by the US and/or Israel, and a quarter don't know.

Where is the truth? Available evidence, and the many contradictions and inconsistencies surrounding the official 9/11 story, suggest that at least some US, Saudi, Pakistani and Israeli officials were aware that a major attack was in the offing in the US on 9 September 2001 using al-Qaeda operatives.

Officially the 19 Arab youth (15 of them Saudi), were operating under their al-Qaeda mentors (notably, Osama bin Laden, Khalid Sheikh Mohammed[3] and Yusuf bin al-Shibh[4]). While 'deep state' conspiracies and false-flag attacks by the CIA and Mossad[5] do take place, this event seems just too complicated to conceive of as a 'deep state' conspiracy, though that possibility remains until convincing answers to the many discrepancies in the official explanation are given.

Bin Laden initially did not claim to be the mastermind of 9/11, condemning the mass deaths in a video message on 16 September 2001: "I stress that I have not carried out this act ... nor do I consider the killing of innocent women, children, and other humans as an appreciable act. Islam strictly forbids causing harm to innocent women, children, and other people".

But could he have done otherwise, given that he was the Talibans' guest, that they were not part of the attack and were not party to Bin Laden's plan to lure the US into Afghanistan? On 7 October 2001 he went a bit farther, saying, "America has been hit by Allah." Khalid Sheikh Mohammed and Yusuf bin al-Shibh finally boasted that they orchestrated 9/11 in an interview with Yosri Fouda in April 2002,[6] and Bin Laden—now presumably in hiding in Pakistan—eventually claimed 9/11 as an al-Qaeda operation in 2004.[7] In 2006, NBC showed a video purportedly made at Bin Laden's compound in Afghanistan in 2000 which included martyrdom messages by hijackers Jarrah[8] and Atta.[9]

At most, only one third of Muslims approve to some extent of the 9/11 attacks,[10] despite justified anger at the US invasions of Afghanistan and Iraq (compare this with Bush's determination for revenge for 9/11, justifying the deaths of millions of mostly Muslims). Whether or not Bin Laden in fact masterminded 9/11, it fit his strategy to hit the enemy at its "center of gravity" and encourage imperial overreach to bankrupt and paralyze the empire's forces. According to Khalid Sheikh Mohammed and Yusuf bin al-Shibh, Zawahiri was not directly involved, but there can be no doubt he too approved of the act. His being out of the loop was probably in keeping with the secrecy of the operation. In any case, after the 1998 fatwa, al-Qaeda thinking concerning the far enemy vs the near enemy and the question of killing of innocents was agreed. The spectacular 'success' of 9/11 meant that it required no encore, and indeed, no such action—apart from dubious plots such as the shoe bomber and the underwear bomber—has been planned on US soil since.[11]

Bin Laden et al were in fact the logical outcome, the apotheosis, of the ascendance of Saudi tribal Wahhabism. Whoever was pulling the strings to produce 9/11, the Saudis as much as the US imperialists produced the charismatic Saudi-Yemeni, now-legendary Bin Laden and, according to the official story, 19 hijackers who were almost all devout Saudi youth.

The Saudis' perversion and destruction of Islam's holy cities,[12] their willingness to mimic and serve the needs of empire and Israel, their promotion of Sunni-Shia enmity, and their embrace of a rigid, shallow Islam unable to address the modern world—all this contributed to Bin Laden's support for, if not his commission of, a plan to destroy the West's most emblematic shrine (the WTC). "Destroy Babylon" was/is a nihilistic version of Islam that welcomed the American military reprisal, engagement and quagmire that was sure to follow, ignoring the primary Quranic injunction that 'the end does not justify the means'.

9/11 also provided a convenient *casus belli* for the empire, blackening Islam in the eyes of the world—the most obvious reason for the imperialists to perpetrate such a false flag operation if they are indeed responsible. Whoever is responsible, 9/11 did, nonetheless, instil in Muslims a burning and urgent purpose: to affirm their religion and to let the world know what Islam and jihad really stand for—which has nothing to do with blowing up innocent people.

The Saudi-Pakistani 'Conspiracy'

Evidence censored from the Joint Intelligence Committee Inquiry of 9/11 (2002)—the 28 redacted pages—was leaked to the US press by ex-Senator Bob Graham, pointing to Saudi officials' involvement in 9/11 and suggesting a scenario involving Pakistan's ISI and rogue (?) Saudis. Some of the actors revealed in the 28 pages (so states Graham, who is among the significantly few officials who have actually seen the pages) include Pakistani and Saudi officials and nationals, including Pakistanis Lieutenant General Mahmud Ahmed and Saudi officials Omar al-Bayoumi, Osama Basnan, Princess Haifa (wife of Saudi US ambassador Prince Bandar), and Saudi businessman Abdulaziz al-Hijji. They all had repeated, direct contact with those directly involved in the hijackings.

Consider Pakistani Inter-Services Intelligence (ISI) Director General Mahmud Ahmed, who was 'retired' on 8 October 2001 by Pakistani dictator Pervez Musharraf. The reason? The next day, *The Times of India* reported that, "US authorities [FBI] sought his removal after confirming the fact that $100,000 were wired to WTC hijacker Mohamed Atta from Pakistan [in fact, the UAE] by British-Pakistani

Ahmed Omar Sheikh at the insistence of General Mahmud". Mahmud Ahmed is now working for the *Tablighi Jamaat* dawa society, proselytizing Islam. The 9/11 Commission's Final Report states that the source of the funds "remains unknown".

Ahmed Omar Sheikh—who transferred the $100,000 to Atta several weeks before 9/11 and received approximately $8,000 (the unspent funds) from Atta a few days before 9/11—was arrested by Pakistani police in February 2002 for the Daniel Pearl kidnapping, sentenced to death, and has spent the subsequent 11 years incommunicado. It appears now that he was not Pearl's murderer (Khalid Sheikh Mohammed confessed to this after his arrest), but Pakistan refuses to permit his extradition to the US in connection with Pearl or 9/11, presumably because he could implicate senior Pakistani officials.[13]

Ex-Senator Graham, who chaired the Joint Inquiry in 2002, told *IBTimes* in 2013: "The Saudi government without question was supporting the hijackers who lived in San Diego. You can't have 19 people living in the United States for, in some cases, almost two years, taking flight lessons and other preparations, without someone paying for it. But I think it goes much broader than that. The agencies from CIA and FBI have suppressed that information so American people don't have the facts."

Two of the Saudi officials in question are Omar al-Bayoumi and Osama Basnan. Bayoumi worked for the Saudi Ministry of Defense and Aviation. They moved to the US in 1994, and in 2000—after a visit to the Saudi Consulate in Los Angeles—invited two of the hijackers, Khalid al-Mihdhar and Nawaf al-Hazmi,[14] to San Diego. Bayoumi found the two future hijackers an apartment and paid their first and last months rent ($1,500). Bayoumi left the US in July 2001, was briefly interviewed in Britain by the FBI after 9/11, but released and never brought back to the US for questioning. As for Basnan, *Newsweek* reported that he received $73,000 over several years from Princess Haifa, wife of Saudi US ambassador Prince Bandar (now Saudi intelligence chief). Basnan apparently took over Bayoumi's responsibilities with the hijackers—whatever they were—but remained at large immediately after 9/11, was never questioned, and was finally deported to Saudi Arabia in November 2002 on a visa-violation charge.

Then there is the Floridian Saudi millionaire Abdulaziz al-Hijji. The Hijji family fled their Sarasota mansion and the country just weeks before 9/11, leaving behind three luxury cars, clothing, furniture and fresh food in the frig. The gated community's visitor logs and photos of car license tags showed that future 9/11 hijackers Mohamed Atta, Marwan al-Shehhi,[15] Walid al-Shehri[16] and Ziad Jarrah visited the Hijji home, which was only a few miles from their flight school. Abdulaziz returned to wrap up his affairs in 2005 but was not detained or questioned.

The Saudi connection ran through the then intelligence chief Prince Turki bin Faisal al-Saud (b. 1945), who had agreed to let Bin Laden leave Saudi Arabia in 1992 and purportedly to provide him with secret funds as long as al-Qaeda refrained from promoting jihad in the kingdom.[17] The Saudis' refusal to accept Sudan's offer to extradite Bin Laden in 1996 suggests the Saudi leadership feared/ respected/ encouraged Bin Laden in his self-styled jihad as long as he left them alone, as he was merely doing what they should have been doing as followers of Wahhab. In *Ghost Wars: The Secret History of the CIA, Afghanistan, and Bin Laden, from the Soviet Invasion to September 10, 2001* (2004), Steve Coll writes that the CIA realized and admitted this.[18]

The idea behind the Saudi-Pakistani understanding was/is a Saudi-led hegemony in the Muslim world (acceptable to the US), where Pakistan would preside in Central Asia. The Pentagon, CIA and FBI lied to the 9/11 Commission, not only to protect their links to their own duplicitous agents, but—more importantly—to prevent the whole Saudi/ Pakistani/ US alliance from collapsing.

The US State Department was encouraging Unocal in its Afghan gas pipeline fantasy right up until 2001, gambling that the Taliban would bow to Saudi-Pakistani pressure to conform to this grand strategy of Saudi-led hegemony with Pakistan as Big Brother to the Taliban. But the US, by inciting a jihad against the Soviets, then departing once its ends were achieved, without establishing stability in Afghanistan, had left a vacuum filled by competing groups, a breeding ground for further terrorists who had no interest in making peace with the US to hand it energy resources, or work hand-in-glove with the US on political issues, as do the Saudis. Hence, the dilemma: either the Taliban would have to buckle, or the US would have to invade Afghanistan (and anywhere else it deemed a terrorist haven) after a "new Pearl Harbor".[19]

There is sharp criticism in the 9/11 Commission Report of the Pentagon, CIA, FBI and Federal Aviation Administration for blatant lying and obstruction, though it seems that this concentrated more on covering up their incompetence, their refusal to share vital information, and the fact that their agents among the conspirators were really double agents. Bayoumi and Basnan may even have been *triple* agents, working, as related above, for the Saudis, very likely the FBI, and possibly al-Qaeda. The fact that they (and Hijji) were not closely questioned at the time and have lived carefree ever since in Saudi Arabia is suspicious. Ahmed Omar Sheikh seems to have been another (much more hands-on) triple agent, working with MI6, ISI and al-Qaeda. In his memoirs *In the Line of Fire* (2006), Musharraf said, "At some point, he probably became a rogue or double agent." We will never know exactly *who* Omar Sheikh was working for, as he will most likely die in Pakistani custody, just as the US government preferred to kill Bin Laden rather than to capture him alive.

US Plans: LHOP?

CIA head Tenet and National Security Council adviser Richard Clarke both supported Bush's *pre*-9/11 plan to invade Afghanistan if the Taliban were to continue to defy the empire,[20] and were just waiting for the go-ahead. In a White House memo a week before 9/11, Clarke wrote that he could not understand, "why we continue to allow the existence of large-scale al-Qaeda bases where we know people are being trained to kill Americans. *You are left waiting for the big attack*, with lots of casualties, after which some major US retaliation will be in order." 9/11 skeptics call this 9/11 scenario LHOP (let it happen on purpose).

Afghanis themselves were among the many who had tried to alert the US to what was coming. Massoud warned the European Parliament in France April 2001 of an imminent large-scale terrorist attack on US soil, and Taliban foreign minister Wakil Ahmed Muttawakil warned the US consul general in Peshawar and the UN in Kabul in July 2001 that al-Qaeda planned to strike the US. Jordanian intelligence said the rumored plan was being called the 'Big Wedding', alluding to a martyr's death as his wedding day in Paradise.

The inconsistencies, loose ends, and blatant lies surrounding 9/11, especially with respect to the security agencies and Israel, made the official story inconclusive. The authenticity of some video pronouncements by Bin Laden are disputed, but even if he didn't plan 9/11, given his shrewd manipulation of media in spreading his ideas, he had every reason to take credit for it or to attribute it to divine justice, as he subsequently did. And Bin Laden's co-authorship of the 1998 fatwa "Jihad Against Jews and Crusaders" opened the gates to a 9/11-type attack involving mass civilian deaths. It tacitly approved the Luxor killings in 1997 and the August 1998 bombings of US embassies in Tanzania and Kenya, in which 224 mostly innocent bystanders were killed, and contradicts Bin Laden's pious self image.[21]

In armed jihad, Prophet Muhammad explicitly forbade killing children, women, slaves, and prisoners of war, restricting killing to enemy soldiers. "You shall not be treacherous, you shall not deceive, you shall not mutilate, you shall not kill children nor their inhabitants of hermitages."[22]

It is just not possible that the US government watched this scenario unfold without tacit approval, since it was US petrodollars that have been paying for it all along. From 1997–2000, Saudi Arabia, the UAE and Pakistan—all US allies—recognized and aided the Taliban, and accepted Bin Laden's presence and activities there. Sudan offered to extradite Bin Laden to both the US and Saudi Arabia in 2006 and they refused.

These neo-Wahhabis waged wars in Afghanistan in the 1980s–1990s, in Bosnia and Kosovo in the 1990s, in Libya and in Syria in 2011. They established 'caliphates', however short-lived, in parts of Yemen and Mali,[23] and continue to inspire terrorist acts, though targeting Muslim collaborators (not to mention innocent bystanders) more often than forces of the empire.

While the debate raging around whether 9/11 was a false-flag act (and if so, what kind) continues, in the final analysis, the 'who' and 'how' of 9/11 is a moot point. Whether it was 100% LHOP or 50% LHOP, by 2011, the empire's plans of invasion and regime change in the Middle East were proceeding apace.

Post-9/11 Terrorism

While Bin Laden had been in common cause with the CIA in Afghanistan, his continued existence over the years—now as enemy—provided an excuse to invade Afghanistan, Iraq and elsewhere after 9/11, acts which were guaranteed to incite further terrorism against the empire. And where genuine terrorist acts were lacking, there was always the possibility of false-flag terrorist acts, which have been a staple of imperialist policy from time immemorial.[24] While formerly—the narrative goes—the perpetrators of terrorism were communists, now they are "al-Qaeda", lumped together with the very different Taliban, Hamas, the Muslim Brotherhood, etc., under a label of convenience to serve as 'the enemy' for the West.

But 9/11 is the terrorist high water mark, when viewed in light of the litter of incompetent genuine terrorist acts by frustrated fundamentalists both before and after. Rather than inspiring greater and greater acts of destruction, the WTC towers' collapse coincided with terrorism's swan song in Egypt. The Islamic Society renounced bloodshed in 2003, and in September 2003 Egypt freed 1,000 members, with Interior Minister Habib el-Adli citing the group's stated "commitment to rejecting violence". In 2006 the Egyptian government released another 1,200 members. Following the Egyptian uprising of 2011, the Islamic Society formed a political party, the Building and Development Party, which gained 13 seats in the 2011–2012 elections (12 in Upper Egypt and one in Suez) to the lower house of the Egyptian Parliament as part of the Islamic Alliance led by the Salafi Nur Party. Terrorism since 2011 has been overwhelmingly the work of the Egyptian army, which tried to put an end to the Egyptian Arab Spring almost immediately, perpetrating unattributed acts of violence intended to turn popular opinion against political reform. This 'succeeded' in the July 2013 coup, but the outlawing, jailing and sentencing of the MB, and the slaughter of peaceful demonstrators protesting these acts can only lead to the rise to retributive acts of violence.

The Saudi-Yemeni Bin Laden was officially killed in 2011 and succeeded by the Egyptian Zawahiri as al-Qaeda's chief, but—apart from the ISIS/IS offshoot after the invasion of Iraq (ISIS/IS is not 'terrorist'[25])—al-Qaeda had been a ghost for years.[26] The terrorist incidents since 9/11 most trumpeted in the West are:

- The 2002 Bali bombing (202 killed), Israeli-owned Paradise Hotel in Kenya (15 dead)
- The 2004 Madrid train bombings (191 killed)
- The 2005 London metro bombings (52 killed)
- The 2005 bombings in Jordan (60 killed)

Like 9/11 they are all attributed to al-Qaeda, though none proved to be directly carried out by al-Qaeda, including the Bali bombing (perpetrated by the Indonesian Islamic Society[27]) and the Jordan bombings (by Iraqi insurgents).

The only comparable attack in recent years involving westerners was not a suicide bombing, but the hostage-taking incident in January 2013 at the gas facility near Amenas, Algeria, where the Al-Mulathameen ("Masked") Brigade, an offshoot of AQIM, took more than 800 people hostage. The hostage-takers demanded the release of Muslim prisoners and an end to French intervention in Mali, but the Algerian authorities refused any negotiations and assaulted the facilities, resulting in the deaths of 39 hostages and 29 members of the Brigade.[28]

Despite the many cries of "Wolf!", terrorism has been on the decline. The South Asia Terrorism Portal estimates that terrorism and insurgency-linked fatalities in South Asia have dropped from a peak of 30,000 in 2009 (of which over half were in Sri Lanka alone and many in Nepal—neither of these related to Islamic militants), to just 6,668 in 2013. In Kashmir, deaths dropped from 4,507 in 2001, to 181 in 2013. Pakistan-backed terrorist attacks outside Kashmir, which resulted in 364 fatalities in 2008, killed 29 in 2013. This of course leaves aside the ongoing drone campaign of terror waged by the US in Pakistan.

Only in Afghanistan, Pakistan, Iraq, Syria, Yemen, Nigeria and Somalia were there increases in terrorist attacks against civilians, military and officials alike, which had more to do with US actions and long-standing local tribal conflicts than with Islam, and only local Muslims suffered. Boko Haram in Nigeria is a throwback to the dan Fodio caliphate of the nineteenth century and resentment of the rapid growth of Christian conversion dating from the colonial period. The violence reflects a long tradition of tribal and colonial violence similar to that in Liberia, Côte d'Ivoire, Guinea, and Sierra Leone. Bin Laden warned Shabab in Somalia not to call itself an al-Qaeda affiliate.[29]

Likewise, the conflicts in former Yugoslavia and the Caucasus (Bosnians and Kosovars in secular Yugoslavia, and Chechens in the Soviet Union) had primarily ethnic roots, and were blatantly fomented by the West. The Yugoslav civil war and Chechen insurgency of the 1990s were not primarily about religion, despite the arrival of jihadists fresh from Afghanistan (who were welcomed temporarily by beleaguered independence movements and who tried to usurp the struggles).

US Chicken and Jihadist Egg

The main scene of post-9/11 random violence against

civilians has been in post-US-invasion Iraq, where as many as 500,000 have died as a result of the 2003 US invasion.[30] And the overwhelming majority killed are Muslims, there and in Afghanistan, Pakistan,[31] and other Muslim-majority countries, so the slaughter is not of great concern to imperial planners. Ironically, Winston Churchill has the dubious distinction of ordering the first terrorist civilian bombings—in Iraq in 1922. That this was no aberration on his part is shown by his cold-blooded decision in 1940 to bomb German civilian targets, despite the fact that Germany was not (yet) bombing British civilian targets. Churchill's rationale was that since they didn't have resources or technology for targeted bombing, civilian bombing was better than nothing, and would show the British people that he was a decisive leader.[32]

So it is 'logical' that the US readily resorts today to massive bombing in the Middle East which largely kills civilians. In 2003, Lieutenant General Tommy Franks, who led the invasions of Afghanistan and Iraq infamously said, "We don't do body counts," referring to civilian deaths. According to the FBI, extremist Muslims commit only 6% of the few terrorist attacks that do happen in the West.[33] The few thousands killed in 9/11 and other terrorist acts pale in comparison with this US-inspired slaughter of hundreds of thousands.

Just as Churchill's terrorist bombings had their inevitable blowback, so does this cold-blooded slaughter today. According to Robert Pape and James Feldman's *Cutting the Fuse: The Explosion of Global Suicide Terrorism and How to Stop It* (2010), based on US Defense Department estimates, while there were only 20 suicide attacks around the world in 2000, and only one (against the *USS Cole*) against Americans, in 2009 there were 300 suicide attacks, 270 of which were anti-American[34] (and since 2006, anti-Canadian).[35]

The exposure of Americans to terrorism abroad remained minimal in 2013, with 16 US citizens killed out of 17,891 globally. Almost 3,000 people were kidnapped or taken hostage by terrorists in 2013, 12 of them Americans. Despite the increase in attacks, the vast majority of terrorist incidents were local and regional, not international in focus. The only incident on US soil was the Boston Marathon bombings in April 2013, killing three. Rapid deterioration of security in Iraq, the grinding civil war in Syria, Egypt's post-coup suffering, and persistent insurgency and terrorism in Pakistan and Afghanistan—all directly connected with US policies in the region—were still the main culprits.[36] ISIS/IS made a surprise transition to governance.

The logical implication of US promotion of Islamic jihad in Afghanistan in the 1970s–1980s—as clear as day to anyone with half a brain—was that the Afghans would seek to institute an Islamic state, and that the mujahideen who travelled to Afghanistan to join the jihad would return to their own countries and seek to foment Islamic revolutions there. The probable result—also as clear as day—would be the triumph of Islam throughout the Middle East when those 'jihads' were successful.

Of course, this is not what was intended by the strategists in Washington; in fact, very much to the contrary. When Bush 'liberated' Iraq in 2003, he called it part of the "global democratic revolution" led by the US, though the US continued to support secular dictatorships throughout the region in the 1990s–2010s. But the democrats turned out to be Islamic: in Turkey, and after 2011 in Tunisia, Egypt and elsewhere. And they were more 'democratic' that the authoritarian secularists they replaced. For all the accusations of secrecy against Egypt's Muslim Brotherhood, it was far more inclusive and tolerant than Mubarak's National Democratic Party or the current military dictatorship.

Certainly, there has been no evidence of any receptivity on the part of the West to 'democratic revolution' when the pro-Islamic results came in. The West tried to stuff the democratic genie back into the bottle, beginning in Algeria in 1992 when the Islamic Salvation Front won at the polls. The election of Hamas by Palestinians led to a blockade on Gaza. Secretary of State John Kerry embraced the coupmaker, Sisi, as the restorer of democracy in Egypt.

Even if the US is innocent of false-flag terrorism, the US-instigated scenario of wholesale retaliation—a kind of neocon takfirism—guaranteed that al-Qaeda and similar groups would spread rapidly, perpetuating the unwinnable cycle of violence everywhere—the "intervention trap", functioning as Bin Laden/ Zawahiri had intended, abetted even by those al-Qaeda who are captured, and who under torture 'confess' lies about al-Qaeda and Iraq to further the goal of chaos,[37] such as Ibn al-Sheikh al-Libi.[38] The momentum from the US-sponsored jihad in Afghanistan continues today. After US and NATO intervention in Libya, the threat has percolated to the Sahel region of Africa, destabilizing Mali, Chad, Niger, Mauritania and even Nigeria,[39] putting pressure on secular governments to allow AFRICOM to 'help' them maintain stability. This will start yet another cycle of violent resistance, another "intervention trap".

Destroying Afghanistan as a base for al-Qaeda and finally killing Bin Laden did not end the threat of terrorist acts, but transformed their context. Disabled as a centralized organization with the ability to function around the world, now the new generation of self-styled jihadists such as Suri calling themselves al-Qaeda, carry forward its long term plan for the region, 'managing savagery', without any direct relation with the remaining members of Bin Laden's original organization. All the causes of the rise of terrorism from the 1970s on—extreme poverty and endemic unemployment, in the face of humiliation by US-Israeli hegemony in the region—are still valid, more so since the 2013 coup in Egypt. In light of this, we are caught in the "intervention trap", and the cycle of violence will continue.

Appendix: Al-Qaeda Spin-offs

- **Al-Qaeda in the Arabian Peninsula** (AQAP, 2009), led by Nasser al-Wuhayshi, a Saudi who served as Bin Laden's personal secretary in the 1990s in Yemen. It supposedly masterminded (and bungled) three incidents since 2009 intended to blow up commercial airliners bound for the US. A fourth attempt in May 2012 was reportedly thwarted when the suicide bomber turned out to be simultaneously working for the Saudi, British and American intelligence agencies.[40] In April 2014, dozens of AQAP militants were killed in US drone attacks in Yemen.

- **Al-Qaeda in Iraq** (2003, also known as Islamic State of Iraq and al-Sham (ISIS, Sham referring to Syria and ISIL, referring to Syria and Lebanon as the Levant, and since June 2014 Islamic State (IS)), formed as a direct result of the US invasion of Iraq in 2003, and is considered responsible for thousands of civilian deaths, especially Shia. Zawahiri ordered ISIS/IS to disband in Syria in 2013. The claim that ISIS/IS merged with the Syrian **Jabhat al-Nusra** (Support Front, 2012) was dismissed by Nusra, but in the ever-shifting sands of this conflict, by June 2014, al-Nusra, along with other resistance groups, had pledged allegiance to ISIS/IS in Iraq. As part of the Syrian insurgency, both had at one point effectively been supported by the western-Saudi-Gulf states. However, in Iraq the story seemed to change, as in June 2014, Mosul and Tikrit fell to ISIS/IS control.

- **Al-Qaeda in the Islamic Maghreb** (AQIM, 2007), which has carried out a few kidnappings for ransom, and received a boost when the West overthrew Gaddafi and opened Libya to western briefcases, AQIM and other local jihadis. To the extent that AQIM is now flush with arms and former political prisoners, it is, again, thanks to western intrigue.

Endnotes

1   Respondents were asked "Who do you think was behind the 9/11 attacks?" and their answers were categorized into four response groups: Al Qaeda, the US government, Israel or Other. Any answers that approximated al-Qaeda, such as "bin Laden" or "Islamic extremists" were categorized along with those who said al-Qaeda. Those who simply characterized the perpetrators as "Arabs" "Saudis" or "Egyptians" (3% on average) were included in the "Other" category. Those with greater education were only slightly more likely to attribute 9/11 to al-Qaeda. A stronger factor influencing beliefs about 9/11 were respondents' attitudes toward the United States and Israel. <http://www.worldpublicopinion.org/pipa/articles/international_security_bt/535.php>

2   At *http://publicpolicypolling.com*

3   Khalid Sheikh Mohammed (b. 1964) A Kuwaiti Pakistani, he planned his nephew Ramzi Yousef's 1993 WTC bombing. He plotted in the Philippines in 1994 to crash US airliners into the sea with Abdul Hakim Murad (who attended 4 US flight schools in preparation), traveled to Bosnia in September 1995, worked as a humanitarian aid worker under an assumed name for Egyptian Relief, and obtained Bosnian citizenship in 1995. He fled to Afghanistan in 1996 and began working with Bin Laden, recruiting Atta and heading al-Qaeda's propaganda operations from 1999 until late 2001. He built alliances with Indonesia's Jemaah Islamiah, Abu Sayyaf and the Moro Islamic Liberation Front (20 bombs simultaneously in ten Indonesian cities in 2000, 5 bombs in Manila two days later, killing 22, the Bali bombing in 2002 resulting in 200 deaths, the Tunisian synagogue bombing in 2002, killing 21.) He was captured in 2003 and rendered to Jordan and Poland and then held in Guantanamo.

Under torture, he confessed to the 1993 World Trade Center bombing, the Richard Reid shoe bombing attempt to blow up an airliner in December 2001, masterminding the September 11 attacks, the Bali nightclub bombing in Indonesia and the murder of Daniel Pearl 2002, and various foiled attacks, as well as numerous other crimes. If his boasts are to be believed, then what looks like a worldwide terrorist conspiracy can be traced largely to a few very energetic 'evil geniuses', provoking the question: is it possible some collection of US officials assisted the orchestration of this scenario to provide the pretext for the endless 'war on terror' (the MHOP 9/11 theory)?

4   Ramzi Bin al-Shibh (b. 1972), the '20th hijacker' who didn't get a visa, a Yemeni citizen held at Guantanamo since 2006. He was captured in 2002 in Karachi, and rendered to Morocco for interrogation, charged in 2008, and began his trial in May 2012. In the mid-1990s, Bin al-Shibh moved as a student to Hamburg, Germany, where he became close friends with Mohamed Atta and Marwan al-Shehhi. He failed to get a US visa in 2000 and took on a coordinator role in 9/11, serving as a link between Atta in the US and Khalid Sheikh Mohammed in Afghanistan. He is suspected of having been involved in the 2000 *USS Cole* bombing, and the 2002 synagogue bombing in Tunisia.

5   The CIA's Operation Northwoods and many instances of Mossad operations, especially in Egypt, are well documented. See Walberg, *Postmodern Imperialism*, 225.

6   See Fouda, Yosri and Fielding, Nick, *Masterminds of Terror: The Truth Behind the Most Devastating Terrorist Attack the World Has Ever Seen*, Arcade, 2003.

7   See "Full transcript of bin Ladin's Speech", *Al-Jazeera*, November 1 2004.

8   Ziad Jarrah (1975–2001), a Lebanese said to have crashed Flight UA93 which was headed for the Capitol. He switched from dentistry to aircraft engineering in 1997 and was friends with Shibh, Shehhi and Atta, going to Afghanistan for training in 1999 and hoping to go to Chechnya. Atta, Shehhi, Jarrah 'lost' their passports at the same time to hide their trip to Afghanistan and they got US visas, except for the Yemeni Bin al-Shibh. Jarrah was detained by a UAE official in 2000 who called the CIA and was told to release him ("we'll track him").

9   Mohamed Atta (1968–2001), an Egyptian architectural student and one of the ringleaders of the September 11 attacks, said to be the hijacker-pilot of AA11, crashing the plane into the North Tower of the World Trade Center. He was a graduate student from 1992 in Hamburg, where he became involved with the al-Quds Mosque, where he met Marwan al-Shehhi, Ramzi Bin al-Shibh, and Ziad Jarrah, who together formed

the so-called Hamburg cell. Atta arrived in the US, together with Marwan al-Shehhi, in June 2000. Both ended up in Venice, Florida at Huffman Aviation where they entered the Accelerated Pilot Program. Atta and Shehhi obtained instrument ratings in November 2000, and continued training on simulators and doing flight training. Beginning in May 2001, Atta assisted with the arrival of the "muscle hijackers", re-entering the US on an expired visa, and obtaining a local driving licence. In July 2001, Atta and Shehhi traveled to Spain where they met with Bin al-Shibh and Khalid Sheikh Mohammed to exchange information and finalize the plot. In August 2001, Atta traveled on surveillance flights to determine details on how the attacks could be carried out.

10 John L. Esposito, Dalia Mogahed, Who Speaks For Islam?: What a Billion Muslims Really Think, Gallup Press, 2008.

11 The shoe bomber was arrested December 22, 2001, the underwear bomber December 25, 2009..

12 Ninety percent of pre-twentieth century architecture in Mecca and Medina has been razed, with more to come. According to the Washington-based Gulf Institute. Saudi authorities maintain they have the sole right to decide what should happen to the historic sites in Medina and Mecca. In 1925, they leveled the cemeteries in Medina (where the Prophet's grandson Hasan and Imam Jafar al-Sadiq are buried), and Mecca (where the Prophet's grandfather and other ancestors are buried). They built the 600m tall Abraj al-Bait (Royal Hotel Clock Tower, second tallest building in the world after the Dubai Khalifa tower) beside the holy mosque of Mecca. It houses luxury hotels and apartments and is located on a five-storey shopping mall, where the Ottoman Ajyad fortress (1781) once stood, built to defend Mecca from Bedouin bandits like the Saudis. Currently, as part of their plans to turn the Masjid al-Nabawi in Medina into the world's largest building (capacity 1.6 million), they are threatening to destroy the thirteenth century green dome which holds the tombs of the Prophet, Abu Bakr and Umar, mosques dedicated to Abu Bakr and Umar, and the Masjid Ghamama, built to mark the spot where the Prophet gave his first prayers for the Eid festival. The Saudis have announced no plans to preserve or move the three mosques, which have existed since the seventh century and are covered by Ottoman-era structures. A pamphlet published in 2007 by the Ministry of Islamic Affairs, and endorsed by Grand Mufti of Saudi Arabia Abdulaziz al-Sheikh, called for the dome to be demolished and the graves of Muhammad, Abu Bakr and Umar to be flattened.

13 The delay in his ongoing appeal has been ascribed to his links with

MI6 and ISI director-general Mahmud Ahmed (who FBI forced into retirement October 2011 because he sent $100,000 to Atta via UAE just weeks before 9/11. Atta sent back $8,000 on 8 September 2011). Former Pakistani President Pervez Musharraf, in his book *In the Line of Fire*, stated that Ahmed Omar Sheikh was originally recruited by MI6 while studying at the London School of Economics and was sent to the Balkans by MI6 to engage in jihadi operations. Obviously Ahmed Omar Sheikh could reveal the extent of Pakistan's complicity in 9/11 and the fact that ISI allowed the Pearl kidnapping and execution (ISI worried Pearl was reporting to Indian intelligence and the CIA and would uncover the ISI/jihadi links).

14 Khalid Mihdhar (1975–2001), said to be the Saudi pilot of AA77 targeting the Pentagon. Mihdhar went to the US in 2000, training at a flight school with Hazmi, left and returned 4 July 2001 (despite being on the CIA watch list and with the FBI looking for him). Nawaf al-Hazmi (1976–2001), also Saudi and said to be co-pilot of AA77 striking the Pentagon. He extended his US visa in July 2001. Both he and Mihdhar attended the Kuala Lumpur summit in 2000.

15 Marwan al-Shehhi (1978–2001), from the UAE, said to be pilot of UA175 which crashed into the South Tower. He and Jarrah trained with Atta in Georgia and Florida.

16 Walid Shehri (1978—2001), a Saudi who is said to have helped Atta hijack Flight AA11.

17 In 2002, Prince Turki bin Faisal al-Saud was named in a multi-billion dollar lawsuit by the families of 11 September victims, alleging that he and other Saudi princes, banks, and charities may have funded the terrorists involved in the attack. In addition to intelligence chief, he also served as ambassador to the UK (2003) and the US (2005) before resigning abruptly. His involvement was also strongly implied in the Michael Moore documentary "Fahrenheit 911". A reporter for the *Baltimore Chronicle* claimed he was flown out of the United States shortly after the terrorist attacks, but the claim disappeared from later versions of the article. Prince Turki described "Fahrenheit 911" as "grossly unfair" to Saudis. Turki won a libel suit against *Paris Match* in December 2004 over claims he was linked to 9/11. Prince Turki maintains that he had had no contact with bin Laden since Iraq's invasion of Kuwait in August 1990.

18 Steve Coll *Ghost Wars: The Secret History of the CIA, Afghanistan, and Bin Laden, from the Soviet Invasion to September 10, 2001*, New York: Penguin, 2004, 511. Cofer Black, chief of the CIA Counterterrorist Center, said they "had to maintain contact with [anti-Taliban Afghan leader] Massoud to prepare for the day—a virtual certainty—when

al-Qaeda pulled off a major attack against the US ... preparing the battlefield for WWIII." Ibid., 518.

Yet more evidence pointing to Saudi involvement is related by Gerald Posner in *Why America Slept: The Failure to Prevent 9/11* (2003), based on testimony by Abu Zubaydah (b. 1971), supposedly Bin Laden's recruiter and writer of al Qaeda's manual on resistance techniques. He is at the center of the ongoing torture scandal. #3 on the US list of terrorists (after Bin Laden and Zawahiri), a Palestinian raised in Saudi Arabia, who was arrested 2002 in Pakistan and handed over to the US (as of 2014, imprisoned in Guantanamo). He was duped by US interrogators masquerading as Saudis, providing them with phone numbers for a senior member of the Saudi royal family who would "tell you what to do." The numbers were traced to Prince Ahmed bin Salman bin Abdulaziz (1958–2002), a nephew of King Fahd, who was murdered shortly thereafter.

Zubaydah revealed more details of Saudi and Pakistani ties to Bin Laden, which the CIA passed on to the related governments, including a 1996 meeting where Pakistani air force officer Mushaf Ali Mir also promised Bin Laden protection, arms and supplies for al-Qaeda. In the space of one week in July 2002, three of the four persons named by Zubaydah were dead:
- Prince Ahmed bin Salman bin Abdulaziz, 43, of a heart attack,
- Prince Sultan bin Faisal bin Turki bin Abdullah, 41, of a heart attack,
- Prince Fahd bin Turki bin Saud al-Kabir, 25, "of thirst".
- Seven months later, a plane crash killed Pakistani Air Marshal Mushaf Ali Mir, his wife and several aides in Pakistan.)

19 Project for a New American Century (PNAC), a neocon thinktank founded in 1997, published *Rebuilding America's Defenses: Strategies, Forces, and Resources For a New Century* in September 2000, calling for the US "to preserve and extend its position of global leadership by maintaining the preeminence of US military forces. ... The process of transformation is likely to be a long one, absent some catastrophic and catalyzing event—like a new Pearl Harbor." Secretary of Defense Donald Rumsfeld issued a paper less than two weeks after 9/11 outlining the strategy. "We're going to take out seven countries in five years," a senior general told General Wesley Clark, "starting with Iraq and Syria and ending with Iran." The hit list included Lebanon, Libya, Somalia and Sudan. Wesley Clark, *A Time to Lead: For Duty, Honor and Country*, Palgrave Macmillan, 2007.

20 As Bush told the 9/11 Commission, to justify invading Afghanistan and get Bin Laden, it was necessary to await "another attack on America".

21	The date of the embassy bombings marked the eighth anniversary of the arrival of American forces in Saudi Arabia. The attacks were linked to the Egyptian Islamic Jihad, brought Bin Laden and Zawahiri to the attention of the American public for the first time, and resulted in the FBI placing Bin Laden on its Ten Most Wanted Fugitives list and Bin Laden's indictment for "conspiracy to attack defense utilities of the United States". Bin Laden was never indicted in relation to 9/11 nor, it should be reiterated, did he make the FBI list for that offense.
22	Hadith reported by Ibn Hanbal, quoted in Ramadan, *In the Footsteps of the Prophet: Lessons from the Life of Muhammad*, UK: Oxford University Press, 2007.
23	Not so bizarre, considering the nineteenth century Oman-Yemen emirate and African jihadi movements of reformist Sufi orders which resulted in Islamic states in the 18th–19th centuries in northern Nigeria, Morocco, Libya, Sudan. See *From Postmodernism to Postsecularism*, Chapter 1
24	See endnote 80.
25	ISIS/IS is not carrying out terrorist acts. The term 'terrorist' is so misused, it has become more of a morbid joke than a meaningful political term.
26	CIA director Leon Panetta told ABC's "This Week": "There are at most 50–100, maybe less. There's no question that the main location of al-Qaeda is in the tribal areas of Pakistan." *ABC News*, 27 June 2010.
27	The 2002 Bali nightclub bombing was supposedly organized by Indonesian Hambali (b. 1964), aka Riduan Isamuddin, "the Osama bin Laden of Southeast Asia", leader of the Indonesian Jemaah Islamiyah (JI). He traveled to Afghanistan in 1983 and met Bin Laden. He fled Suharto's "New Order" in 1985 for Malaysia. After Arab visitors began funding JI, he founded a front company, Konsojaya, in 1994, as an import-export company trading in palm oil between Malaysia and Afghanistan. Hambali planned and attended the January 2000 al-Qaeda summit in Kuala Lumpur, attended by 9/11 hijackers Khalid al-Mihdhar and Nawaf al-Hazmi. This gathering in Kuala Lumpur was observed by the CIA and Malaysian authorities, but what specifically was being said at the meetings was not picked up. Hambali also provided money and documents to Zacarias Moussaoui in October 2000. Although JI operated independently of al-Qaeda, Hambali was considered third in command of al-Qaeda by the US following the 2003 capture of Khalid Sheikh Mohammed until Hambali's capture in 2005. He was interrogated secretly for three years and still awaits trial in Guantanamo.
28	<http://www.eurasiareview.com/19042014-south-asia-terror-

assessment-2014-analysis/?utm>

29   In a message supposedly seized during Bin Laden's capture in 2011. (Mahmoud Mohamed, "Bin Laden letter reveals strained relations between al-Qaeda and al-Shabaab", *Sabahi*, May 7 2012.) In 2013, the Somali militant group al-Shabab launched an assault on Nairobi's Westgate Mall., killing 67, an attack on a Mogadishu courthouse that killed 29, and a twin suicide bombing at Mogadishu's UN compound that claimed 22 lives.

30   According to *owni.eu*, from 2001–2011, there have been more than 300,000 deaths, half civilian, resulting from the War on Terror. According to a study by US and Iraqi academics, 500,000 have died in Iraq alone since the 2003 invasion. Kerry Sheridan, "Iraqi Death Toll Reaches 500,000 Since Start of US-Led Invasion, New Study Says", *AFP*, 15/10/13. The ongoing bombings of security, officials and civilians, killing dozens almost daily in Iraq are too many to list.

31   Terrorist attacks in Pakistan from 2007–2011 killed 35,000, including:

- in December 2007 the bombing after the return of Benazir Bhutto to Karachi (23 deaths) by Tehrik Taliban Pakistan (TTP), plus 56 suicide bombings across the country, killing 865 security and civilians
- in 2008 17 suicide bombings (300+ deaths) including Marriott Hotel Islamabad (53 deaths), plus the Mumbai bombings by Lashkar-e-Taiba (164 deaths)
- in 2009 TTP attacks in Lahore (150 deaths), Rawalpindi army mosque (37 deaths)
- in 2010 87 suicide attacks (3,000+ deaths) including Lahore (95 Ahmedi deaths)
- in 2011 May army barracks by TTP and al-Qaeda (160 deaths) following the assassination of Bin Laden + NATO killed 24 Pakistani soldiers in "friendly fire"
- since 2007 250 drone strikes (2,000+ deaths, at most only 1/3 being terrorist leaders).

Ahmed Rashid, *Pakistan on the Brink: The Future of America, Pakistan, and Afghanistan*, Viking, 2012.
The Pakistan Taliban (TTP) continues to conduct mass bombings (attacks on Hazaris in Quetta and Christians in Peshawar in 2013, and a school in Peshawar in December 2014, killing 145), which are revenge for the killing of more than 3,000 by US drones and untold numbers by the Pakistani army in the tribal areas since 2002.

32   This of course was instrumental in prompting Germany to bomb London in the famous 'Battle of Britain'. Illogically, Britain prides

itself on withstanding this terrorist civilian bombing, insisting it did not dampen British morale, though Britain (joined by the US) stubbornly continued the policy of civilian bombing throughout the war (were Germans more cowardly/ resigned than British?). Germany caused only a fraction of the same civilian damage as did Britain and the US. Only 40,000 Londoners were killed in Battle of Britain (vs hundreds of thousands in Allied bombings of Dresden, etc.).

33   Sabrina Park, "Only 6 percent of terrorists are Muslim", *http://dailytitan.com*, 13 September 2010.

34   Between 1981 and 2006, 1,200 suicide attacks occurred around the world, constituting 4% of all terrorist attacks but 32% (14,599 people) of all terrorism-related deaths. 90% of these attacks occurred in Iraq, Israel, the Palestinian territories, Afghanistan, Pakistan or Sri Lanka. Since 2006, al-Shabaab and its predecessor, the Islamic Courts, have carried out major suicide attacks in Somalia. See Riaz Hassan, "What Motivates the Suicide Bombers?" Yale Center for the Study of Globalization, September 3 2009.

35   An intriguing footnote to the shooting of a Canadian soldier on Parliament Hill in October 2014 by Michael Zehaf-Bibeau is the fact that his step-father was Libyan-Canadian businessman Bulgasem Zehaf, who joined US-backed jihadists to overthrow Libya's Muammar Ghaddafi in 2011. Such blowback is also seen in the fate of Somali-Canadian Mohamud, a young jihadist who actually made it to Syria in mid-2014, only to die there. Youths such as Mohamud are denounced as misguided and naïve. But they are really just responding to the West's cynical call to overthrow the Syrian government, a decades-old western policy and still the goal of the US government, despite President Bashir Assad being the main force resisting IS.

36   <http://www.theguardian.com/world/2014/apr/30/global-terrorism-rose-despite-al-qaida-splintering>

37   The Al Qaeda Handbook, purportedly an al-Qaeda document found by British police in 2000, instructs members of al-Qaeda how to lie to captors during interrogation, and falsely claim they are being tortured.

38   Ibn al-Sheikh al-Libi (1963–2009), who in Afghanistan was head of the Khaldan training camp, was captured in November 2001 in Afghanistan. False information he gave under torture to Egyptian authorities was cited by the Bush administration in the months preceding its 2003 invasion of Iraq as evidence of a connection between Saddam Hussein and al-Qaeda, although reports from both the CIA and the Defense Intelligence Agency strongly questioned its credibility, suggesting that al-Libi was "intentionally misleading" interrogators, a fact confirmed by many credible sources, including

Omar Nasiri in *Inside the Jihad: My Life with Al Qaeda A Spy's Story* (2006). In 2006, the US transferred al-Libi to Libya, where he was imprisoned. He was reported to have tuberculosis, and in 2009, he reportedly committed suicide.

39 See Chapter 10 Appendix, Al-Qaeda spin-offs.
40 Ewen MacAskill, "Underwear bomb plot: British and US intelligence rattled over leaks", *Guardian*, 11 May 2012.

| Chapter Eleven |

PERILS OF COOPERATION

Saudi Arabia

As noted in the introduction, the idea behind the Saudi-Pakistani-US understanding that led to the Afghan collapse in the 1990s and on to 9/11 was/is a Saudi-led hegemony in the Muslim world (acceptable to the US), where Pakistan would preside in Central Asia. What are the results of a century of Islamic rule in Saudi Arabia, and 70 years in Pakistan?

Saudi Arabia (28 million, 85% Sunni, 15% Shia), founded in 1932, and the Gulf states (approximately 10 million, mostly Sunni), which achieved 'independence' in the 1970s, claim to be the first countries in recent times to be governed by Islamic principles, at the same time satisfying the demands of empire to keep the Muslim world operating within the imperial order.

Given its prominence as guardian of the holy places and its ability to project influence, including its Wahhabi version of Islam, with its immense oil wealth, it is not surprising that many Muslims look to Saudi Arabia for guidance in implementing Islam in their daily lives. Despite disapproving of the Saudi 'pact with the [US] devil', most Egyptians see Saudi Arabia as a better model than Turkey for the role religion should play in government (61% vs 17%).[1]

This derives from the overwhelming desire for some kind of sharia governing daily life (92% in the above poll), and longing for a Saudi-style safety net for the broad population. The oil windfall through the twentieth century has allowed the Saudi and Gulf 'states' (really tribal principalities) to undertake ambitious modernization programs in conformity to the strictures of Wahhabi Islam. (Turkey was not so 'lucky'.) The Saudis gave western corporations blank checks to build state-of-the-art infrastructure, and the kingdom guaranteed its people free health care and education, its men jobs—a kind of medieval Islamic socialism—even as it imported tens of thousands of experts, laborers and domestic help from abroad. The Wahhabi doctrine to keep women covered and chaperoned or out of sight, the encouragement of polygamy, the beheadings and other hadd punishments have continued to the faux disapproval of western governments.

There is still no genuine parliament (let alone universal suffrage)[2] or an independent judiciary among these 'states', but only the feudal-style process of negotiations among king, tribal leaders and ulama. There is virtually no culture—music, creative literature and art are essentially banned. The Saudis are "as indifferent and even opposed to traditional Islamic art as are the partisans of modernism". They are the worst per capita polluters in the world. In effect, they are in the same position with respect to re-emergent Islamic civilization as liberal assimilationists (viz., their common wholesale adoption of western technology), with the difference that they get their western science and life style paid for by oil, in the process, fueling imperialism's war machine against Islam.

The main Saudi opposition is the Shia minority.

Since 1979, dozens of Qatif protesters have been killed (the US uses the nearby Dhahran Air Base). There were large demonstrations in Qatif from February 2011 on, demanding the release of political prisoners (there are thousands in Saudi Arabia, mostly Shia, and torture is the norm). There are also semi-clandestine groups of MB supporters, including the Brotherhood of the Hejaz, part of a broader Sahwa (awakening) social movement which began in the 1970s, and which Bin Laden joined.

Among Sunni Saudis, there are a few Saudi voices, such as Muhammad Abd al-Karim, assistant professor of Islamic jurisprudence in Riyadh. He represents underground critics who reject the absolute rule of the monarchy, and calls for reinterpreting Islamic texts, criticizing traditional Salafis who prohibit engagement with politics and outlaw activism. He argues that Wahhab-inspired jihadists are like the rulers they rebel against in the sense that both build their legitimacy on a rigid interpretation and application of sharia. He calls for peaceful jihad, a struggle against oppression that relies on civil disobedience, strikes, demonstrations and activism.[3]

Saudi King Faisal (r. 1964-1975) was the best of the Saudi monarchs—intelligent, competent, uncorrupt, sincerely promoting his conception of Islam, assassinated by a relative under suspicious circumstances following the 1973 oil embargo. He founded the (anti-communist) Muslim World League (1962), the Organization for Islamic Cooperation (1969), the International Islamic News Agency (1972) and the Islamic Development Bank (1975) (disparaged as "American Islam" by Khomeini).

Qatar

Qatar (1.9 million, 75% Sunni) was headed until 2013 by Prince Sheikh Hamad bin Khalifa al-Thani, who overthrew his laid-back father in 1995, set up Al-Jazeera TV a year later, and used his power as absolute monarch sitting on one of the world's largest supplies of natural gas to guide the Arab secular dictatorships towards some kind of Islamic democracy, promoting the more traditionalist, democratic Muslim Brothers everywhere as the logical heirs of the Caliphate. All the while he is hosting the main US-British air base in the region, and portraying Qatar as a kind of model, orthodox (Wahhabi) Islamic state. (Qatar is hosting the World Cup in 2020.)

It is hard to know what to make of Qatar. Sheikh Hamad

- acquiesced to the West's overthrow of Libyan President Muammar Gaddafi in 2011 and the ongoing insurgency against Assad in Syria (following Turkey's lead)
- finances Doha thinktanks and conferences where western liberals debate the future of the Arab world with likeminded Arabs, and yet,
- supports the Muslim Brotherhoods[4] and other Islamic activists, despite the fury of the West and the Saudis.

His courage in defying Saudi Arabia to address the project of promoting a more responsive approach to implementing Islam in today's world is certainly to be commended. It is not popular in Riyadh or Washington. According to leaked US State Department documents, Qatar's record of counter-terrorism efforts was the "worst in the region" and its security service was "hesitant to act against known terrorists out of concern for appearing to be aligned with the US and provoking reprisals".[5]

Qatar's shifting alliances at present put it more in league with Turkey than Saudi Arabia, even as Saudi Arabia tries to bring Morocco and Jordan into the Gulf Cooperation

Council fold and cement Arab monarchy (including Qatar's) as the preferred political path. The sheikh's juggling act—accommodating the empire and trying to keep the different Islamic activists onside—is every bit as perilous as Turkey's and the Saudis'. It finally exploded in his own overthrow by his son Tamim bin Hamd al-Thani in 2013, who bowed to Egyptian and western pressure to oust Hamas and MB members from Qatar in January 2015. Qatar remains the intriguing odd man out in the Salafi camp, the only one willing to take steps in defiance of empire, however tentative.

Are the Saudis et al craven or farsighted? They are against engaging meaningfully with the current global capitalist culture, only grudgingly complying with the minimal demands of western modernity domestically (though leaving their economic affairs in the hands of western banks and US advisers). The elite live a luxury western lifestyle. No doubt, the Saudis reason that they might as well sit back and enjoy the fruits of capitalism, waiting it out as it declines and Islam prevails. And the Saudis' dawa, financing mosques around the world and providing free study trips to foreign Muslims to study Wahhabism, have had their effect. There is a substantial Salafist minority presence everywhere in the world among Muslims, though their role in governance is minimal. But the Saudi strategy is really just 'the end justifies the means', allowing un-Islamic means in the pursuit of Islamic goals, a contradiction in terms.

In summary, despite the free ride their oil wealth provides, the Wahhab-inspired Saudis and Gulf monarchies have provided little in the way of a meaningful intellectual contribution to the debate about how Islam can accommodate modernity, or how modernity can accommodate Islam (other than to fence off Muslims 'lucky' enough to have lots of oil money). Instead, they produced over time the neo-Wahhabi "obscurantists".

Pakistan

Pakistan (178 million, 80% Sunni, 15% Shia, 5% Ahmadis, Hindus, Christians), Indonesia[6] and Malaysia[7] were shaped by their imperial occupiers and were left in the hands of secular elites after they were granted 'independence' after WWII. Strong Islamic movements were co-opted in the face of the looming Cold War rivalry between the militantly anti-religious communists and the imperialists.

Pakistan uniquely was founded as a Muslim state by the British, the first leader, Muhammad Ali Jinnah, himself a secularist in the mold of Turkey's Mustafa Kemal. Just as imperialism's support for the Saudi Wahhabis and its attempts to manipulate Muslims against leftists was a wild gamble, the earlier (post WWII) imperialist project to divide India by creating a state whose sole justification lay in religion, Islam, was equally fateful. It was clearly part of British attempts to control what was left of its empire, just as was the creation of that other religious state—Israel—at precisely the same time.

It was/is a two-way street. The Muslim League, like the Zionists, loudly supported the British in WWII, gaining crucial training in the art of war. Both the (secular) 'Muslim nationalists' in India and the (secular) 'Jewish nationalists' in Palestine and Europe used a desperate British imperialism on its last legs to get their otherwise unattainable goals, goals which conveniently served the long term imperial interests— an alliance of Saudi Arabia, Israel and Pakistan to govern the Muslim world in league with imperialism—and had nothing to do with reviving Islamic civilization (or genuine Judaism). In fact, a kind of anti-caliphate. And both came with a steep price tag which would keep costing long into the future.

The patina of Islamic governance promoted by largely secular (military) regimes in Pakistan gave way in the

1970s to a more serious effort under the newly 'pro-Islamic' General Zia ul-Haq (r. 1977–1988), who responded to the rising tide of Islamization in the Muslim world. In December 1984, sharia law was established in Pakistan, even as Zia was feted by Reagan and showered with money and arms for the 'jihad' in Afghanistan. Zia boasted he would Islamize Pakistani society *a la* Iran, even as he became America's trust ally in the region against India, Afghanistan, but above all, the Soviet Union. The main effect of Islamization under Zia was to increase the number of traditional madrassas from 900 to 33,000. Funded largely by Saudi Arabia, they became indoctrination centers for Wahhabi-style extremism.

Islamization did not affect politics, the economy remained integrated in the western imperial order, the plans for Pakistani hegemony over the eastern half of the Muslim world in alliance with Saudi Arabia in disarray. 'Islamic' Pakistan became ever more a tool of both the US and al-Qaeda types, a chaotic, unstable state, waging constant war with India over Kashmir, plagued by tribal separatist movements and millions of Afghan refugees. The situation has only degenerated since then. Pakistan's shaky democracy is now headed by the Pakistani Muslim League under Nawaz Sharif, Pakistan's richest capitalist and noted for his corruption.

Forced by circumstances to work closely with the US since it was founded, Pakistan joined Saudi Arabia as a negative example for Muslims. Britain and then the US wanted to have their cake and to eat it—to have a Muslim, anti-socialist ally of empire, but like Saudi Arabia, a nonthreatening one.

Turkey

Turkey (75 million, 73% Sunni/ 25% Alevi[8]) has

been working closely—and openly—with the empire since the collapse of the Ottoman Caliphate and the consolidation of power by militantly secularist army officer Mustafa Kemal in the 1920s. He launched an anti-Islam campaign and aligned Turkey with the West, making it the first Muslim-majority country to recognize Israel (1949), then joining NATO in 1950.

Turkey played a key role in the empire's war against communism, but after decades of repression, the assumed close cooperation between Turkey and the US weakened, as Islamic proponents were elected as soon as relatively free elections were instituted in the 1950s—only to be suppressed by military dictatorships. In the end Turkey's westernized elite could not prevent "restoring the natural flow of history"[9] when the political advocates of Islam finally came to power, beginning in fits and starts in the 1990s. Their experience highlights the dilemma facing those intent on renewing Islamic civilization: how to confront imperialism through the existing systemic avenues for participation without being compromised in the process.

The ideological founder of Turkish Islamism, Necmeddin Erbakan (1926–2011), issued a manifesto, "Milli Gorus" (1969, National Vision). "National" refers not to Turkish ethnicity, but to the ummah, a sharp departure from Kemalist western-style nationalism. His aims were to further Turkey's relations with the Arab 'nations', downgrade relations with Israel and the EU, create a neo-caliphate D-8 or the Developing Eight (Turkey, Iran, Malaysia, Indonesia, Egypt, Bangladesh, Pakistan and Nigeria, constituting 14% of the world's population, 800 million people), and institute a broad economic welfare program. Islamic means and Islamic ends.

He shattered the secular aura that Kemal had built in Turkey, and insisted that people should have "the right to live in accordance with their religious beliefs". By subordinating religion and separating it from the political realm, Kemalism had ironically "promoted the politicization of Islam and the struggle for the control of the state".[10]

Erbakan's political heir, Recep Tayyip Erdogan (b. 1954), founded the Justice and Development Party (AKP) in 2001 His forceful pragmatism allowed him to avoid Erbakan's fate, and stare down the generals, winning an absolute majority in the 2002 elections, thus beginning a new era for Turkey and Islam, implementing the "Turkish model of Islamist-led democratic capitalism".[11] He advocated a watered-down version of Erbakan's project,

- reaffirming Turkey's EU membership aspirations, NATO membership,
- continuing the neoliberal policy of privatization,
- promoting globalization, and
- cultivating an alliance with the Turkish liberal elite.

Encapsulating the philosophy of the AKP, Finance Minister Mehmet Simsek said: "In issues such as family we are conservative. In economy and relations with the world we are liberal. And in social justice and poverty we are socialist."[12] In a 2010 interview with *The Times*, President Abdullah Gul rejected any notion that Ankara had turned its back on the West. Turkey "was now a big economic power that had embraced democracy, human rights, and the free market." It had become a "source of inspiration" in the region. "The U.S. and Europe should welcome its growing engagement in the Middle East because it [is] promoting western values in a region largely governed by authoritarian regimes."[13]

At the same time, the Islamic majority refused use of Turkey's NATO base for the invasion of Iraq in 2003, and severed relations with Israel following the latter's attack on a Turkish boat, *Marmara*, bringing aid to Gaza in 2010 (infuriating Washington). In terms of economics, Turkey remains integrated in the global market, though it is also trying to position itself as a leading proponent of Islamic banking,[14] alongside Saudi Arabia, Malaysia and Iran.

Referring to Turkey's "strategic depth" in former Ottoman lands, then-foreign minister Davutoglu said in Sarajevo in 2009 (after the devastating war there): "We will reintegrate the Balkan region, Middle East and Caucasus ... together with Turkey as the center of world politics in the future."[15] However, as indicated above, this policy has run into problems as the Turks pursue their own hegemonic interests in the region and at the same time try to keep in American good books. The decision to drop the alliance with Syria's Assad and support the largely Sunni insurgents in Syria reflects the AKP's decision to accede to the Saudi/ Gulf Salafi agenda, and the US desire to overthrow Assad for his hostility to Israel and alignment with Iran. Syria's ill-fated uprising of 2011 attracted al-Qaeda militants, upset Turkey's delicate domestic balance involving the Kurds and Alawites, and resulted in a bloody civil war which has spilled across the border into Turkey.

What was meant to be the crowning touch to the new Turkish role—Erdogan's co-founding of the Alliance of Civilizations with Spanish Prime Minister Zapatero at the UN General Assembly in 2005—is now exposed as at best premature, at worst, a cruel joke by the West, with Turkey emerging not at the center of a peaceful new Islamic order, but alone at the center of a vipers' nest of inter-ethnic fighting and international intrigue. The Turkish Muslims' 'map' has run off the page, so to speak. Whether or not Assad survives in Syria, and the Kurds are able to wrest some form of independence, the Turkish Muslims will have to face up to their mistake in trying to 'have *their* cake and eat it'—maintaining their active participation in NATO while pursuing their own neo-Ottoman regional ambitions.

For all his apparent cooperation with the West, as his project to move away from empire unravels, Erdogan is not backing down. He realizes the US is the "mastermind" trying to marginalize all Islamic actors in the Middle East, from the Muslim Brotherhood in Egypt to the Justice and Development Party in Turkey, willing to

> resort to any means, even those we cannot think of. This mastermind will be behind the provocation that will shake our resolve. Actions will be taken to directly target the reconciliation process [with the Kurdistan Workers Party]. But they will not succeed. ... Colonialist minds will always exist, but no power will be able to make Turkey backtrack from its own path. This includes the mastermind at the top and its partners.[16]

The current US-Turkish tensions are not unprecedented: the US imposed an arms embargo on Turkey after Turkish troops invaded Cyprus in 1974. And it is clearly time to revise an alliance born in a different era, when Cold War fears—from both the West and capitalist Turkey—seemed to justify Turkey's NATO membership. "There are growing doubts over whether the US and Turkey share the same priorities and even whether they share the same goals," Washington-based analyst Bulent Aliriza said. "Even when it comes to defining the enemy—there is no common enemy."[17]

Endnotes

1 Three-quarters of Egyptians see the US as hostile to Egypt. More than

60% said Egypt's laws should strictly adhere to the Quran, and another 32% say the country should follow the values and principles of Islam but not strictly follow the teachings of the Quran. However, most also endorse specific democratic rights and institutions which do not exist in Saudi Arabia, such as free speech, a free press and equal rights for women. Among those who choose Saudi Arabia over Turkey as the best model for Egypt, two-thirds also said democracy is preferable to any other kind of government, and a free press is important. Pew Research Center's Global Attitudes Project poll based on 1000 face-to-face interviews conducted in 2012. "Egyptians choose Saudi Arabia over Turkey as model: poll", *Hurriyet Daily News*, May 10 2012.

2   In Kuwait (3.6 million, 64% Sunni, 21% Shia) in 1991, the reinstalled Kuwaiti Sheikh Jaber al-Sabah (r. 1977–2006) was pushed to institute a more meaningful elected consultative assembly, curb the religious police and give more freedom to women. His US patrons, after all, had to justify the costly invasion with a pretense of bringing democracy. Women were finally given the vote in 2006 and in 2009 four women were elected. There are no parties in Kuwait, only parliamentary blocs (Salafi, Popular {Bedouin, Shia}, Liberal), and elections are marred by vote buying and tribalism. The Salafis have dominated the elections and began impeaching ministers in 2010. Emir Sheikh Sabah has dissolved the unruly parliament four times, but the opposition are demanding a constitutional democracy, much as the MBs are in Morocco, Jordan and Bahrain. The era of absolute monarchies is almost over.

3   See<http://www.al-monitor.com/pulse/originals/2014/01/saudi-writers-offer-islamic-liberation-theology.html?utm>

4   Sheikh Hamad gave Salafi/MB exiles such as Egypt's Qaradawi the chance to reach a worldwide satellite audience on the understanding that "they could speak to the world and arouse the fury in Egypt or Libya, but they would have to leave their revolution outside of Qatar." Felix Imonti, "Qatar - Rich and Dangerous", *Oilprice*, 17 September 2012.

5   Scott Shane, Andrew Lehren, "Leaked Cables Offer Raw Look at U.S. Diplomacy", *The New York Times*, November 28 2010.

6   Indonesia, the world's largest Muslim nation (203 million, 87% Sunni, 9% Christian, 3% Hindu), and Malaysia were incorporated into the post-colonial order in the 1950s after bitter civil wars led by the communists, nationalists and Muslims. The British handed over power to the nationalists (as the French did in Algeria), and the communists and Muslims fought each other in opposition.

Indonesia's Sukarno tried to incorporate Islam into the otherwise secular constitution at independence through the Pancasila five principles—moral and ethical norms derived from Islam acceptable to the nation's Christian, Buddhist and Hindu minorities. But communism was at its peak of popularity in the 1960s, and Suharto's US-backed 1965 coup was against them rather than Muslims, who joined in the slaughter of up to a half a million. (This contrasted with Nasser's coup in Egypt in 1952 and his embrace of socialism against the empire, though the Muslims suffered in the same way.) After Suharto's fall in 1999, the Muslims quickly asserted political authority, and the first president of Indonesia was Abdurrahman Wahid, the head of the Islamic Nahdlatul Ulama (1923, NU, renaissance scholars), the largest Muslim organization in Indonesia (with 30 million followers today). However, Wahid was quickly pushed aside, and so far pro-Islam activists are ineffectual, divided into various political parties, some regional. Another negative example for Muslims.

7   Malaysia (30 million, 61% Sunni, 20% Buddhism, 9% Christianity, 6% Hinduism) had a less traumatic post-colonial history, where Muslims were successfully incorporated into the liberation movement. The United Malaysia National Organization (UMNO), the main political party in the National Front (a coalition of three parties representing Malays, Chinese, Indians), has governed Malaysia ever since. UMNO from the start represented the interests of the Malays and Muslims, and Islamic dress code and a nod to non-interest bearing bonds have been developed. Mahathir bin Mohamad became prime minister (r. 1981–2003), and pursued various Islamic initiatives, including founding the International Islamic University Malaysia and an Islamic bank (1983). He is alone among Sunni Muslim leaders strongly critical of Israel. He also advocated ending US dollar hegemony and for Muslim nations to establish a gold dinar as their common currency.

In both Indonesia and Malaysia, Islamic advocates are active in politics, though as a respected opposition. Both countries have struggled with the activities of more radical jihadists—Malaysia's capital Kuala Lumpur was the site of the summit of 9/11 planners in January 2000, and Indonesia suffered the 2002 Bali bombing (202 killed). The al-Qaeda threat has abated, though Indonesia faces powerful separatist movements.

8   Turkish Alevis are not directly associated with Syrian Alawis, though both venerate Ali. They are specific to Turkey and are seen as more secular and syncretic, combining Sufism and a Turkified version of Islam where men and women can pray together.

9   In the words of Turkish Foreign Minister Davutoglu. See Eric Walberg, "Turkey and the Middle East: Carpe Diem", *Al-Ahram Weekly*, 24 March 2011.

10 Hakam Yavuz, "Political Islam and the Welfare Party in Turkey", *Comparative Politics*, vol. 30, no. 1 (October 1997), 65.
11 David Kirkpatrick, "Turkey's Erdogan nurtures new role in the Middle East", *New York Times*, 13 September 2011.
12 "Turkish Finmin says EU needs Turkey to retain importance",<http://europeanunion-platform.org>, 19 September 2011.
13 Svante Cornell, "What Drives Turkish Foreign Policy?" *Middle East Quarterly*, Vol. XIX: No. 1, Winter 2012.
14 The goal is to replace interest with charges mitigate risk for both lender and borrower. Just how Islamic what has developed is, is still in dispute.
15 See Cornell, "What drives Turkish foreign policy?"
16 Mustafa Akyol, "The Middle East 'mastermind' who worries Erdogan", *Almonitor*, October 31 2014.
17 Liz Sly, "For Turkey and U.S. at odds over Syria a 60-year alliance shows signs of crumbling", *Washington Post*, October 30 2014.

| Chapter Twelve |

PERILS OF IMPLEMENTATION

Saudi Arabia, Pakistan and Turkey have been more-or-less successfully managed under western sponsorship—so far. Other Muslim-majority countries —Iraq/Afghanistan, Lebanon, Palestine, Tunisia, Morocco, Sudan, Libya, Egypt, Iran—have proved more problematic for the empire. Where not devastated by civil war and subversion, they have provided some experience of Islam in politics. In both Iraq and Afghanistan, there was no equivalent of the Islamic movements as represented by the Muslim Brotherhood and Iran[1] offering a nonviolent alternative to Saudi Wahhabism without being compromised. This meant that the collapse of the secular regimes—Afghanistan in the 1990s and Iraq in 2003—quickly gave way to extremist neo-Wahhabi insurgencies, which found common cause with al-Qaeda, and promoted the al-Qaeda agenda.

Afghanistan

Afghanistan (31 million, 85% Sunni, 15% Shia), following the communist coup in 1978, had became the only Muslim socialist state apart from the People's Democratic

Republic of Yemen (South Yemen).² This had led to ten nightmarish years of a proxy civil war between the US and USSR, ending in a brief truce from 1989–1992 under President Najibullah, followed by three more years of civil war as an "Islamic state", and six austere but relatively peaceful years under the neo-Wahhabi Taliban as an emirate, where Osama bin Laden was given safe haven after he was forced to leave Sudan in 1996.

The period from 1991–1994 was one of intrigue and open fighting among the various factions. The US did not 'forget' about Afghanistan—now, the official Washington line—but on the contrary, tried to install Afghan liberal émigrés who had sat out the civil war, and when that failed, let the country descend into turmoil. This was reprehensible, as after financing the *destruction* of Afghanistan, the US had a clear responsibility to help their allies, the mujahideen factions, to form a government, however unpalatable to the West, and provide massive aid to *rebuild* the country's infrastructure—the roads, irrigation systems, etc. As Secretary of State Colin Powell warned on the eve of the invasion of Iraq, "You break it, you own it."³

US maneuvering alienated not only the mujahideen—now the Taliban, but prompted US allies Saudi Arabia and Pakistan to support the hardest-line factions (Sayyaf and Hekmatyar) to forestall US plans, and to keep Afghanistan within the Saudi-Pakistani fold.

The Taliban's success in disarming all warring factions quickly gave them control of all but a small territory in the north controlled by the Tajik military leader, Ahmad Massoud (who was working with the CIA until his assassination on 10 September 2001). The Taliban organized an emirate and began implementing its primitive version of sharia, which derived more from tribal traditions, excluding women from public discourse, and relied on traditional punishments (lashes, limb-chopping and beheading). Western media and politicians at the time demanded a stop be put to this or at least crippling sanctions imposed on an already desperate nation, but it must be emphasized that Saudi Arabia routinely uses these punishments (60 beheadings from January–September 2014, approximately seven per month), including many foreigners, without any repercussions.[4]

The Taliban did not prevent disinterested aid, but they were not going to accept US advisers, consultants, 'NGOs'—the army of briefcases—intent on westernizing the country, imposing western ideas about the role of women and how children should be educated. Realists in the West calling for recognition of the Taliban as the legitimate government were drowned out.[5]

In the West, the Taliban are best known now, not for their laudable accomplishments—eradicating opium production, disarming and bringing order to a population awash in arms—but for their massacre of 8,000 Shia Hazara in 1998, blowing up the Buddha statues in Bamiyan in March 2001,[6] and, of course, providing a home to Bin Laden. Recognized only by the Saudis, the UAE and Pakistan, the Taliban outdid the Saudis in their attempt to emulate a seventh century Islamic lifestyle as they conceived it (thanks to their Saudi-financed education in Pakistani madrassas in the 1980s), including a ban on all music and modern media except for recitations from the Quran and lectures on Islam. A decade of occupation and civil war made Afghanistan an extreme version of what imperialism can lead to—a genuinely premodern society, but one stripped of its rich premodern culture, brutally occupied, fragmented, starving, with no prospect for extricating itself except by yet further armed struggle. Any notion of Islamic cultural richness had been obliterated by the machinations of imperialism and the now entrenched Sunni-Shia divide.

Though the Taliban had nothing to do with acts of terrorism such as the African embassy bombings in 1998 and 9/11, their guest Bin Laden did, and their reluctance to hand him over to a third party (let alone the US), without being provided with evidence of his guilt in 1998 and again immediately following 9/11, provided the US with a pretext to bring the Taliban experiment in Islamic governance to an end. It's hard to imagine the Taliban continuing to shield Bin Laden if the US had been able to provide evidence of his culpability. But that would mean revealing the US-Saudi-Pakistan conspirators behind 9/11, which the US could hardly be expected to do.

Given the devastation of the country when they took power in 1994, the Taliban's crude interpretation of sharia, and their subsequent isolation from all assistance except for a handful of relief organizations, it is impossible to pass judgment on their governance, except to note that they abruptly ended opium production, and brought a cruel peace and penurious social justice to the country. As it turns out, many Afghans still believe that Taliban rule was better than the alternative of US invasion and prolonged occupation, not terminated even now, though officially declared by the US to be over.

Their subsequent insurgency against the imposed Karzai government, like that of their later counterpart in Syria-Iraq, ISIS/IS, attests to the resilience of Islamic belief and jihad, when aggression has reduced Muslims' resistance to its starkest form. In a hopeful sign, since the US invasion and contrary to earlier practice, the Taliban have almost never targeted Shia, but rather the occupiers and their local representatives.[7]

In May 2014, Afghans sleepwalked to the polls to replace Karzai, with disputed results declaring US-educated ex-World Bank official Ashraf Ghani (and his warlord VP

Dostum) the winner, and the Tajik Abdullah Abdullah, follower of Massoud, a reluctant "chief executive officer". The current Iraqi scenario appears to be the future scenario for Afghans, where a bitter ethnic divide threatens the unity of the country, and a resilient Taliban aims to reassert control as soon as troops leave (now slated for 2015—if ever).

Iraq

US strategy after invading and destablizing both Afghanistan and Iraq (33 million, 63% Shia, 33% Sunni) was to promote "surges" (Iraq 2007–2008, Afghanistan 2010–2012) to defeat growing insurgencies, which were themselves the direct result of US actions, whether intentional or not.[8] It is clear in both cases that the surges were unsuccessful. Iraq's April 2014 national elections and subsequent disintegration parallels the situation in Afghanistan, where the official political process is paralyzed despite (or rather as a result of) western-style elections, and where American plans for withdrawal have been reversed.

ISIS/IS[9] stunned the world in 2014 by capturing Fallujah in January and then most of Sunni Iraq in June, declaring a nascent caliphate on 'liberated' territory spanning Iraq and Syria.[10] Iraqis are now living through a variant of the 1990s Afghan scenario, when the Taliban quickly took over most of a country in the grips of sectarian violence with the promise to disarm militias and provide security. In Iraq's Sunni majority areas, a population exhausted by war and violence, resentful of a Shia government in Baghdad, now accepts a harsh rule by Sunni extremists who promise security.

ISIS/IS is heir to Al-Qaeda in Iraq (AQI), formed as a direct result of the US invasion of Iraq in 2003. ISIS/IS leader Abu Bakr al-Baghdadi, successor to AQI leader Abu

Musab al-Zarqawi and Abu Omar al-Baghdadi (d. 2010), has suddenly emerged as figurehead of a movement which is attempting to shape the future of Iraq, Syria and the wider Middle East along the lines proposed by Osama Bin Laden.

In 2006, AQI created an umbrella organization, the Mujahideen Shura Council, in an attempt to unify Sunni insurgents in Iraq, and AQI spokesman Abu Ayyub al-Masri declared the self-styled Islamic State of Iraq (ISI) as a front which included the Shura Council factions. AQI seemed in decline in 2010, as the resistance to the US occupation was supposedly collapsing due to the US surge of 2007–2008. But the US decision to disband the Iraqi army and ban Saddam Hussein's Baath Party in 2003 also preordained the destruction of the Iraqi state, which meant that the insurgents merely had to wait until the occupying troops departed.

AQI's transformation into a homegrown organization covering the Levant is reflected in its name change to ISIS in April 2013 (as of July 2014 Islamic State (IS)). The Syrian Jabhat al-Nusra (Support Front, 2012) functioned in parallel to ISIS/IS, and supposedly merged with it in 2013. ISIS/IS leader Baghdadi is arguably the real heir to Bin Laden, rather than Ayman Zawahiri, who in vain told Baghdadi to leave Syria to Nusra, and has shown no real initiative since Bin Laden's assassination in May 2011. It was Baghdadi who took the initiative to avenge Bin Laden, which included:

- 24 attacks near Baghdad immediately afterward the US announcement of his death in May 2011;
- a wave of ISI suicide attacks beginning in Mosul in August 2011 resulting in 70 deaths;
- a series of coordinated car bombings and IED attacks in Baghdad in December 2011, killing 63 just days after the US completed its troop withdrawal from the country.

How far Baghdadi is directly responsible for the military strategy and tactics of ISIS/IS is uncertain. Former Iraqi army and intelligence officers from the Saddam era are said to play a crucial role. ISIS/IS is reviving the spirit of the 1980s, attracting jihadists from Muslim countries such as Tunisia, Morocco, Turkey, Saudi Arabia, Indonesia—but also from Canada, France, the United States, Australia, Finland, Ireland, Denmark, Belgium, Chechnya ...[11]

Suddenly the musings of Zarqawi as related by Fouad and Naji above—the "management of savagery" and al-Qaeda's long term plan to 2020—are taking on a chilling reality. The year 2014 witnessed both the 'second stage of the management of savagery' (transforming the chaos of insurgency into an interiorly-ordered Islamic caliphate), and the third stage (extending the jihad wave to the secular countries neighboring Iraq).

Afghan Taliban leaders congratulated their "brothers" in Iraq and Syria, though they continue to pledge allegiance to Mullah Omar as emir. A former spokesman for Pakistan's Tehreek e-Taliban (TTP) even shifted his allegiance to ISIS/IS.[12] Indeed, ISIS/IS's experience recapitulates that of the Taliban in the 1990s, though IS 'caliph' al-Baghdadi is said to hold an Iraqi university degree in Islamic sciences and has shown greater flexibility in implementing sharia than did Taliban leader Mullah Omar. Fears are that ISIS/IS would follow the Taliban lead and conduct mass killings of Shia and state officials, but an NBC report from IS-controlled Mosul suggested that residents generally prefer ISIS/IS rule, that ex-soldiers are encouraged to join in the defense of the city, that Shia are generally treated as Sunni, and the main problem is a lack of electricity.[13] However, most western reports emphasize the targeting of Shia. In an interview with a Pakistani journalist, Baghdadi reaffirmed plans to destroy mosque-shrines where Shia and Sufis worship,[14] and the UN reported the killing of 670 Shia prisoners in Mosul in August 2014.

As was the case in Afghanistan under the Taliban, the project of ISIS/IS to consolidate a nascent caliphate out of chaos and devastation after decades of war, and in the face of concerted opposition from both imperialism, neighboring Saudi Arabia and Iran, make its implementation extremely difficult. Nonetheless, though besieged and attacked, IS has managed to keep order and maintain a functioning economy. The ability to collect taxes and to control and sell oil has provided a financial base. Indications are that it is serious about Islamic governance:

- It has put the caliphate project back on track after almost a century of Muslim humiliation
- It has made sharia (at least its version) the basis of its social order, and there is evidence that it enjoys popularity[15]
- It has (correctly) targeted Saudi Arabia as the font of corruption and decadence, the Muslim world's 'enemy at home'

It is set to become the only 'state' to back its currency with gold coinage. IS says the new currency will take the group out of "the oppressors' money system".[16]

Speculation that IS is in cahoots with the US and Israel is not credible (though Mossad is no doubt infiltrating ISIS/IS). Until 2012, anti-Assad fighters—some now identified as IS members—were being trained at a secret US base in Jordan, but that proves nothing beyond the usual US scheming to manipulate Muslims. Similarly, the Saudis have poured arms into the hands of various rebel factions in Syria, but have failed in attempts to seduce IS and encourage it to target Shia in Yemen (al-Houthis) instead of the Saudi monarchy.[17]

Apart from its anti-Shia sectarianism, the major stumbling block in coming to terms with ISIS/IS is its insistence that while its ultimate goal is to dismantle Israel, the first step in this process is for Muslims to rid the Muslim world of its fifth column, recalling Russian ultra-leftists after the Russian revolution who rejected political compromises with other groups determined to resist capitalism—who Lenin attacked as "an infantile disorder".[18] Baghdadi cites the tradition that asserts that only the caliph can declare war against the enemy, and since the Ottoman Caliphate collapsed, there has been no caliph—until now.

That flies in the face of 70 years of official resistance by Arab governments (put in place by Britain-US) and the Palestinian support movement (dominated by soft Zionists, urging acceptance of Israel as a Jewish state). It is an argument that deserves to be taken seriously. The Arab governments are corrupt and compromised, and prop themselves up with pious words in defense of the Palestinians. The Palestinian support movement is timid and ineffectual. The PLO is more like Israel's policeman in the Occupied Territories—though at least Mahmoud Abbas has sought and achieved admission for Palestine to the International Criminal Court. Uncompromised supporters of the Palestinians realize that Saudi-led 'resistance' to Israel will never lead to a liberated Middle East. So IS has a point, and its strategy cannot be dismissed as irrational. Its phenomenal success is because of its zeal and belief in its project, making it unlikely to waver in its beliefs and commitment.

That said, the project of creating a sectarian Sunni caliphate violently, based on a narrow sectarian Islam is not likely to succeed. If anti-Shia sectarianism grows ("Killing a Shia is better than killing a Jew" is supposedly an IS refrain), this takes the heat off Israel and helps justify US intervention on human rights grounds (reminiscent of the dubious R2P Right to Protect doctrine which facilitated NATO's devastation of Libya). It is possible that the US, Israel and/or Saudi Arabia use agents to whip up anti-Shia sectarianism, or even atrocities and killings, then blamed on the Shia.

On the other hand, if the Shia and Christian minorities do not wish to be viewed as tools of the enemy, they must make it clear that they are not enemies of the ISIS/IS project, must call for their recognition in the time-old way as 'people of the Book', perhaps accommodated through payment of the traditional protection tax (jizya). At present, as dissidents, they are sitting ducks, and the crocodile tears of western leaders and the media are making things worse for them. This cynical use of dissidents has long been ammunition in the western arsenal to confront imperialism's enemies. They are self-made martyrs for western media—and quickly discarded when the West's armies and carpetbaggers are welcomed as liberators.

Together, Afghanistan under the Taliban and Iraq under ISIS/IS could provide a glimpse of the neo-Wahhabi 'utopia', if it weren't for the extreme devastation and subversion they both suffer(ed). Overall, the experience in these two states is less notable for Muslims looking for a new dispensation, than for the empire, should it show any genuine interest in learning from its previous mistakes (unless the actual goal of the West is indeed genocide and chaos).

Just as aggressively waging war to try to wipe out the Taliban in Afghanistan has failed,, so it remains futile to duplicate the same 'policy' in Syria/ Iraq against ISIS/IS, which is, despite its violations of human rights, now carrying the mantle of 'revolutionary justice'. Bombing and invasion only make things worse. The way to improve the situation is massive, disinterested aid to rebuild these countries, channeled through Muslims. 'You break it, you own it.'

Lebanon

Lebanon (4.3 million, 27% Sunni, 27% Shia, 5% Druze, 39% Christian), from 1948 onward, host to Palestinian refugees (now numbering half a million), suffered a decade and a half of civil war from 1975–1990. Stoked by Israel, it led to 120,000 deaths and a million refugees. Israel then invaded in 1982, briefly occupied Beirut, driving the PLO into exile, and abetted a Maronite militia-led massacre of 1,000–3,500 Palestinian refugees and Lebanese, Iranian, Syrian, Pakistani and Algerian civilians at the Sabra and Shatila camps. Following the civil war, Israeli occupation of southern Lebanon continued until 2000, when Israel abandoned its client South Lebanon Army and withdrew. Syrian troops left Lebanon in 2005.

Hizbullah (1982, Party of God) emerged in response to the Israeli invasion of Lebanon, inspired by the Iranian Revolution and the Palestinian resistance. A Shia organization, it inspired the Sunni Palestinian Hamas. It helps the poor and resists Israel through militant MB-type grassroots organizations. Its continued popularity, deriving especially from its effective defense of the country against the Israeli 2006 aggression, has led to its participation in coalition governments since 2005. Its current leader is Sheikh Hassan Nasrallah (b. 1960), a follower of the Iraqi Mohammad Baqir al-Sadr.

Under the intense pressures of threatened and actual invasion during the past four decades, Hizbullah has evolved as a more horizontal, secretive cell structure, establishing "communities of capability"[19] as a form of resistance to western power based on the nation-state. There is relative freedom from hierarchy through decentralized networks.

Hizbullah's social activities repoliticize culture by stressing collective community as a set of Islamic social values, norms and role models to be emulated by Shia living their day-to-day lives.

The ideal is Islamic, envisioning a just community, where there is respect to counter the dehumanization and alienation of contemporary society—to turn anger from a destructive course into something politically useful, socially constructive, encouraging "personal responsibility and initiative and service to community."[20] Resistance is not revenge, but self-defense; it is neither expansionary nor focused on gaining power. In fact Hizbullah has stepped back from taking governmental leadership in Lebanon, which it might easily have achieved.

The evolution of Hizbullah contrasts with jihadists such as ISIS/IS, who have set out to seize and hold territory, and create a new political entity, the Caliphate. But the Caliphate is about more than just territory. ISIS/IS conducts little popular mobilization beyond vague slogans of world Muslim unity, 'shock and outrage' consciousness-building via the internet, and fear among about-to-be conquered peoples. ISIS/IS criticizes Hizbullah (and Hamas, which has built on Hizbullah's experience, despite the Shia/Sunni differences) for participating in democratic processes, while the US attacks Hizbullah, even labeling them as "terrorist" though they are duly-elected participants in Lebanon's government, because Hizbullah presents a significant bulwark against their hegemony.[21] But this development within Islam is a genuine step towards a new social order not just blindly replicating electoral democracy and reliance on the (larger, alienating) nation state. On the contrary, ISIS/IS's obsession with conquering territory in a sense emulates the imperial project in reverse (with all that entails).

Gaza

In Gaza (1.8 million, 99.8% Sunni, 0.2% Christian),

Hamas[22] was founded in 1987 based on the Palestinian MB, and evolved along the lines of Hizbullah, mobilizing Palestinians under the banner of Islam in a way that addresses the lacuna left by ongoing PLO inaction, if not complicity with Israel. Like Hizbullah, Hamas boldly turned to armed resistance, not so much to defeat the far stronger enemy, but as a psychological tool to build a sense of self-worth and sacrifice on behalf of the community. It joined other Palestinian resistance groups to conduct suicide bombings in the 1990s (300 Israelis died), but abandoned them after the second Intifada (2000–2005).

Instead it focused on creating disciplined military structure, and building the elements of a popular culture of resistance, calling for negotiations with Israel to avoid civilian casualties. Rather than concede to Hamas' call, Israeli Prime Minister Ariel Sharon charged ahead with his unilateral withdrawal from Gaza in 2005, forcibly removing Israeli settlers, who destroyed the Israeli infrastructure in Gaza in a 'slash and burn' retreat.

US democracy promotion in the Middle East then took a remarkable turn. Genuine elections were held in Gaza and the West Bank in 2006, and Hamas won. This was yet another affirmation that honest elections in the Arab world, whether in Egypt in 1952, Algeria in 1991, or as later happened in Tunisia and Egypt in 2011, would result in Islamic governments. The US and Israelis were horrified, and every obstacle was put in the way of the new Hamas administration led by Prime Minister Ismail Haniyeh, including the total blockade of the 1.8 million Gazans (still in place at this writing), including random but unremitting bombing and three full-scale invasions (2008-2009, 2012, 2014).

As has been the case with Iran and Afghanistan after the Soviet withdrawal, Israel and the West have worked to undermine the Muslims by intensive external subversion.[23]

The Palestinian Authority under President Mahmoud Abbas and his Prime Minister Salam Fayyad was recognized by the West as the sole Palestinian government, and continued to work with Israel, now in league with it against Hamas and the people of Gaza, further discrediting the PA as a corrupt, ineffectual puppet administration.

Following the Arab Spring in 2011 and the rise to power of the Muslim Brotherhood in Egypt, the situation in Gaza eased somewhat, a situation which ended with the Sisi coup in Egypt in 2013. Fearing Hamas's example as an honest, no-nonsense government, Sisi's Egypt, Saudi Arabia, the UAE and Jordan have openly sided with Israel against Hamas. Egypt and Saudi Arabia's fight against political Islam mirrors that of Israel. Diatribes against Hamas on Egyptian TV are even broadcast by Israel into Gaza.

> The Arab states' loathing and fear of political Islam is so strong that it outweighs their allergy to [Israeli Prime Minister] Benjamin Netanyahu. I have never seen a situation like it, where you have so many Arab states acquiescing in the death and destruction in Gaza.[24]

Perversely, this is confusing cause and effect. Sisi et al accuse the MB/ Hamas of allowing terrorism, whereas, in fact, it is the unjust secular oppression of Muslims that abets terrorism. The best security move for Egypt/ Gaza would be to support the popularly elected Shia Hamas (as the Sunni Morsi government did), rather than to try to undermine them (as Sisi does).

In addition to external subversion, Hamas was plagued by internal al-Qaeda-affiliated groups such as Jund Ansar Allah (Army of Supporters of Allah), which carried out their own operations (rockets, mortars, abductions), forcing Hamas to crack down on them. In June 2013, Hamas deployed a 600-strong force to prevent rocket fire into Israel from Gaza; however, as happened in Egypt following the 2013 coup, militant groups have continued to carry out their acts of resistance despite the Muslim Brotherhood commitment to nonviolent protest. There is no question that Hamas is the best guarantee for keeping the loose-cannons under control.

ISIS/IS condemns the Hamas government as insufficiently Islamic, justifying its call to overthrow Hamas as a first step toward confrontation with Israel.[25] Some ISIS/IS fighters even burned the Palestinian flag during the Israeli invasion of Gaza in July 2014 because they consider such nationalist symbols indicative of the decline of the Islamic world, which succumbed to national divisions through the creation of an independent "nation-based" political state. One tweet stated, "The Hamas government is apostate, and what it is doing does not constitute jihad, but rather a defense of democracy" [which Salafists oppose]. Another tweet said, "Khaled Meshaal: Hamas fights for the sake of freedom and independence. The Islamic State: it fights so that all religion can be for God."[26] On the other hand, Hamas Prime Minister Haniyeh condemned the killing of Osama bin Laden by the US, calling him a "martyr" and an "Arab holy warrior". (The US government condemned his remarks as "outrageous".)

Hamas has three wings: the social welfare and political wings, which are responsible for social, administrative and political activities respectively, and the military wing, which is engaged in covert activities, such as acting against suspected collaborators, gathering intelligence on potential targets, procuring weapons, and carrying out military attacks. The Majlis al-Shura (consultative council), the top political and decision making body, includes representatives from

Gaza, the West Bank, Israeli prisons, and the exiled external leadership, the Political Bureau, elected by regional councils. Before the beginning of the Syrian civil war, chairman of the Hamas Political Bureau Khaled Mashaal operated in exile in Damascus, Syria. He operates from Qatar.

In the tradition of the Muslim Brotherhood and Hizbullah, 90% of Hamas's activities revolve around social, welfare, cultural, and educational activities—services not provided by the PA despite its collection of Palestinian tax revenues—including running relief programs and funding schools, orphanages, mosques, healthcare clinics, soup kitchens, and sports leagues. It supports families of those who have been killed or imprisoned while carrying out militant actions or supporting such actions.[27]

Hamas is well regarded by Palestinians for these services, as well as for its efficiency and perceived lack of corruption compared to the PLO. Despite the blockade and the 2008 Israeli invasion of Gaza intended to cow Palestinians into abandoning Hamas, Palestinian public opinion polls have consistently shown Hamas maintaining its popularity with 52% support compared to 13% for Fatah.[28] The PA, fearing its complete discrediting, has prevented any further 'national' elections since 2006.

Since Hamas took control of the Gaza Strip in 2007, some of its members have attempted to impose the hijab head covering on women, though it has passed no laws regarding dress and moral standards. The government's Islamic Endowment Ministry has deployed Virtue Committee members to warn citizens of the dangers of immodest dress, card playing, and dating. Hamas officials argue that Islamic law is the desired standard but that they would rely on persuasion. Ahmad Yousef and Ghazi Hamad, advisers to Prime Minister Haniyeh, have stated that their role model for Islamic government is Turkey's AKP rather than the Taliban.

Most of the Gaza Strip administration funding comes as aid, delivered by UN organizations directly to provide education and food. Most of the Gazan GDP of $700 million comes as foreign humanitarian and direct economic support, including from the Arab League, the US, Europe, Turkey and Iran, though a breach with Iran due to the civil war in Syria disrupted Iran's aid (a rupture healed when Iran and Hizbollah sided with Hamas in face of the 2014 Israeli invasion).[29] All aid from the West is funnelled through the UN, as they officially consider Hamas a terrorist organization (though western governments and Israel have been negotiating with Hamas officials all along).

Despite a decline in GNP under Hamas, in 2012, Gazan official Mahmoud Zahar said that Gaza's economic conditions were better than those in the West Bank. In 2011, Hamas began buying cheaper fuel from Egypt (rather than from Israel), bringing it in via a network of underground tunnels. This ended with Egypt's coup. Now Israel and the post-coup Egyptian government are working together to destroy the tunnels, precipitating a fuel crisis.

No analysis of the Middle East would be complete without mentioning these legendary tunnels Gazans have continued to build both to Egypt and under the separation wall into Israel. The tunnels, made from cement, mud and wood, mostly go to Egypt to bring life-saving food and drugs. Like the Vietnamese, faced with overwhelming firepower from above, Hamas has gone underground—literally. Hundreds of Gazans have died building and operating them. They have been bombed day after day both by Egypt and Israel. And yet they endure.

Despite the blockade and invasions of Gaza, Hamas remains popular, and was credited with defeating Israel in the invasions (or rather, for preventing a clear-cut Israeli victory), despite the massive death toll of Palestinians (more than 2,000 each time). Israel is outraged by the fact that

Palestinians are repeatedly able to penetrate Israel via tunnels under the separation wall, even successfully launching a drone over an Israeli military installation and briefly closing the Tel Aviv international airport in 2014.[30] Asmaa al-Ghoul, a Gazan journalist who used to refer to Hamas's "terrorism", stated that with its July 2014 invasion, Israel had "created thousands—no, millions—of Hamas loyalists. Never ask me about peace again."[31]

Tunisia

In an irony of imperialism witnessed throughout the region, Islamic activists in Tunisia (11 million, 98% Sunni) were repressed more after 'independence' in 1956, than before under the French. The French handed power to secularist President Habib Bourguiba, who was pushed aside in a coup in 1988, and his even more corrupt successor, Zine al-Abidine Ben Ali, was president for 23 years. Just as Egypt's Nasser, Sadat and Mubarak all initially courted the Islamic activists only to turn against them, members of Tunisia's MB-linked group al-Nahda (1981, renaissance) were allowed to participate in the 1989 elections as independents and, despite blatant repression and vote rigging during the elections, garnered 17% of the vote. This show of electoral democracy by the dictator Ben Ali was cynically used two years later, when Ben Ali had 25,000 of these publicly-declared supporters of Nahda imprisoned.

The self-immolation of a fruit vendor, Mohamed Bouazizi, in December 2010, was the spark that set off the 2011 Arab Spring uprising. Nahda won 89 of the 217 seats in the elections of October 2011 to lead a left-Islamic coalition government. Prime Minister Nahda Hamadi Jebali, leader of Nahda, and President Moncef Marzouki, a former dissident exiled in France, headed the new government, in a power-sharing deal between Nahda and its secularist leftist coalition partners Takkatol and Marzouki's Congress for the Republic. Marzouki, author of *Dictators on Watch: A Democratic Path for the Arab World*, argued during the election campaign that progressive forces should unite with moderate Muslims in recognition of the importance of Islam in the Arab world. During the election campaign, he criticized the "old left" as "secular and Francophone, and totally disconnected from the real problems of Tunisian society".

Tunisia's army is much weaker than Egypt's, and the secular political system was entirely discredited (unlike Morocco's enduring monarchical tradition), so there has been no coup, though assassinations and secular-Salafi frictions show that underlying tensions remain. The secularists are well entrenched, and the MB-dominated government was careful to accommodate them, producing a constitution which was broadly accepted. The new constitution passed by the parliament in January 2014 (200-12 with 4 abstentions):

- calls for a more decentralized and open government,
- recognizes Islam as the official state religion, but protects freedom of belief,
- provides for some restrictions on free speech, most notably in banning attacks on religion and accusations of being a non-believer,
- provides for gender equality,
- protects the nation's natural resources,
- demands the government take steps to fight corruption, and
- divides executive power more evenly between the president and prime minister.

In the October 2014 parliamentary elections, the secularist Nidaa Tounes ("Tunisian Call") won 38% of the popular vote (85 seats in the 217-seat parliament). Ennahda Movement, which had won the 2011 elections with 37% of the vote, came second with 28% (69 seats). Nidaa Tounes portrays itself as a return to the secularism of Habib Bourguiba, who was Tunisia's first president (1957–1987). The 87-year-old Beji Caid Sebsi, who served under Bourguiba three times as a minister, was elected president in the second round of voting in December 2014 as the Nidaa Tounes candidate.[32] This retrenchment was disappointing to the Islamic activists, but understandable in light of the hostility and continued chaos next door in Egypt and Libya.

Tunisia's MB-led government managed to issue a "law on transitional justice" in its last days in office, prepared by the Ministry of Human Rights and Transitional Justice, setting up a 15-member Truth and Dignity Commission to hold hearings during the next five years to expose the repression of citizens since 1956, similar to Morocco's Truth and Reconciliation Commission (see below). Caid Sebsi wants to amend the transitional-justice law that was approved by the constituent assembly finding it unacceptable that it is retroactive. As it stands, the law covers actions carried out in the 1960s, when Bourguiba repressed dissent harshly. Caid Sebsi headed his interior ministry for part of this time, from 1965-69.

The MB was forced to backtrack on the gains of the post-uprising period. To placate secularists, the MB-headed government resigned after the constitution was agreed in 2014, giving way to a caretaker government in preparation for parliamentary and presidential elections. Virtually all those convicted for their crimes under the Ben Ali regime have been freed from prison (Ben Ali lives in luxury in Saudi Arabia). Mohamed Ghariani, the former secretary general of

Ben Ali's Constitutional Democratic Rally party, was released and has returned to politics as an adviser to Caid Sebsi. Even as the secularists bounced back, over a thousand Tunisians have gone to fight on the side of ISIS/IS, and prior to the parliamentary elections in October, 1,500 Tunisian "terrorism suspects" were arrested. Caid Sebsi faces a tough challenge, though not as grim as Sisi's in Egypt. Hopes to paper over the legacy of the Arab Spring are unlikely to be realized.

The Arab Spring manifested itself in radically different forms across the Arab world. It has barely touched Algeria, which has suffered two civil wars—the 1950s against the French and the 1990s following a coup to prevent an Islamic movement from coming to power. Syria and Yemen have similarly suffered from civil wars which have devastated the Islamic cadres.

Morocco

Morocco, (35 million, 99% Sunni), became the most westernized Arab state after 'independence' in 1956, and continues to be a tourist playground for Europe, a "major non-NATO ally" with free trade agreements with the US and EU. King Mohammed VI (r. 1999) moved quickly to contain spontaneous demonstrations, offering a more open political order, allowing the supporters of Islamic government to gain a modicum of power. He criticized the "years of lead" (1960–1990s), when his father King Hassan II had thousands of oppositionists tortured and "disappeared", and instituted a Truth and Reconciliation Commission in 2003, which paid over $100 million in compensation to victims and their families (though no government officials were prosecuted).

The MB's Popular Democratic and Constitutional Movement existed in Morocco from the 1960s but was persecuted along with all the other opposition. It was finally able to register its Justice and Development Party (JDP) in 1998. Large and persistent public protests in 2011 suddenly made genuine elections an important weapon in King Mohammed VI's arsenal, and he immediately announced a process of constitutional reform and promised to relinquish some of his administrative powers. A referendum on constitutional reforms

- required the King to name a prime minister from the largest party in parliament;
- handed a number of rights from the monarch to the PM, including dissolution of parliament;
- allowed parliament to grant amnesty, previously a privilege of the monarch;
- made Berber an official language alongside Arabic.

The changes were reportedly approved by 98.5% of voters, government officials claiming turnout was 72.7%. Following the referendum, early parliamentary elections were held on 25 November 2011, the Islami JDP won a plurality of seats, and, in alliance with center-leftists, its head, Abdelilah Benkirane, was appointed prime minister, in accordance with the new constitution. There is still widespread cynicism, as the king retains real power; only about 25% of Moroccan adult citizens actually voted in the elections.

As in Tunisia and Egypt, the new government was committed to economic growth, improved education and greater Arab and Muslim unity, but has no chance of making any major changes in economic direction. Morocco was invited in 2012 to join the Gulf Cooperation Council along with Jordan, clearly an attempt by the absolute monarchies to help put the brakes on Morocco's Islamic advocates. (Jordan's post-'independence' history has paralleled Morocco's as a monarchy and tourist playground for the West, though less corrupt. Persecution of leftists and Islamists has followed a similar course, and Jordan's MB has had even less political input.)

The political situation post-Arab Spring is fluid. Muslims such as Mohamed al-Marouani, founder of the moderate Islamic movement al-Oumma in 1998, sentenced to twenty-five years in prison for "conspiring against state security", were released. Al-Oumma was finally registered as a political party. The voices of Morocco's Sufi orders and Salafis have also joined the more open debate about Morocco's future.

Benkirane's government has taken some modest steps, boosting funding on social programs, taking on the powerful drug lobby to lower some drug prices and launching a major public Medical Assistance Regime (RAMED) aimed at the most underprivileged. At the same time, he has pursued elements of the neoliberal agenda, reducing the amount spent on fuel, electricity and water subsidies, and moving to raise the retirement age and pensions contributions.

So far, the monarchy has managed to contain unrest and keep Morocco's 'pact with the devil' on-track, counting on its historical prestige and the insoluble economic problems Islamic movements face to discredit them. But, as in Tunisia, unsolvable economic problems and the clash with western tourist culture continue to produce frustrated Muslims and recruits for AQIM. The genie can't be put back in the bottle except by Islamic governance.

Saudi/ Emirati banning of all the MBs—in Egypt, Syria, Jordan, Morocco and Tunisia—has now become a farce, given they must deal with Moroccan and Tunisian governments, and provide *de facto* support for the Syrian

MB as part of the insurgency there. Tunisia and Morocco show how evolution can take place (very slowly) under imperialism, under both republicanism and a monarchy. While hardly inspiring so far, given Egypt's experience of extreme subversion, their experience is worth considering. The reconciliation committees in both countries are important developments.

Sudan

Sudan emerged after a protracted independence struggle in 1956, riven from the start by ethnic rivalry and a majority Christian/ animist population in the south. The 1972 truce between north Sudan (35 million, 97% Sunni) and south Sudan (8.2 million, 18% Sunni) was undermined by President Jamal al-Nimeiri's insistence that Islamization include the application of sharia in the south in 1983. Northerners argued, not without reason, that Christianity was mostly a legacy of imperialism, and tried to turn the clock back to make Islam the unifying principle for a truly independent 'Islamic state'. This did not convince the animist-Christians, who looked back on colonial days with nostalgia, as they were the privileged ones then. This stand-off finally resulted in the creation of an independent south Sudan in 2011.

Hassan al-Turabi, Nimeiri's attorney general from 1979–1985, presided over the implementation of sharia in both north and south. At the same time Turabi supported women's right to vote—his Muslim Brotherhood ran women candidates—and he proposed a broad understanding of the ulama to include professionals in every science and discipline, who must be inculcated with an Islamic responsibility for ijtihad. He argued that "hudud were applicable only in an ideal Islamic society from which want had been completely banished."[33]

There is no end to the simmering civil war across artificial, porous borders where the many tribes share traditional pasture rights and where oil wealth and unused, potentially irrigable land make Sudan a pawn in imperial games. Though hardly much worse than other third world dictators in human rights terms, Nimeiri's successor, Omar al-Bashir, became a target for the West, as he had harbored Bin Laden from 1992–1996 (Bashir offered to extradict Bin Laden to the US in 1996 in an effort to reduce Sudan's isolation, but Clinton refused, in a still-unexplained move). Sudan is also boycotted because of the suffering of Christians in the civil war. It is pilloried in the West precisely because it has played a worthwhile role in exploring Islamic implementation and maintaining a (precarious) anti-imperialist stance.

Libya

In Libya (6.5 million, 90% Sunni, 7% Ibadi[34]) in the 1980s, quasi-socialist military dictator Muammar Gaddafi ruled from 1969, modelling himself on Egypt's Nasser, but with his own Islam-inspired Green Book as ideological prop. Apart from post-revolutionary Iran, Libya was the sole Muslim country to wrest itself from the imperial clutches in the post-WWII period, and should have been a model for Muslims and secular anti-imperialists. But Gaddafi's attempts to improve on the Quran and democracy pleased no one and he remained isolated until his ouster in 2011, as a result of the wave of protests in the region, but more importantly by a massive bombing campaign by NATO.

Chaos reigns in the post-Gaddafi vacuum, now flooded by arms, with rebel holdouts and al-Qaeda active as evidenced in the assassination of US Ambassador Chris Stevens in September 2012. Post-Gaddafi governments are under western tutelage, as their precarious existence is solely due to the West, reversing the quixotic gains of the Great Socialist People's Libyan Arab Jamahiriya.

Abdelhakim Belhadj (b. 1966), who represents the Salafist Islamic trend as leader of the Salafi al-Watan Party, is a veteran of the Afghan jihad, ex-emir of the Libyan Islamic Fighting Group (which carried out three assassination attempts on Gaddafi in the 1990s), and ex-Taliban member, 'rendered' to Libyan jail by the US in 2004. He was freed in 2010 under a "de-radicalization" drive championed by Saif al-Islam Gaddafi, and a few months later became a military leader of the insurgency against Gaddafi.

The Libyan MB modeled its new Justice and Construction Party (JCP) after Egypt's Freedom and Justice Party and came a distant second with 10% to the liberal National Forces Alliance (48%) in the July 2012 elections (which can hardly be considered honest, given the invasion and occupation).(The al-Watan Party did not gain many votes.) The collapse of Gaddafi's Libya allowed western businessmen and EU state-builders to flood the country and give it a make-over a la Kosovo. This will shape Libyan society for many years to come, with western 'security' firms, NATO training missions and EU administrators and educators weaving close ties to the new Libyan elite.

Gaddafi's strict neutrality in the Cold War, his defiant support as a Sunni for Shia Iran in the 1980–1988 war with Iraq, his attempt to unite Africa in opposition to imperialism, and his financial support and even token weapons support to the PLO, the Irish Republican Army and other groups he deemed anti-imperialist, were well-intentioned, but he was an erratic, wilful, and ineffectual leader for Arab nationalists, and a ruthless persecutor of genuine Muslims.[35] More a lesson on how not to oppose empire and implement Islam.

The above experience provides some lessons—both positive and negative—on what Islam manifested in real life means, how resistance to imperialism can be consolidated and eventually help re-establish a unified ummah. But the main actors here must remain Egypt and Iran.

Egypt

Following the Arab Spring in 2011, Islamic activists in Egypt (90 million, 85% Sunni, 15% Christian) quickly moved to the forefront of political life, for the first time able to freely practice their social networking and build their movement in preparation for assuming political authority. In no other Muslim country were the pro-Islam forces so well organized and powerful, except in Iran in the 1970s and Algeria in the 1980s. However, in contrast to Iran in 1979, and paralleling Algeria in 1990, they were confronted by a powerful military with a patriotic, anti-imperialist track record to fall back on, and its own powerful political and economic position to maintain. While the US—Egypt's close ally since the 1970s—was careful not to arm it to the extent that it could threaten Israel, the US provided Egypt's military with crowd-control weapons and training, thoroughly infiltrating and westernizing its officers.

By 2010, the generals were looking for a way to prevent Mubarak from passing on power to his ineffectual son Gamal and inaugurating a pseudo-monarchy *a la* Saudi Arabia. When a popular uprising took place in January 2011, they allowed it to proceed, pushing aside Mubarak in a benign coup, opting to go with the flow, at least long enough to control and co-opt events.

The seizure of power from Mubarak by the military in February 2011 was neither a anti-people coup nor a US-instigated color revolution in the mold of Serbia in 2000 or Kyrgyzstan in 2005. It caught President Obama by surprise, though with the writing on the wall, the US moved quickly to capitalize on the popular nature of the uprising, endorsing the coup and interpreting it as the fruit of Obama's call for democracy on his trip to Cairo in 2009.

In the aftermath of the 2011 uprising, the Egyptian military portrayed itself as the hero but was acting far more like the villain. It was desperately trying to short-circuit the revolution and leave the system in place, *sans* the corrupt dynasty at the top. For the masses, with memories of Colonel Nasser's socialist dictatorship in the 1950s–1960s (despite his ruthless victimization of Islamic activists), it was still heroic. This duplicitous role of the Egyptian military was not clear to many at the time, who continued to support it, in the face of its violence against demonstrators, as it at times was seemingly working with the MB and/or the secular revolutionaries, even as it acted to undermine them. The military's anti-democratic agenda became much clearer with its bloody coup in July 2013.

Notable secularists such as Mohamed ElBaradei and Hamdeen Sabahi, anxious to break the military's undisturbed monopoly on power, made cautious overtures to the MB. Their own lack of popular support was clear from the start. They needed the MB much more than the latter needed them.

This contrasts with Iran in 1979, where a much weaker army collapsed as the Shah fled, quickly exposing the irreconcilable rift between secularists and those pro-Islam. But the faith of the masses there was in Ayatollah Khomeini as the revolution's inspiration, and without the equivalent of Egypt's powerful national army backing them up, the westernizers (including the army) were forced to give way to an openly anti-western Islamism culminating in the Iranian students' seizure of the US embassy in 1979 and the ensuing hostage crisis.[36] The army was quickly reconstituted and a structure of Islamic revolutionary guards put into place, which meant no turning back for the revolution.

Egypt's MB, locked into its commitment to democratic process, had no such room to maneuver, and was forced to accommodate and even praise the unreconstructed military, even as the MB witnessed and experienced first-hand its acts of violence. And when the secularists realized that they would never gain more than a handful of seats in any free elections, and the MB made clear they intended to pursue (as much as possible) an independent, Islamic agenda, the ElBaradei sector 'lost it', betrayed the revolution and threw their lot with the Mubarakite establishment, preferring the neoliberal nightmare of yesteryear, where they could indulge their petty privileges and maintain their cultural dominance.

The MB were loudly condemned for not being 'inclusive', for pursuing their own agenda without regard for the noisy opposition. But, commented MB official Gehad el-Haddad shortly after the July 2013 coup, "If the National Salvation Front [the anti-MB coalition that called for the July 2013 coup] were to send the president a list of their demands on NSF letterhead, and the president were to remove the NSF letterhead and put it on a presidential letterhead, and issue it as a decree, they [the NSF] would go to the street protesting against it."

Until the last minute, the military's intent was unclear. They kept flipping back and forth between their traditional thuggishness and flagrant violations of human rights while at other times showing signs of genuine interest in establishing a more democratic order. For instance, they openly killed dozens of Christian Copts at Maspero in October 2011,[37] then supervised genuinely democratic elections a few months later.

In league with the judiciary, they carried out a postmodern coup,[38] one which hid behind a craven judiciary, annulling that parliament and stripped the presidency of any real power six months later, even as they bowed to the popular will and allowed the MB President to take office and begin to flex some political muscle, retiring the bungling Field Marshall Mohamed Hussein Tantawi and appointing what he hoped were less compromised officers. The police were more consistently against the revolution—basically refusing to work at all after the initial uprising, failing to protect the new president from assault, allowing a collapse of law and order. The police refused to stop demonstrators threatening to invade the presidential palace on December 4 2012, and the MB was forced to call on its own supporters to resist the demonstrators. The resulting altercation was later used to accuse Morsi of murder of three unidentified protestors, though eight MB supporters died defending the president.

Egypt's erstwhile 'allies', the US, Saudis et al, were also fence-sitters, wondering what the MB would actually do. Could it be pressured by the economic crisis, the noisy secular spoilers and the still powerful old guard, with its stranglehold on the economy, into acting as a new face for neocolonialism? Would it accept the pillars of the old order—support for Israel, the craven Arab monarchies, and the global capitalist market system, and continued hostility to the only genuine Islamic government (Iran)?

Unlike the revolutionary movement in Iran led by Ayatollah Khomeini, the MB was handicapped by

- the hegemony of western neoliberalism (vs the Cold War raging in 1979, which gave Iran's Islamic movement some breathing space);
- the greater relative power of the Egyptian military (which gave it control of the revolution in its early, crucial unfolding);

- the greater power of the Egyptian judiciary (which allowed them to annul the pro-Islamic elections and block serious reforms);
- the weakness of the Egyptian 'soft state', which had been captured by the pro-West cronies of Sadat and Mubarak, who were able to manipulate the privatization program to facilitate a huge transfer of wealth to themselves, in the process undermining the credibility of the state—the state which the MB inherited with the seeming collapse of Egypt's neoliberal experiment;
- the weakness of the Egyptian ulama (vs the much greater role of the Shia ulama, which made them the dominant force both before and after the Iranian revolution);
- the significant Christian minority in Egypt which was generally supportive of Mubarak and had its own sectarian, largely secularist agenda in the revolution.

Thus, the MB's seeming weakness and caution was in fact reflective of its sensitivity to democratic norms and processes, being under intense scrutiny for any infringement of same. This fostered its need to be part of a broad coalition including secularists to forestall a coup, and march to a different drummer in the face of significant and strong, pro-West liberal/ Coptic opposition.

In retrospect, it is clear that from 2011 on the military and secular establishment were doing their best to sabotage the MB.[39] The initial coup overthrowing Mubarak had allowed "the restoring of the natural flow of history" in the Middle East, confirming the popular will for an Islamic democracy. This was reaffirmed the next year when the Muslim Brotherhood's Freedom and Justice Party and its Salafist 'allies' gained 2/3 of the seats in what was recognized as the most democratic elections in Egypt's history, undistorted by voting-rigging and unfair financing.

Stripping the MB president of real power was intended to ensure that the hamstrung Morsi would fail, discrediting the notion of Islamic government. This was a kind of postmodern coup, which would take the place of the old-style brutal modern coup to restore precarious US hegemony, without the Pinochet-style murder of the president and torture of his socialist following.[40] (The last time the world witnessed a 'modern' coup to oust an anti-empire leader was against Hugo Chavez in Venezuela in 2002, and it backfired for the US with a vengeance.)

The murder of 16 Egyptian border guards in early August 2012 provided early fuel for the anti-MB forces, but Morsi turned the tables, shifting the blame for the crisis onto the incompetent military, forcing the retirement of Tantawi and other top generals, appointing as "minister of defense with revolutionary taste"[41] Abdel Fattah el-Sisi, director of the military intelligence and reconnaissance department.

Sisi, like the entire army leadership which matured over the past 40 years under presidents Sadat and Mubarak, was trained in the UK/ US (Sisi at the UK Joint Command and Staff College in 1992, and the US Army War College in 2006). But Sisi also had close ties to Saudi Arabia, and his thesis at the US Army War College argued that democracy in the Middle East and North Africa would only take root if it sought "public support from religious leaders (who) can help build strong support for the establishment of democratic systems," and sustained "the religious base versus devaluing religion and creating instability."

As Morsi forged on, it became clear that his was not a US "Islamic client regime," as accused by many on the left. His steps towards independence included:

- an attempt to assert control over the military through dismissals and appointments,
- forcing Israel to put another slaughter in Gaza on hold,
- refusing to sign an IMF loan which would require the government to cut the public sector and food subsidies (instead mobilizing MBers to end corruption in the delivery of bread),
- rejecting intense pressure to join Turkey and the West in invading Syria,
- making overtures to Iran on normalizing relations and finding a peaceful solution to the Syrian civil war,
- using the Shura Council (senate) in place of the disbanded parliament as the last legitimate elected body left by the Mubarakite judiciary and military, whose broad-based Constitutional Constituent Assembly wrote a fine constitution, incorporating much sharia,
- announcing a major economic project for Sinai and to upgrade the Suez Canal,[42] programs which would eventually be taken over by the post-coup Sisi government, and then alluded to by some as evidence of its forward-looking competence,
- completing the drafting of a new constitution which was passed in a referendum with 64% approval, despite the protests of the secular establishment and its control of the mass media, which uniformly denounced it.

Founded two months before the Sisi July 2013 coup, the opposition Tamarod (rebellion) group resorted to fomenting a color revolution *a la* Kyrgyzstan, and in a few weeks made the ludicrous claim to have gotten 22,134,460 signatures to its petition, and attracted 30 million demonstrators on 30 June. The wildly exaggerated claims were blindly repeated by the Mubarkite and western media. They demanded that Morsi resign and if he refused, called upon the military to overthrow him. Even the Salafis were swept up in the hysteria, broke ranks with the MB and joined the secular opposition, hoping to survive what could clearly be seen as an impending coup.

The scenario of the 1973 US-funded coup in Chile was repeated in Egypt, right down to gasoline shortages and disruption of transportation. The Saudi princes withheld promised financial aid to the MB, clearly with the blessing of Washington, and welcomed Egypt's Pinochet with open arms, as he carried out the classic 'modern' coup with lots of (US-made) bullets and tanks. The only difference with Chile is that Allende died with a rifle in his hands, defending the cause. Though Egypt's Morsi was arrested and spirited away, thousands of unarmed MBers launched huge protests, holding to their principle of nonviolence day after day even as they continued to be mercilessly gunned down, many by army snippers, captured on video with impunity. Whether or not Tamarod was funded directly by US dollars, there is no doubt that Sisi and the Egyptian military were encouraging them and at the same time were in daily contact with US officials about what to do. And on 1 July, the US issued an ultimatum demanding Morsi resign or expect a military takeover. One of Morsi's aides texted: "Mother just told us that we will stop playing in one hour."

The MB was not reading from Tamarod's script. They knew they had popular support and refused to back down. The secularists fell back on Plan B and greeted coupmaker Sisi as Egypt's savior. When leading liberal Elbaradei refused to lend his name and reputation to Sisi's slaughter when president, the media promptly called for him to be tried for "betrayal of trust". But there were lots of unscrupulous liberals eager for the limelight. Qatar analyst Larbi Sadiki asks in Al-Jazeera,

> Who are these Arab liberals? Who amongst them has one iota of Mill or Locke's political creativity? They have an obsession with bombing Iran, bashing Islamists, and being bedfellows with the enemies of democracy. It's not their political rhetoric but their relationship with the generals of security forces and intelligence services that is cause for most concern. Instead of learning about constitutionalism or putting together theories about legal and democratic governance, they unfortunately seek satiation of their hedonism.[43]

With Egypt's coup in July 2013, all traces of the post-2011 attempts to reform and clean up the corruption of the previous 40 years were systematically erased. All appointees under Morsi were replaced by military officials and old-guard Mubarakites. A state of emergency and trials by military courts were re-instituted. Complete disregard for legal norms—presided over by the Mubarakite head of the Supreme Constitutional Court and interim President, Adly Mansour—became the order of the day.

President Morsi was accused of treason—for conspiring against Egypt with the hapless Palestinians. Among the thousands of MBers arrested was the 70-year-old Muslim Brotherhood (MB) Supreme Guide Mohammed Badie, sentenced to life imprisonment in September 2014 along with 682 other MB members, while the fate of MB Secretary General Mohammed el-Beltagi, whose daughter Asmaa was murdered by a soldier obeying orders, is still pending after three panels of judges refused to convict him. Badie and Beltagi were themselves accused of murder. Documented murders, like the gassing and shooting of 36 Muslim Brotherhood prisoners in a truck by police in 2013, and death sentences for 528 MB supporters accused of murdering a single policeman by a Cairo judge in March 2014, are ignored or applauded in the press and on TV, now safely back in the hands of Mubarakites. Remarkably, the unarmed, peacefully protesting MBers were/are slaughtered like sheep, then impuned on TV as murderers.

Post-coup presidential elections took place in Egypt in May 2014, intended to legitimize the event. When turnout was revealed to be 15%, Sisi ordered two more days for voting, declaring the first a national holiday, and ordering free bus/ train transportation to allow voters to go to their home constituencies to vote, or face a $70 fine. He then won 96% of the vote (with an official turnout of 45%) against 4% for the socialist Sabahi, whose participation had made the electoral farce possible. All this occurred in an atmosphere of surreal media frenzy, where abstainers were labeled traitors.

The election was boycotted by the Carter Center due to the "restrictive political and legal context".[44] The US and Britain, however, warmly congratulated Sisi on his 'election', legitimizing the coup and renewing cooperation and aid. Sisi ominously vowed it would take 25 years to achieve democracy, a stark reminder of Chile's experience under an equally ruthless military dictator, whose rule lasted 17 years before it collapsed and the (now toothless) Socialists were returned to power.

By not even waiting until the assorted pressures and destabilization forced the MB to sell out to Washington, as its critics—left and right—never tired of charging they had done, and by mowing them down—unarmed—as soon as Ramadan ended on August 14, the army inadvertently restored and cemented the MB's aura of incorruptibility. Of course, it is the army that long ago sold out to the US, taking its $1.5 billion yearly bribe to leave Israel in peace, killing Egyptians rather than Egypt's enemies.

Pro-coup and anti-coup proponents are making unlikely bedfellows around the world. The coup was enthusiastically welcomed by the Saudi sheikhs, Israeli leaders, Syria's embattled Bashar al-Assad, and Iraq's lame duck, soon to be removed, Nouri al-Maliki (albeit the latter two fighting their own civil wars against Sunni fundamentalists). At the same time, Iran, Turkey, Europe were critical, and the US wishy-washy, as Sisi tilts slightly toward Russia. The latest anti-coupers include even some of the most pro-Zionist Zionists, not only "Bomb, bomb, bomb Iran" Senator John McCain (whose visit to Cairo shortly after the coup to admonish coupmaker Sisi was followed a few days later by the slaughter of a thousand MBers), and Brookings Institute neoconservative Robert Kagan, calling for suspending military and economic aid to Egypt.

> Suspending aid now is not merely a matter of principle or even of abiding by our own laws—although that ought to count for something. As a practical security matter, we may pay a heavy price down the road for our complicity—a whole new generation of Islamist fighters, some percentage of whom will turn to terrorism. The United States should acknowledge that Morsi failed utterly as Egypt's first freely elected president. But the reliance on military intervention rather than a political process to resolve crises severely threatens Egypt's progression to a stable democracy.[45]

Yes, "Morsi failed utterly", though Kagan doesn't say why: Morsi never had a chance, having been reluctantly installed by the military following his election, which on the surface gave Morsi the reins of office, but without any power to reign.[46]

Much like the old Communist International, Kagan and the 'democracy promoters' in Washington have created a "Capitalist International", according to Steven Weissman, through which they engage in 'democracy promotion', 'color revolutions' and now 'color coups'. The formula for responding to the color coup: slap Sisi's wrists, paper over the massacre, and restore the safe Mubarakite order.

Pinochet was humiliated in the end, but died under house arrest before he could be convicted of anything.[47] That may be Sisi's worst-case scenario—leaving aside the fate of Mubarak's predecessor, Anwar Sadat, who was assassinated. He still has an ace, however threadbare: he has tried to drape himself in Gamal Abdel-Nasser's nationalist cloak and turn to Russia-China for support. The US quickly lost interest in protesting human rights violations and the illegality of the coup, and renewed military aid, resigning itself to a few more wintry decades subsidizing their Pinochet-on-the-Nile.

As of 2014, Egypt's US Ambassador Robert Ford, with experience in Iraq 2004–06, Algeria and Syria, is a clear sign that Obama will continue to back the coupmakers with all the dirty tricks in the bag, including death squads, to maintain US hegemony in the region. Kagan can rest assured.

Iran

Islamic Iran (75 million, 93% Shia, 5% Sunni) should be a beacon of hope for those striving for a return of Islam as the determining force guiding world events, but as the communist revolutionaries in Russia found after 1917, a genuine threat to imperialism faces unremitting subversion—both hard and soft power.[48] Combine that with the inexperience of revolutionaries in wielding power at a state level, and it is hardly surprising that the Soviet post-revolutionary experience was troubled. The Soviet Union finally imploded under western pressure 72 years after the revolution—much to the regret of the majority of its citizens, including (especially) its Muslim citizens in the 'stans'.[49]

Iran's post-revolutionary experience in many ways recapitulates that of other revolutions, for example Cuba, where unremitting US hostility and the inevitable post-revolutionary disarray resulted in 'revolutionary justice',[50] an alarming exodus of the (mostly western-trained) elite, and a largely negative image pushed by the western media, which claims violation of human rights of those who would undo the revolution. The unremitting sanctions against Iran by the US are much like its blockade of Cuba, which is supported only by Israel.

Not only the overwhelming domestic support initially for the Islamic revolution leading to the declaration of Iran as an Islamic republic in 1979–1980, but other events—the US embassy hostage crisis, Iran's invasion by Iraq in 1980,[51] and just about any moves by the Iranian government since (notably Iran's development of nuclear power)—have been distorted in western discourse in an effort to turn both non-Muslims and Sunni Muslims everywhere against the Iranian experience. For almost four decades, the Iranian economy has suffered western-led and enforced boycotts and sabotage.

The ousters of Hosni Mubarak in Egypt and Zine al-Abidine Ben Ali in Tunisia and the Arab Spring in these Sunni-dominated countries were hailed in Shia Tehran as the "Islamic Awakening", as echoes of Iran's 1979 ouster of the Shah. Western media dismissed this comparison, though the parallels were unmistakable—both countries' leaders were corrupt, secular, pro-US, and the leadership that won popular support was Islamic. Instead, the media tried to draw a parallel between the youthful, westernized urban Facebook activists in Cairo in 2011 and their Tehran equivalents calling for a 'Green Revolution' during the presidential elections in 2009, intent on rapprochement with the West whatever the cost. The latter represent a large faction in Iranian society— the westernized urban elite who indeed had brought to power the reformers of the 1990s under Muhammad Khatami in 1997. But at that time, the conservative ulama prevailed, undermining the weak president and chipping away at the liberals' support, and by 2002, liberalization was dead. However, the brain drain (3 million educated Iranians have emigrated) and capital flight continue, bleeding the economy and undermining the Islamic state.

The populist Tehran mayor, Mahmoud Ahmadinejad, was elected president in 2005. He was identified as a 'conservative', though this is misleading, as in economic terms, he was more socialist (his supporters would simply call him more Islamic), refusing to implement the neoliberal agenda of privatization, instead using oil revenues to subsidize food and fuel. He appealed to both nationalists and supporters of Islamic government, pursuing Iran's legitimate right to nuclear power, strongly supporting the Palestinians and attempting to dispense with dollars in the oil trade.[52] He went to Cairo to hail the revolutionaries in 2011 and gave enthusiastic interviews there to an equally enthusiastic press.

Charges in the western media that his re-election in 2009 was rigged had little basis in reality. To imagine that the iPod uprising by westernized urban youth could have toppled the regime and ushered in a 'post-Islamic' era flies in the face of reality. Recall the defiant words of Ayatollah Ali Khamenei, now Iran's supreme leader, during the hostage crisis in 1979: "We are not liberals like Allende and Mossadeq, who the CIA can snuff out."

Iran's social and economic problems continue to plague it. The current president, Hassan Rouhani, was elected on a reform platform in 2013, intent on lessening domestic and international tensions. Nonetheless, there is much to admire in post-revolutionary Iran. Despite the war with Iraq and the constant subversion and boycotting by the West:

- Peasants were given land and created thousands of cooperatives.
- Agricultural prices were raised and the country became self-sufficient in cereal production.
- The literacy campaign meant all Iranians can now read and write.
- Roads, electricity, clean water, and health clinics came to villages.
- The poorest peasants now have some access to modern consumer goods.
- Life expectancy went from less than 56 in the 1970s to 70 in 2000.
- Infant mortality went from 104 per 1,000 to 25 per 1,000.
- The UN praised Iran's birth control program which began in the 1990s.
- For workers, basic goods are subsidized, there are labor laws regulating the work week and providing job security, and May Day rallies are celebrated with socialist slogans.[53]

At the same time, the Iranian economy is far from being consistent with a truly Islamic order, as it is still allowing the exploitation which is inherent in capitalism to endure, including a stock market and extremes of wealth. As was the case in the Soviet Union, external subversion of the system is resisted by the majority, though not necessarily by the economic elite. Vigilance in defense of the revolution is essential.

Iran's support for the Palestinians, continues to impress the Muslim and anti-imperialist worlds. Iranian leaders from Ayatollah Khomeini to presidents Khameni, Rafsanjani, Khatami and on to Ahmadinejad and Rouhani have all pursued peace initiatives with the West, without bowing to western arrogance. 2001 was declared the UN "Year of Dialogue among Civilizations" as a result of a resolution by Khatami. It was followed immediately after 9/11 by Iranian overtures to help track down al-Qaeda members. This offer was rebuffed, and President Bush instead attacked Iran in his State of the Union address in 2002 as part of an "axis of evil" which Washington intended to overthrow.

Despite the campaign in the western media accusing Iran of a conspiracy to build nuclear weapons, despite a bill of health by the International Atomic Energy Agency, and Iran's membership in the Non-Proliferation Treaty, Gellhorn Prize winner for investigative journalism, Gareth Porter, exposed the real conspiracy behind this in his *Manufactured Crisis: The Untold Story of the Iran Nuclear Scare* (2014). "Through painstaking checking with experts and an IAEA official, I discovered that the documents submitted to the IAEA, which supposed showed Iranian plans to put nuclear warheads on their missiles, were fabricated by Mossad and passed on to the IAEA by the terrorist group People's Mojahedin of Iran. Mossad was sloppy. They were contradictory—clearly doctored blueprints for an obsolete missile system."

Despite the torrent of lies about nuclear bombs, at least some intelligent western analysts have a more nuanced approach to Iran these days—perhaps due to the perceived need for US policy changes in the region. Graham Fuller, former vice chairman of the National Intelligence Council of the CIA, makes the case that Iran has a largely western-style constitution, including democratic elections, that the Supreme Leader is the equivalent of the US president (above the political fray), selected by senior ayatollahs as an "unelected moral leadership".[54] The political philosophy behind Iranian democracy is corporative, seeking to homogenize various interest groups rather than promoting conflict, as in the West. He describes the positive view current that Iran's experience is central to modern Islamic governance, that "the debate is more creative than anything taking place elsewhere in the Muslim World [with] great impact on other Islamic movements."[55] Iran has been able to interpret sharia to improve the treatment of women with respect to inheritance, divorce and child custody.[56]

Just as some imperial strategists in Washington, following the Egyptian coup in 2013, rejected supporting the coupmakers, seeing the MB as a necessary 'evil' to control the al-Qaeda types, so there are realists who favour burying the hatchet with Iran, in the interests of preventing a collapse of the Afghan regime if and when the US forces pack up, and of stabilizing Iraq under a Shia government not directly hostile to the US. Threats to invade Iran by Israeli and US hawks have receded, and what look like genuine negotiations continue to foreshadow the possibility of Iran returning to the western-controlled global order.[57]

The road forward for West-Iranian détente is rocky. Post-revolutionary problems have heaped up, as they did for the communists in post-1917 Russia, resulting in violations of principles (communist in the case of Russia, Islamic in the case of Iran) or their too rigorous enforcement. Protecting the revolution was/is not for the faint of heart, and many Soviet communists lost faith, while others took cynical advantage of the situation. Similarly, saving the Islamic revolution in the face of permanent subversion and opposition by the imperialist world and by accommodationist Muslim governments has been an uphill battle for Iran.

Fuller cites Kalim Siddiqui's criticism of Iran's post-revolutionary experience:

- nationalism,
- the continuance of a bloated bureaucracy,
- lack of thorough land reform, and
- the emphasis on Shiism,

as post-revolutionary features that have harmed Iran's image and its way forward.[58] Inevitably, power corrupts, and Iran's religious institutions and the reality of Islamic governance continue to provoke debate. However, these are criticisms that could be addressed to almost any government. The real reason for the worries about Iran is the fear of what Turkish Prime Minister Davutoglu called "the restoring of the natural flow of history" in the Middle East: the re-emergence of a Middle East united by Islam.

Despite the unremitting sabotage, Iranian politicians have shown remarkable cool and ability to adapt to circumstances, embracing other dissenting nations such as Cuba and Venezuela, helping Iran's neighbors, holding anti-Zionist conferences attended by prominent western Jews,[59] actively building a broad anti-imperialist alliance with BRIC countries such as Russia, India and China, and taking on leadership roles in such organizations as the Non-Aligned Movement (NAM).

Iran has provided considerable aid to Afghanistan

(including a new rail link from Herat to the Persian Gulf) and built its section of the gas Peace Pipeline with Pakistan.[60] It strains to work with rivals Saudi Arabia and Egypt before-and-after the 2013 coup. In 2012, there were two conferences—OIC and NAM—where Iran's increasing international prominence was on display. The Organization of Islamic Cooperation meeting in Mecca saw Iranian President Mahmoud Ahmadinejad sitting next to Saudi King Abdullah bin Abulaziz, and frank discussion about Syria. Iran made the decision to expel Syria look foolish and pointless, arguing that the Syrian leadership should have been invited to make its case first, insofar as expulsion is a violation of the OIC charter. "By suspending Syria's membership, this does not mean you are moving towards resolving an issue. By this, you are erasing the issue," said Iran's Foreign Minister Ali Akbar Salehi. And making things worse, he could have added.

Iran had every reason to boycott the OIC meeting, or to come and denounce its hosts for supporting the ruthless suppression of the Bahraini uprising. Instead, Iranian officials came to the OIC to try to mend fences with the Saudi and Gulf states (and to encourage their attendance at the NAM conference in Tehran),[61] and to try to bring the bloodshed in Syria to an end. "Every country, especially OIC countries, must join hands to resolve this issue in such a way that will help the peace, security and stability in the region," said Salehi.

Just as with the MB in Egypt, the Iranian heirs to Ayatollah Khomeini find they face an evolving playing field, where the imperialists no longer have the luxury of targeting Iran without the threat of blowback. The revolution in Iran, the rise of Shia power in Lebanon as a result of the 1975–1990 civil war, the formation of a Shia-friendly government in Afghanistan and a predominantly Shia government in Iraq have created a new constellation of forces in the Muslim world—the so-called Shia crescent. This, combined with Iran's perennially good relations with neighbors and third world countries, strengthened Iran's position and caused great worry in Washington, Tel Aviv and among Saudi/ Gulf accommodationists, supposedly over the possibility of increased terrorism, even though the impulse for and commission of terrorism in the Muslim world comes not from Shia, but from Wahhabi and neo-Wahhabi Sunnis, to say nothing of US-Israeli instigated false flag operations fingering/ targeting Muslims.

If necessary, the imperialists will revert to 'détente' with Egypt's MB and Iran, just as they used détente with the Soviet Union, where greater openness to the West led to the collapse of the anti-imperialists and the bankruptcy of the communist belief system. The situation in the Soviet Union was undermined by the fact that insofar as the communists were appealing primarily to material motives to inspire Soviet citizens, western mass culture proved the easy winner there, with its ability to make false promises of affluence appear realistic. Islam is the 'secret weapon' of the Iranian revolution, and by implication re-emerging Islamic civilization, accounting for the ability of Muslims to defy the overwhelming power of the empire, and their willingness to die for their beliefs.

In line with the post-WWII imperial strategy to destroy communism and to build up Europe as a common market adjunct to the US world empire, tentative US support for the MBs, combined with accommodation with Iran, might portend its ability to stave off the worse option of unending al-Qaeda-type insurgency and terrorism.

When color revolutions and invasions no longer work, this is the new alternative for salvaging something of the imperial project in the region. A Twitter statement by US Department of Homeland Security official Mohammed

Elibiary in June 2014, warning against the rise of an Islamic Khilafah, said that America's only option was to contain it in order to make it like the European Union: "As I've said b4 inevitable that Caliphate returns ... Choice only whether we support [European Union-] like Muslim Union vision or not."[62]

But it takes two to tango, and the extent to which the MBs in Egypt and throughout the region or Iran would be willing to adjust their policies to align with US demands in reciprocity for such support can't be foreseen. Will Muslims be able stave off the pressures that led to pro-empire color revolutions elsewhere?

Lessons from Egyptian, Iranian and other experience:

- No revolution can succeed based on Sunni-Shia sectarianism. This common characteristic shared by both Wahhabis and neo-Wahhabis dooms their respective rump caliphates. Western-style nationalism also undermines the chances of unifying the ummah.
- Relations with the military and judiciary are fraught with danger. An unreconstructed military and judiciary can overthrow popular governments, and Egypt's recent experience shows that they will stop at nothing. Iran moved quickly in 1979 to purge both—its period of 'revolutionary justice' immediately following the revolution when many Iranians opposed to the revolution were killed or fled. This period of virtual civil war is inevitable in a revolution, but given a lessening of external threats over time, a new order can evolve which is not so hard on citizens' human rights.
- Truth and Reconciliation Commissions such as in Morocco and Tunisia can help heal the wounds of past repression once Islamic activists are recognized as an

essential element in the political process. But they do not preclude some reckoning with the crimes of the past. If the military and judiciary are not reformed, there can be no true reconciliation.

- Electoral democracy is a two-edged sword, but not to be dismissed, given the context of empire, where this is a bedrock. Opinion polls and ballot boxes can be manipulated behind the scenes and by foreign powers, promoting divisiveness and bigotry, and electoral schedules are arbitrary, discouraging honest politicking in favour of false promises and short-term palliatives instead of long-term rebuilding and renewal. But Turkey, Egypt (2011–2013), and Iran show that they can play a positive role in allowing the expression of popular opinion and move the Islamic project forward.

- More important than voting rituals is community organizing and promotion of social welfare on the grassroots level, as shown by the MBs, Hamas, Hizbullah and Iran. Resistance is as much for promoting dignity as actually overthrowing the still powerful empire. Care must be taken with western NGOs—some are fine, some are a direct weapon of the empire, as best exemplified in color revolutions.

- Beginning to confront banker hegemony in the world economy has already started, if tentatively, with so-called Islamic banking, promoted by all sides, from Saudi Arabia, to Malaysia and Indonesia, Turkey and Iran, and attempts to establish a gold dinar for the Muslim world. This movement must work in tandem with SCO/BRICS efforts to reform the world's monetary system.

- In general, the historical, political and economic contexts must be recognized and relations of mutual respect with the West established. Islamic forces have greater leverage today than in the past. It is in the West's interests to work with, or at least cease subverting, MBs and Iran if it wants to divert Muslims' energies away from more radical groups.

Endnotes

1 Iran experienced violence following the revolution, primarily the persecution of the liberal and communist opposition, though both sides were to blame for this. Policies to implement social justice following the revolution were in fact in many respects socialist, despite the suppression of the communists. The revolution itself was almost unanimous and was able to consolidate itself quickly. See endnote 56 above.

2 With the collapse of the Soviet Union, the (socialist) People's Democratic Republic of Yemen was forced in 1990 to join north Yemen, run—with the empire's blessing—by secular autocrat Ali Abdullah Saleh (r. 1978–2012) in what became the Republic of Yemen (25 million, 53% Sunni, 45% Shia). The Muslim Brotherhood (Islah, 1990, reform), is the largest opposition party. After a grueling year of demonstrations and virtual civil war in 2011, culminating in the resignation of Saleh and the 'election' of his vice president, Abd Rabbah Mansur al-Hadi, Islah became part of the interim government. Al-Qaeda is strong in this failed state, and US drones regularly kill supposed terrorists and innocent civilians.

3 This aphorism went viral at the time, known as the Pottery Barn rule.

4 Dane Fallon, "Saudi Arabia Has Beheaded 59 People This Year Yet No Coverage", *Business 2 Community*, October 2014.

5 Despite protests from human rights groups, a State Department official said, "The Taliban will develop like the Saudis ... no parliament, and lots of *sharia* law. We can live with that." There was little likelihood of Russia regaining any influence in Afghanistan and it was very much in US interests to work with the Taliban, which it did from 1994–98 mediated by the Saudis, as the US never recognized the Taliban government. George Monbiot, "Oil, Afghanistan and America's pipe dream", *www.dawn.com*, 25 October 2001.

6 The West was eager to move in an 'army' of restorers to preserve the Buddha statues in Bamiyan, which the Taliban were threatening to destroy, and which they finally did in March 2001. According to the

New York Times (18 March 2001), as well as Taliban ambassador-at-large Sayed Hashemi, the Taliban were furious that foreign aid groups were more interested in restoring the statues than helping starving Afghans.

7   Unlike the Pakistani Taliban, who have targeted and continue to both.

8   When extrajudicial killings and indiscriminate bombings in Iraq peaked in 2006, this was blamed by the US on insurgents, and torture was blamed on rogue elements in the Interior Ministry. The impression created was of senseless violence initiated by the Iraqis themselves, but the "sectarian violence" that engulfed Iraq "was not an unintended consequence of the US invasion and occupation, but an integral part of it" to target Iraqis who rejected the illegal invasion and occupation of their country, the so-called Salvador Option. US Special Forces and Pentagon-hired mercenaries like Dyncorp helped form the sectarian militias that were used to terrorize and kill Iraqis and to provoke civil war. See Walberg, *Postmodern Imperialism*, 137–138

9   Islamic State in Iraq and Syria, since June 2014, Islamic State (IS).

10 Syria's post-WWII experience is not dealt with in detail here. The current civil war has its roots in persecution of the MB in the 1960s–1980s, pushing Islamic activists to armed resistance. Its current situation more or less parallels that of Egypt. See my *From Postmodernism to Postsecularism*, 229–230.

11 See "Syria's Foreign Jihadis: Where Do They Come From?" CNN, September 1, 2014 <http://www.cnn.com/interactive/2014/09/syria-foreign-jihadis/> The parallel between Iraq today and Afghanistan in the 1980s also extends to the Spanish Civil War that preceded World War II, a war of the committed against the entrenched, awash in the betrayals and conflicting agendas of erstwhile backers.

12 Jon Boone, "Isis ascent in Syria and Iraq weakening Pakistani Taliban", *Guardian*, October 22 2014. Shahidullah Shaid was expelled as a result.

13 Yuka Tachibana, "What Life Is Like in Iraq's City of Mosul Under ISIS Rule", NBC, 9 July 2014.

14 He also vowed to overthrow the Saudi monarchy and to liberate Palestine, and along with his nemesis Zawahiri, condemned the Egyptian coup against the MB. Interview with *Let Us Build Pakistan*, 3 July 2014. <http://informationclearinghouse.info/article39058.htm>

15 See for instance "Enforcing Sharia in Raqaa The Islamic State (Part 3)", news.vice.com, August 11 2014 <http://youtube/watch?v=jOaBNbdUbcA>

16 November 16 2014 http://www.cryptocoinsnews.com/isis-announces-new-gold-dinar/ This has enraged the US. The US undermined both

	Saddam Hussein and Gaddafi for their financial independence and in the case of Libya, its metals-backed currency.
17	See endnote 180.
18	Vladimir Lenin, *"Left-wing" Communism: An Infantile Disorder,* Communist International, 1920.
19	Crooke, *Resistance,* 152.
20	Ibid., 183. This is in line with both Islam and the social psychology findings about the 'social mind' and the optimal size for the cohesive group (see endnote 34).
21	Ibid., 190. Since the Quran is explicit on governance, the only slogan needed is the MB's 'Islam is the solution'.
22	Hamas is an acronym of Islamic Resistance Movement, as well as the Arabic for devotion and zeal in the path of Allah.
23	Israel has worked to undermine Hamas by • refusing to recognize it as the legitimately elected government of the Palestinians • instituting a drastic blockade, allowing only arbitrarily-determined humanitarian aid (many medical goods and construction materials are banned) • firing the 120,000 Gazans employed in Israel or in joint projects • paying all Palestinian tax revenues to the Palestinian Authority invading (2008, 2014) and bombing Gaza, killing more than 3,600, and destroying homes and infrastructure almost daily.
24	So Aaron Miller, a former Middle East negotiator under several presidents, told *The New York Times.* See, David Kirkpatrick, "How Arab leaders' 'loathing' of Hamas has kept them quiet on Gaza war", *The New York Times,* July 31 2014.
25	They justify this by appealing to the struggle against apostasy under the first caliph Abu Bakr, and Salah al-Din's assertion of Sunni Islam over the Shia Fatimids prior to evicting the Crusaders in the twelfth century. Egyptian Salafist sheikh Talaat Zahran condemns Hamas as equivalent to Shia, since they receive funding, arms and training from Iran and Hizbullah.
26	Ali Mamouri, "Why Islamic State has no sympathy for Hamas", *Al-Monitor,* July 29 2014.
27	Families typically receive a one-time grant of $500 to $5,000, and those whose homes have been destroyed by the Israel Defense Forces have their rent paid for temporary housing.
28	Danny Rubinstein, "Hamas leader: You can't get rid of us", *Haaretz,* April 14 2005.
29	<http://www.al-monitor.com/pulse/originals/2014/07/nasralla-relation-renewed-hamas.html#>

30	<http://en.alalam.ir/news/1612118>
31	Jodi Rudoren, "In Gaza, Grief, Anger - and No Small Measure of Pride", *The New York Times*, August 10 2014.
32	Caid Sebsi won 55% of the vote in a run-off against incumbent Moncef Marzouki (45%). Marzouki was head of the incumbent coalition that included the MB.
33	John Esposito and John Voll, *Makers of Contemporary Islam*, UK: Oxford University Press, 2001, 132.
34	Ibadism is a branch of Kharijism, with beliefs in between Sunni and Shia, like the Shia, denying the legitimacy of the Caliphs after Ali, and believing the Quran was created by God at a certain point in time.
35	Gaddafi most notoriously 'disappeared' Iraq-Lebanese Shia Sheikh Musa al-Sadr in 1978 supposedly at the request of Syrian President Hafez al-Assad. The suppression of a riot at the Abu Salim prison in Tripoli in 1996 claimed over 1,000 deaths according to Human Rights Watch.
36	The US embassy in Iran was the center of US espionage in the Middle East. 52 American hostages were held for 444 days, and US diplomatic documents were revealed and published by the students. It was resolved peacefully without any torture or deaths of US citizens.
37	<http://www.wikipedia.org/wiki/Maspero_demonstrations>
38	I.e., if worse comes to worse, let the real winner win, but get the courts to give you the power.
39	"The Square", the Academy Award-nominated Egyptian-American documentary film by Jehane Noujaim, depicts events in Egypt from January 2011 focusing on Tahrir Square. The film uses actual footage of security force atrocities to document the unceasing and unapologetic recourse to murder and torture by the military and police. It has interviews with senior military figures, one of whom smugly admits that the so-called revolution was actually carried out by the military itself to prevent Mubarak from passing on the presidency to his son Jamal, and that when it is time, it will be cut short.
40	Though in reality, the violence following the coup was just as bad as in the case of Chile.
41	According to the MB's Freedom and Justice Party website.
42	The MB made development of the Sinai a plan from the start, intending to take back Egyptian control over the peninsula and reduce the threat of terrorism by raising the standard of living. The Suez development plan was announced in October 2012, which Sisi copied as his own Suez project in 2014 as part of his presidential election campaign in May 2014.
43	Ironically, in 2014, as Egypt's presidential election got underway, the

	CIA finally admitted its role in Iran's coup in 1953, which gave Iran's liberal elite another generation to enjoy its privileges.
44	Canada sent four observers who were able to assure Foreign Minister John Baird that the election was fair (it took 500 Canadian observers to judge Ukraine's presidential election shortly before Egypt's to do the same).
45	Robert Kagan, "American aid makes the US complicit in the Egyptian army's acts", *Washington Post*, 1 August 2013.
46	Kagan was founder of the Project for a New American Century (PNAC). See endnote 150.
47	There were 300 charges against Pinochet on human rights violations, and others on embezzlement and tax evasion. He was arrested in 1998 in Britain, returned to Chile in 2000, and died under house arrest in 2006.
48	See Walberg, *Postmodern Imperialism*.
49	Ibid.,148 (endnote 141).
50	From 1979–1981 Iran's revolutionary courts executed 500 political opponents. The first post-revolutionary president, Abulhassan Bani-Sadr, and Mujahideen-e-Khalq tried to overthrow the government in June 1981 at the height of the war with Iraq, resulting in assassinations and leading to a new purge. From 1981–1985 8,000 oppositionists were executed (keep in mind the context of internal insurrection, concern of treason against the state during wartime). In 1988 a final mass execution of 2,800 was ordered by Khomeini after the war with Iraq ended in a UN-mediated ceasefire, which Khomeini compared to "drinking from a poisoned chalice". Shortly before he died in 1989, Khomeini issued the fatwa against Salman Rushdie as an apostate. See Abrahamian, *A History of Modern Iran*, 182. Ayatollah Hussein Montazeri, who had been groomed to be the next Supreme Leader, resigned in protest and went into retirement in Qom, dismissed from his position by Imam Khomeini after people within his inner circle were found to be involved in anti-state activities as well as over his public disagreements with Khomeini. Severe, peremptory justice seems to be an inevitable part of genuine revolutions as they face attack by external forces seeking a return to the status quo ante..
51	Supported by the US, the Soviet Union and the Sunni leaders.
52	The Iranian oil bourse was opened in 2008, and by 2012, Iran managed to conduct all sales in non-US dollar currencies, including the yuan, yen, rupee, euro and a basket of currencies, as well as gold.
53	See Ervand Abrahamian, *A History of Modern Iran*. UK: Cambridge University Press, 2008.
54	Graham Fuller, *The Future of Political Islam*, Palgrave Macmillan,

2003.
55 Ibid., 104.
56 Ibid., 106.
57 See, for example, Stephen Kinzer, "US-Iran detente will be biggest geopolitical story of 2014", *Aljazeera America*, 6 January 2014. "Dempsey says Iran influence in Iraq could be 'positive'", Almonitor, January 12 2015. Dempsey is chairman of the US Joint Chiefs of Staff.
58 Siddiqui, *Stages of Islamic Revolution*, 62, 82–91.
59 The "New Horizon Conference of Independent Thinkers" in 2012 and 2014 was denounced in the western media as anti-Semitic, though in fact the conferences were merely anti-Zionist, and as such were attended by prominent anti-Zionist Jews. Ahmadinejad attended the first conference, and was accused of "holocaust denial" for suggesting the figure of six million as the number of Jews who died in the holocaust was exaggerated, and mocked for suggesting that 9/11 was a conspiracy.
60 Pakistan bowed to US-Saudi pressure and delayed finishing its portion of the pipeline, though it intends to finish construction as soon as the sanctions end.
61 Saudi Arabia and the Gulf states all sent officials.
62 "Communique to the Islamic Ummah", *english.hizbuttahrir.org*, 28 June 2014.

| Chapter Thirteen |

RETURN OF THE CALIPHATE

The seventh century message of Muhammad was to spread Islam around the world —not by conquest but peacefully—with the goal of achieving a loosely-organized caliphate[1] composed of communities united in faith, relating through trade and sharing their wealth. This is still the vision that Muslims have,[2] though the overpowering might of the imperialists has put it on a back burner, requiring a more complex strategy for unification today.

The three unified caliphates were:

1. the four Rightly Guided Caliphs Abu Bakr (Muhammad's father-in-law, father of Aisha), Umar ibn al-Khattab, Uthman ibn Affan (Muhammad's son-in-law, married to both Ruqayya and Um Kulthum) and Ali ibn Abi Talib (Muhammad's cousin and son-in-law, married to Fatima) (632–661),

2. the Umayyad Caliphate (661–750), and

3. the Abbasid Caliphate (750–944, though it formally existed until 1258).

The various Muslim political formations after the Abbasid Caliphate were not empires comparable to those established under capitalism by the West from the sixteenth century on, which used private property and the market to thoroughly change and exploit their colonies. Caliphate rule was much less invasive.

The Caliphate differed from previous empires by its largely peaceful expansion, with almost no destruction of infrastructure or mass killing of natives. The Muslim armies were mostly welcomed by the subject peoples as new (better) masters who brought peace and lighter taxation, as well as establishing principles that were more universally accessible. "The new doctrine did not seem strange, and indeed increasing numbers found it quite a logical further step in their own religious development."[3] The new rulers provided more flexible and tolerant rule than the Byzantines and Persians, tolerating Christian heterodox sects which had previously been persecuted by both Byzantium and Rome. The Muslims were seen as builders, not destroyers. Suddenly across the continent, there arose a *pax islamica*.

Imperial rivalries and sectarian bloodletting were suppressed as the new legal system based on the Quran was formulated. The Muslims ruled, but did not force conversion, because forced conversion could never result in sincere adherence to Islam. The promotion of conversion was even discouraged as it meant losing the poll tax levied on non-Muslims (*dhimmi*), who were freed of obligations such as military service. The protected religions later came to include Zoroastrians, Hindus and Buddhists. Eventually, the Hanafi school of Islamic law applied this term to all non-Muslims living in Islamic lands. As an example of the distinctions between Muslims and *dhimmis*, sharia law permits the consumption of pork and alcohol by non-Muslims living in Islamic countries, although they may not be openly displayed. Modern Hanafi scholars do not make any legal distinction between a *dhimmi* and a Muslim citizen.

But as noted above, both Salafis and Shia reject the post-Rightly Guided caliphates as illegitimate, having degenerated into absolute monarchy, where model caliphs were few and warfare was common. The last caliphs, the Turkish Ottomans, were sultans; they did not preside over a unitary caliphate. The title caliph was adopted by Abdulaziz II (r. 1861–1875) to add more authority as the Ottoman rule became more precarious. Still, the collapse of the Ottoman Caliphate, disbanded by Turkish dictator Mustafa Kemal in 1924, was a devastating blow to the world ummah, comparable to the effect of the collapse of the Soviet Union and socialist bloc in 1991 on the world socialist movement. Both these monumental events were brought about by the capitalist/ imperialist steamroller that was intent on creating a new, flat playing field for its 'great games'.

Those who approve of, or at least are resigned to, our postmodern moral flatland see the collapse of the Caliphate and the Soviet Union as proof of Thatcher's TINA—there is no alternative, no room for a multi-ethnic world order which is not based on profit and interest.

But critics of the post-imperial world, if it is to survive at all, realize that, on the contrary, we must move towards a political and economic map with justice at the center, moving beyond the material concerns of existence, returning humanity to the natural order. Capitalism, based on exploitation, is the root cause of the current world financial crisis, characterized by massive currency speculation (90% of all financial transactions),[4] and weak and unstable governments blackmailed by the interests of empire, leading to environmental devastation and outright war, piracy, and chaos. As more and more states are undermined and 'conquered' by the American empire and chained to the international financial system, and the threat of war continues, we are slowly being brought to the brink of the Armageddon preached by fundamentalist Christians, Muslims and Jews.

The collapse of the Caliphate did not end Islam as a unifying anti-imperialist force, just as the collapse of the Soviet Union did not end the appeal of socialism as the secular anti-imperialist counterpart to Islam. When given the chance, Muslims have overwhelmingly voted for the return of Islam to the central role in governance. The Arab Spring is the latest manifestation of this, where the advocates of Islam soon dominated political discourse, despite intense pressure by both local secularists and the empire.

There are more than 60 million Central Asians, with rich resources and ethnically close peoples. When combined with Turkey's 75 million, Iran's 75 million, the Indian subcontinent's 480 million, the Middle East's 230 million and southeast Asia's 220 million, it is easy to envision a superpower in the making second only to China and more diverse, based on a unifying belief system grounded in social justice, not ethnicity, greed and violence.

Now, with mass literacy—only a prospect in the Muslim world in the 1970s—and instantaneous worldwide communications via the post-1990 rise of the internet, there is the possibility of more widespread debate and *ijtihad*, and the possibility of creating many and then one government inspired by Islam as a "crystallization of political idealism based on religious community and concord".[5]

The project for a renewed caliphate seeks to take the place of the imperialist project, which left a painful trail of tribal and linguistic divisions, disrupted trade routes, declining local economies, and quisling local leaders tied to the imperial center, caught in a vicious circle of war and exploitation. What better argument for the logic of a renewed caliphate today: dissolve the artificial borders (already effectively removed for capital by global neoliberalism), provide a common, truly just legal code, and protect minority communities of belief,[6] as was the practice under the original caliphate more than a millennium ago?

A Rump Caliphate

As he led his jihadists triumphantly into Mosul and declared an emirate on Iraq-Syrian territory, self-declared ISIS/IS 'caliph' Abu Bakr al-Baghdadi announced that the 1916 secret Sykes-Picot Agreement between Britain, France and imperial Russia, which effectively abolished the Ottoman Caliphate (Turkey's new secular leader formalized this in 1924), was at last being dismantled.

All of the Middle East states, including Saudi Arabia, emerged as a result of the disintegration of the Ottoman Caliphate at the end of WWI, when the Ottoman Caliphate was divided into British-French "mandates" and eventually nation states. The prickly Saudis did not suffer the humiliation of direct occupation, but they followed the imperial agenda.

But Saudi control of the Arabian Peninsula was not what the British had in mind, preferring that the more malleable Hashemites could consolidate power over the holy cities Mecca and Medina. They nominally ruled Mecca at the time—Hussein as Emir of Mecca (1908–1917) and his son Abdullah, as deputy for Mecca from 1909–1914 in the Ottoman legislature. In 1917 Hussein was internationally recognized as king of the Kingdom of Hejaz.

Against all odds, the Saud tribe, followers of the ultraconservative Wahhab, defied the British and occupied Mecca in 1924, using an elite corps of jihadists—the Ikhwan—which Saud leader Abdulaziz organized in 1912 for this purpose (not to be confused with the Egyptian

Muslim Brotherhood founded in 1928). The British had no choice but to accede to this *fait accompli*, and abandon their original plan involving the more westernized Hashemites.

However, the Ikhwan jihadists were then betrayed by King Abdulaziz and his new patrons—yes, the very same British—in 1929. The Ikhwan were not happy with Sykes-Picot, which the Saud leader accepted, as it allowed him to establish a tribal monarchy (under imperialist hegemony) to govern the Muslim world.

The Sauds and even more so, the Ikhwan, were the ISIS/IS of their day—ruthless fighters who slaughtered their enemies as 'unbelievers', determined to impose their Wahhab-inspired austere Islam on all Muslims. The Sauds were known for their thorough plundering and merciless killings, their raids being "deadlier than traditional Bedouin raids, which usually avoided killing for fear of triggering a blood feud,"[7] according to historian Vernon Egger.

For almost a century now, the Sauds have been able to square the circle, reconciling their role within the empire with their primitive Wahhabism, seeing themselves as the head of a kind of rump caliphate. But they have had their day, having failed to unite Muslims in any meaningful way around their sectarian, rigid Wahhabism, in league with empire. Al-Qaeda and now ISIS/IS derive their historical inspiration not from the compromised Saudis but the Ikhwan rebels, the first neo-Wahhabis. Just as the first Saudi King, Abdulaziz, supported by the Ikhwan, swept away the more complacent Hashemites and Ottomans/ British, both Bin Laden and now ISIS/IS would sweep away the now complacent Saudi royal family, grown fat on its oil wealth, and its US sponsors. Saudi control of the holy cities provides a poor echo of the once powerful Islamic civilization, and the neo-Wahhabis know it.

The yearning for a revival of a genuine caliphate

is predominantly a Sunni one. Hizb ut-Tahrir (HuT, Party of Liberation) was founded by Palestinians and Jordanians in 1953, advocating the revival of the Ottoman Caliphate. It was at least initially supported by Saudi Arabia, always eager to associate itself in the eyes of devout Muslims with its implicit self-image as heir to the Ottoman Caliphate, though HuT does not openly operate there.[8]

Rump Caliphate II

The whole nineteenth century reform thrust in Islam appeared to be Sunni, though reformer Jamal al-Din al-Afghani was himself Shia and his Sunni Egyptian ally Muhammad Abduh was nonsectarian, campaigning for an end to the Sunni-Shia animosity. After the Caliphate was abolished in 1924 and replaced by colonialism, Shia and Sunnis cooperated in the revivalist Khilafat Movement. Iraqi Shia ulama supported the Sunni rebellion against the British, and Persian religious scholars went to the Caliphate Conference in Jerusalem in 1931. Sunni extremists like ISIS/IS accuse Shia of being American agents, acceding to the US occupations of Iraq and Afghanistan (they likewise dismiss Sunni rulers). This is hardly fair. No Shia parties inside Afghanistan or Iraq supported these invasions; Muqtada al-Sadr, whose father was murdered by Saddam Hussein, led a powerful insurgency, the Mahdi Army, against US-British forces after 2003, coordinating with the Sunni insurgency. Nour al-Maliki, Iraqi Prime Minister (2006–2014), had fled Iraq for Iran in 1979 under a death sentence as an official of the Islamic Dawa Party (1957), which aims at establishing an Islamic state where the authority is from the ummah rather than the ulama (Mohammad Baqir al-Sadr was a founding member). Dawa opposed the 2003 US invasion from its then headquarters in Tehran.

The Shia really had no alternative but to accept the occupations as *faits accomplis*, naturally attempting to improve their lot under the circumstances. The charge of being agents of imperialism is belied by the fact that Iran is the only outspoken Islamic critic of imperialism and is subjected to unrelenting subversion for its stand.

However, the imperial strategy of divide and conquer—turn local groups against each other using favouritism or subversion—has worked, and Sunni-Shia sectarianism has been consolidated to the extent that in order to achieve their goal of a new caliphate, ISIS/IS is collaborating with their secular foes of yesteryear, Baathists and former military personnel, who operate in tandem in Iraq as the Iraqi Islamic Army and the 1920 Revolution Brigades.

The caliphate revival, the goal of Bin Laden, of HuT, and stretching back to the Ikhwan in the 1920s and Afghani in the nineteenth century, should have ended with the US invasions following 9/11, which aimed at destroying al-Qaeda and consolidating US hegemony in the region. However, the US invasions of Afghanistan and Iraq proved to be a boon to these neo-Wahhabis, and all Obama's horses and all of his men now look quite helpless. By backing the Syrian insurgency, hijacking a peaceful protest movement and turning it into a civil war as was done in Libya, the US gave at least free rein (if not actual support) to the Muslim "rebels" from among whom ISIS/IS emerged. Presumably they were only intended as spoilers to weaken Assad, possibly split up Syria and Iraq; the US certainly had not intended for them to gain power and keep it to forward their own objectives. With that now a possibility, the US is panicking, as well it should.

The Saudis are beginning to panic, outlawing Saudi citizens fighting in foreign lands and cracking down on local dissidents, at the same time moving against Sunni extremists who have targeted Shia Saudis to destabilize the monarchy. The cravenness of their selective use of sectarianism is exposed by CIA double agent Morten Storm, who cites a letter from the Saudis to AQAP leader Nasir al-Wuhayshi in 2011 proposing a deal: "They would pardon Wuhayshi and donate weapons and money if they stopped fighting the Saudis and the Americans and focused instead on fighting Shia rebels in northern Yemen."[9]

Can the US drone ISIS/IS out of existence and replace them with pro-US Sunnis? This no longer looks like an option either. ISIS/IS types are prepared to die in their jihad, like the Ikhwan insurgents a century ago, and it is unlikely that ISIS/IS will be seduced by either the empire or a bankrupt monarchy.

Acceding to ISIS/IS's version of a rump caliphate would certainly be new territory for the empire, the equivalent of the British making peace in the 1920s with the Ikhwan. The main thing, now, as then, is preserving Saudi hegemony. Now, as then, Saudi collapse would mean an end to imperial control over the vital region. Turkey could be a possible spoiler here. It is more concerned with Kurdish separatism as a threat to the integrity of the Turkish state, and it is not inconceivable that it might accept ISIS/IS's continuation, given that it is impossible to mend fences with Assad now.

The West and Israel have underrated the power of Islam to mobilize the masses, assuming that overwhelming military force to suppress Muslims is all that is necessary. Recalling Stalin's dismissive "How many divisions does [the Pope] have?" Uri Avnery argues

> It is ideas that change the world. Like those of the legendary Moses. Of Jesus of Nazareth. Of Muhammad. Of Karl Marx. How many

divisions did Lenin have, when he crossed Germany in the sealed train? ISIS has an idea that can sweep the region: to do what Muhammad did, to restore the Caliphate which ruled from Spain to India, to wipe away the artificial borders that divide the Islamic world, to drive away the pitiful and corrupt Arab rulers, to destroy the infidels (including us). For millions upon millions of young Muslims in their impotent and impoverished failed states, this is an idea that straightens their back and swells their breast. Ideas cannot be detected by spy drones. They cannot be blown out of existence by heavy bombers. The American conviction that you can solve historical problems by bombing from the air is a primitive illusion.[10]

ISIS/IS's astounding success in 2014 highlights the role of the Salafi doctrine within Sunni Islam, indeed, Islam in general. After 2011, the Salafi in Egypt had an uneasy relationship with the MB, criticizing them from the 'right' for compromising with the secularists. They are at best impractical in their political program, at worst, willing to undermine the MB to promote their own agenda, as appeared to be the case when they supported the July 2013 coup toppling the MB. Today, ISIS/IS's success is a threat to both the West, the Arab secular world, and above all, to the Saudis, who spawned and nurtured them. Just as the Taliban are a kind of grim conscience for Afghans, so the Salafis such as the 1920s Saudi Ikhwan and their incarnation today as ISIS/IS act as a corrective to backsliding in the Arab world.

From Many Into One?

Spurred on by this sectarian 'rump caliphate' in Iraq and Syria is an alternative, recalling Siddiqui's Muslim Parliament, and Turkish Prime Minister Ahmet Davutoglu's vision of Turkey as a "litmus test of globalization". Muslims in the West can unite to pursue the implementation of sharia in their personal lives, and Muslim-majority countries such as Turkey and Iran can work towards a nonsectarian political alliance. Eventually Africa, the Levant, Central Asia, the Indian subcontinent and southeast Asia could join. This was Siddiqui's intent in establishing the Muslim Parliament. With cyber grassroots activism picking up steam in the West and with the continued renewal of Islam around the world, this could eventually lead to a coalition of forces determined to bring justice and ethics back into the world.

The major stumbling blocks are the unholy pact of the Saudi/Gulf monarchies with imperialism, and the continued colonial enterprise of Israel. Overcoming these will depend on when the US dollar loses its hegemony and how the US will adapt to the collapse of its empire.

Abdurrahman Dilipak argues that Turkey is the legitimate heir of the Ottoman Caliphate, and should work to restore it.[11] So far, the US and Israel have dominated the Middle East. Once their influence is removed, the main contender for the base territory of the Caliphate is indeed Turkey. The revival of Islam in Turkey could put it in a position to both bring Islam to Europe as a moral force, and at the same time, embrace the Muslim world to the south and east. The only solution to the ethnic conflicts in Central Asia (Turkestan), for the Kurds, and the externally exacerbated Sunni-Shia divide is to base society on the region's one common denominator: Islam.

Turkey's recent renewal of ties with both Iran and the Arab world under the AKP has been dubbed "neo-Ottoman". Davutoglu's vision, where the imperial periphery reasserts its authority and unity, and begins its 'soft invasion' of the imperial center through immigration, bringing with it Islam, anticipated such a process more positively. The EU would be transformed through this multiculturalism, including a renewal of Christianity in dialogue with Islam, where Islam acts as an "inoculation" against moral disease, and Turkey acts as a catalyst for world civilizational change.

At the Leaders of Change summit (2011) in Istanbul, Davutloglu said, "Islam and democracy are side by side" now, and Turkish entry into the European Union will show that "Europe can have a Muslim country." At the sixth Al-Jazeera Forum "The Arab world in transition: Has the future arrived?" in Doha, Qatar a few days earlier, he condemned the colonial divide-and-conquer policies of the 1930s–1950s, carving up the Middle East and cutting the organic relations of Arab countries, and the subsequent Cold War, which distorted and weakened the region and turned nations like Turkey and Syria, which had lived together for centuries, into enemies. We are not witnesses to the end of history, Davutoglu stated, but, on the contrary, to the return of the Middle East to "the normal course of history" after a century of distortion, when ancient civilizations were torn apart by the invaders. He further advised:

> We need to reconstruct and restore the political systems in our region, just as we would rebuild our houses after a tsunami. We must become subjects of change, like the people in Tahrir Square. Turkey understands the region better than others precisely because it is part of the region,

but the people of each country must lead the way. Davutoglu endorsed Erdogan's call to eliminate visas, envisioning a day

> when people can pass from a free Palestine through Istanbul to London. That's our vision. Not building walls around Turkey, but opening up to share with our neighbors. In Cairo, we are the Middle East, in Europe we are Europeans. We must shape history with all the nations around us.

Turkey envisioned the equivalent of the European Union or the North America Free Trade Agreement for a reconstructed caliphate, but not based solely on economic relations. Istanbul/ Constantinople as the last seat of the Caliphate had been the natural center and capital of the Middle East since the fourth century, with its long history of ties to the Middle East, the Balkans, North Africa, and as a crossroads of Christianity, Islam and Judaism. Its visa-free regime with Albania, Jordan, Lebanon, Libya and Syria in 2009 and in 2010 with Egypt was a first step.

But this path to regional hegemony projected by Turkey in 2011 is proving to be perilous. Its high stakes geopolitical intrigues in Syria may derail its neo-Ottoman pretensions, and even turn Turkey into another Pakistan, plagued by neo-Wahhabi insurgents and independence-seeking minorities, next door to a failed Syrian state. Whatever happens in Syria now, Turkey will have a difficult time incorporating it into a Turkish-led neo-Caliphate, much as Germany has faced severe indigestion after swallowing up the remains of civil-war victim Yugoslavia (not to mention Greece) in the EU.

What alternatives to an Islamic Caliphate grounded in Turkey are there? Egypt is by far the largest Arab country, but it has been under secularist leadership since Nasser, and though briefly after 2011 the Muslim Brotherhood seemed a possible focal point, its current disarray has knocked it out of the equation for the foreseeable future.

Then there are the Sauds. But "[h]istorically, the holy cities of Mecca and Medina were unable to keep the seat of Caliph to themselves; probably they will fail this time, too, unless they are willing to moderate their goals and play second fiddle to Turkey."[12] The premodern Sauds are nothing without the empire behind them. Their monarchical rule and their Wahhabi brand of Islam cannot unite the various Islams around the world, and they have already criminalized any association with their neo-Wahhabi offspring (ISIS/IS and others), who will not be easily placated. Threatened on their religious flank, they have been exposed as incompetent and illegitimate 'custodians of the holy places'.[13] They are on the defensive, and the pressure is on to patch up relations with Iran and work with Turkey to end the civil war in Syria and to contain ISIS/IS, the new spoiler in the jockeying for leadership of a reconstituted caliphate.

What about ISIS/IS? Might it paradoxically be the catalyst for uniting the Muslim region—albeit against it? As neo-Wahhabism, it offers a sectarian, rigid Islam, differing from the Saudis' only in its sincerity and rejection of empire. Its sectarian success has prompted calls for a nonsectarian alliance between governments in Syria, Iraq, Iran, Egypt and possibly Turkey opposed to its project. Turkish support for the insurgency in Syria is already being seen as a mistake, encouraging Kurdish separatism, and Turkey's Islamic leaders have no truck with ISIS/IS. A proposal by Diako Hosseini of the Iranian Ministry of Foreign Affairs Institute for Political and International Studies is the establishment of a rapid deployment force by the neighboring countries of Iraq, centered on Iran and Turkey, which would act on the request of the Iraqi government. Iran is already supporting (Shia) Iraq in its fight with ISIS/IS. Such a regional alliance would stabilize the US-installed regimes in Iraq and Afghanistan, though no longer under US hegemony. The rapprochement between Sunni and Shia that it implies would bring Muslims together in a way that ISIS/IS and its sectarian caliphate cannot do, a necessary step on the road to a new caliphate. Neither the Saudi Wahhabis nor the ISIS/IS neo-Wahhabis are capable of making this 'leap of faith'.

IS is more of symbolic significance in the long run, prompting Muslims to look to their past for inspiration. It's like Muslims are living through a conflagration and will have to sift through the rubble soon.

Other Forms of Unity

The most enduring intergovernmental organizations uniting countries in the Middle East and Central Asia in the era of imperialism are the Arab League, formed in 1945 in Cairo (consisting of heads of state of the 6 founding members, now 22 plus 4 observers) and the Organization of Islamic Cooperation (OIC), set up in 1969 with Saudi support, prompted by the 1967 war and occupation of Al-Quds (Jerusalem). The 57-member OIC, representing almost two billion Muslims worldwide, is charged with "promoting solidarity among members and upholding peace and security". Neither it nor the Arab League has played an important role in opposing imperial diktat. Both effectively acknowledge US-Israeli hegemony in the Middle East.

The Gulf Cooperation Council (GCC) set up in 1981 as a political and economic union of the six Arab states of the Persian Gulf—Bahrain, Kuwait, Oman, Qatar, Saudi Arabia and the United Arab Emirates—in reaction to the Iranian revolution, behaves similarly. Yemen hoped to join by 2016, though given the chaos there, this is on the back burner. The GCC has a relationship with NATO similar to the Mediterranean Dialogue and the intent is for the GCC to coordinate with NATO in the region. The policy of the GCC and NATO countries in Syria confirms this.

There are other Saudi-backed international Muslim groups such as the World Muslim League (1962) and the Islamic Development Bank (1975) which all accept Saudi (and hence western) hegemony. None have credibility as heirs to the caliphates of old.

One can only marvel that for over 60 years Israel's neighbors—with more than 30 times the population of Israel—have failed to mobilize their collective power to impose a just regional order without any kowtowing to Washington.[14] Experience shows that they can easily be sabotaged by a ruthless US-Israeli "empire-and-a-half"[15] which can orchestrate a currency collapse, false-flag terrorism, boycotts and regime changes through overwhelming global military and economic power.

Interestingly, there is nostalgia for the Soviet Union especially among Muslims who grew up there, as there was genuine equality among the various ethnicities and economic development which benefited the broad masses, in a kind of stern secular caliphate. After the collapse of the Soviet Union in 1991, many of these Muslims joined Hizb ut-Tahrir. The fact that many of HuT's supporters come from the ex-Soviet Union (Uzbekistan, Tajikistan, Kyrgyzstan, Kazakhstan) shows that members are hoping to revive the spirit of solidarity of the flawed utopian Soviet Union in an Islamic context. But nostalgia alone is not a political platform.

Another grouping of countries with non-imperialist motives and an Islamic element is the Non-aligned Movement (NAM), which held its 16th summit in Tehran in 2012, where Egypt's President Morsi handed the reins of power to Iran's then President Ahmadinejad. (Egypt hosted the previous NAM conference in 2009.)[16] NAM was founded in Belgrade in 1961 by Yugoslav president Josip Broz Tito, Indian prime minister Jawaharlal Nehru, Ghana's first president Kwame Nkrumah, Egyptian president Gamal Abdel Nasser, and Indonesian president Sukarno, the latter two Muslims, and all legends of national liberation movements, who advocated a middle course for the developing world between the western and eastern blocs in the Cold War. Its principles, like those of the Organization of Islamic Cooperation, are solidarity and peaceful resolution of conflicts, though it was founded specifically as a counterweight to both the American and Soviet superpowers, abjuring big power military alliances and pacts.

NAM went into decline after the collapse of the Soviet Union. Nonetheless, NAM represents nearly two-thirds of UN members and 55% of the world's population. At the seventh summit held in New Delhi in 1983, the movement described itself as "history's biggest peace movement", placing equal emphasis on disarmament.

During the 1970s and early 1980s, NAM sponsored a campaign for restructuring commercial relations between developed and developing nations—then billed as the New International Economic Order along with its cultural offspring, the New World Information and Communication Order—orientations which still have relevance today. However, since the end of the Cold War, NAM has struggled to find relevance.

By hosting the conference and taking on the responsibility for NAM leadership, Iran (which as a Shia nation has no pretensions to found a neo-caliphate) is clearly intent on injecting new life into the most important anti-imperialist international organization, given that the UN, the OIC, and the Arab League are all more or less subservient to the US Middle East agenda. NAM summits have traditionally been held every few years. Of the last three, two were hosted by Muslim countries—Malaysia (2003) and Egypt (2009).

NAM's experience demonstrates that Muslims can work with non-Muslim anti-imperialists, based on principles consistent with those revealed by Prophet Muhammad fourteen centuries ago.

Overshadowing NAM's anti-imperialist clout these days are the Shanghai Cooperation Organization (SCO), founded in 1996 by China, Kazakhstan, Kyrgyzstan, Russia, Tajikistan, and Uzbekistan as a security organization, and the BRICS, founded in 2008 by Brazil, Russia, India, China, and as of 2010 including South Africa as an economic grouping, to act as a counterweight to the sole remaining superpower, not based so much on ex-colonial status or any ethical principles, as on a desire to resist Western hegemony and achieve global multipolarity, in the first place by replacing the US dollar as the world's reserve currency.

In 2014, the SCO approved India, Pakistan, Iran and Mongolia for membership (they are observers), giving it a greater Muslim presence. Turkey is a dialogue partner and has applied to join. The SCO has real meaning, a solid economic platform that the toothless Saudi-sponored OIC or World Muslim League can't pretend to. There is more hope in overcoming Sunni-Shia sectarianism in such an independent organization, even if secular, where an anti-imperial agenda is consistent with Islam. The SCO has already begun trading in the members' currencies, minus the US dollar as world reserve currency, a policy in line with Islamic thinking about money, evidenced in the gold dinar advocated by both Malaysia's Mahathir and ISIS/IS.

Color Revolutions and the Arab Spring

The yearning for a caliphate is in direct opposition to

imperial policy, which traditionally has worked to unite all countries under a kind of secular market-driven 'caliphate', using techniques of 'divide and conquer' to keep Muslims at odds with each other. Muslims understand this. Four out of five believe the US seeks to "weaken and divide the Islamic world," and view the ongoing War on Terror as in fact a war against Islam.[17]

The post-Soviet New World Order that the West is trying to impose in Afghanistan, Iraq, Egypt, Ukraine, etc. reflects this imperial policy. Based wherever possible on 'soft power', it seeks to establish obedient "postmodern states" open to "free trade" (in US dollars) and "free" elections (preferably with short terms making for weak presidents), the whole process monitored by a "free" media (read: privately controlled) and western NGOs (key ones like the NED, not at all 'nongovernmental'). It's a very expensive racket—the winner is generally the best-funded and most widely advertised in the "free" media. Sometimes it's even a military dictator, as long as he can arrange to be elected.

Occasionally things go awry—a populist like Venezuela's Hugo Chavez gets elected and re-re-elected, Hamas is elected in Gaza. They must be subverted through media, 'NGO' targeting, boycotts and worse. Some countries, such as Afghanistan, Iraq, Libya and Syria, require the old-fashioned invasion-and-occupation to make them fit the mould. Rarely does a country (such as Iran, Cuba and North Korea) succeed in opting out of the whole circus and survive to tell the tale.

In pursuit of this 'soft power' scenario, the US incorporated into its arsenal a seemingly peaceful, populist strategy of orchestrating mass uprisings, coordinated by social media—the color revolutions of the 1990s–2010s (Serbia in 2000, Georgia's Rose Revolution in 2003, Kyrgyzstan's Tulip Revolution in 2005, and Ukraine's Orange Revolution in 2004 followed by Ukraine's Euromaidan in 2013).[18] The goal has been to weaken central governments through US government-financed NGOs which then act as watchdogs to keep these states on the 'straight and narrow', cementing them as weak, ethnically-based postmodern states within the imperial order.

Kyrgyzstan's coup was openly coordinated via the US embassy, overthrowing probably the most democratic and intelligent of the post-Soviet leaders, with tragic consequences as the new president, Kumanbek Bakiyev, quickly moved to plunder the treasury and create a virtual khanate with his clan in charge, leading to yet another coup in 2010, hundreds of deaths and the image of Kyrgyzstan as a failed state.

In 2009, the western-backed Green Revolution in Iran (deceptively dubbed Green for Islam even as the movement itself sought to move away from the Islamic government and towards the West), relied on the use of demonstrations protesting presidential election results. It failed, though it rattled the Iranian government.

This was followed in 2010–2011 by a surge of spontaneous revolutionary fervor in the Arab world, which owed much to western influence, in particular pro-democracy NGO activity. Tunisia's popular uprising, which overthrew the government on 15 January 2011, has even been dubbed the Jasmine Revolution. However, the scale of this, Egypt's Tahrir Square uprising, and subsequent protests in Bahrain, Yemen, Morocco and Jordan came as an unwelcome surprise to western governments: they proved not as open to manipulation, being on the contrary anti-western and Islamic in orientation, despite their gloss as led by westernized, computer-savvy middle class youth movements.

The strategy generally is in disarray today, with Ukraine descending into chaos following its latest Orange

Revolution, and bringing the world dangerously close to world war. Mistaken in its assumption that these color revolutions can work in Muslim countries in the same way that they did in non-Muslim ones, the US was forced to abandon any pretense to this strategy in Egypt where the US is now backing a blatantly Pinochet-style dictator, 'General' Abdel Fattah el-Sisi[19] who brought a bloody end to Egypt's flirtation with both western-assisted democracy and Islamic governance.

The bankruptcy of the color revolutionary strategy was starkly revealed in 2011 in Libya, where the overthrow of Gaddafi by western-backed ex-al-Qaeda rebels eventually led to the assassination of the US ambassador, and where chaos now reigns. An almost identical scenario unfolded in Syria, where US and Saudi Arabia-backed jihadists linked to al-Qaeda in an attempt to overthrow Bashar al-Assad.

The apparent western contradiction in the case of Egypt and Syria—supporting one ruthless dictator ("our bastard" Sisi) and undermining another (Assad)—makes sense (though not a lot) only in the context of the broader imperial strategy for the region. Iran and Russia are committed to the support of the dictator Assad and opposed to the Islamic insurgency, worried respectively about the sectarian agenda of the insurgency and the possibility of Islamic uprisings internally; the West, Turkey, Saudi Arabia and the Gulf, and Egyptian and other advocates of Islam, all have supported various actors in the Syrian insurgency, though for very different reasons.

As the grip of the US on the Middle East continues to weaken, and what are now seen as blatant color revolutions continue to spin out of control, their usefulness to advance the imperialist agenda continues to decline. However, the imperial legacy of a market-driven new world order, kept in line by 'divide and conquer', endures, abetted by western-style nationalisms, weakening the project of reviving the caliphate.

Endnotes

1. Adam is called "God's caliph" in the Quran—God's appointed steward of the Earth. The term caliphate (stewardship) came into use only after Muhammad's death.
2. Two-thirds of Muslims see the return to a caliphate as the ultimate goal. Three out of four agree with seeking to "require Islamic countries to impose a strict application of sharia," and to "keep Western values out of Islamic countries." At the same time, most view globalization positively and favor democracy and freedom of religion. *WorldPublicOpinion.org*, April 2007. <http://www.worldpublicopinion.org/pipa/articles/brmiddleeastnafricara/346.php>
3. Marshall Hodgson, edited and introduction by Edmund Burk, *Rethinking World History: Essays on Europe, Islam and World History*, Cambridge University Press, 1993,105.
4. <http://www.leftfootforward.org/2012/10/financial-transaction-tax-an-idea-whose-time-has-come/>
5. Dale Eickelman and James Piscatori, *Muslim Politics*, USA: Princeton University Press, 1996, 27.
6. This traditionally involved payment of a tax by non-Muslims (jiziya) in lieu of military service.
7. Vernon Egger, *A History of the Muslim World since 1260: The Making of a Global Community*, New Jersey: Pearson, 2008, 274.
8. HuT operates openly in the UAE, Yemen, Lebanon, Indonesia, Malaysia, Australia and Denmark. Its status is unclear in the US, Britain and Saudi Arabia. No political parties are legal in Saudi Arabia, and HuT's mild criticisms of Saudi policy and its platform calling for an elected caliph put it at odds with the Saudi monarchy.
9. Morten Storm with Paul Cruickshank and Tim Lister, *Agent Storm: My Life Inside al Qaeda and the CIA*, Atlantic Monthly Press, 2014, 274.
10. Uri Avnery, "Is ISIS Coming?" *Counterpunch*, November 7 2014.
11. <http://www.al-monitor.com/pulse/originals/2014/11/turkey-growing-support-for-isis-caliphate.html>
12. Israel Shamir, "The Arab Autumn", israelshamir.net, 2012.
13. See endnote 168 on the destruction of historic Mecca and Medina.
14. Eric Walberg, "Turkey redraws Sykes-Picot", *Al-Ahram Weekly*, 30 September 2011.
15. See Walberg, *Postmodern Imperialism*, Chapter 4.
16. Egypt also hosted the NAM conference in 1964, and Gamal Abdel-

Nasser headed the organization from 1964–1970.

17 WorldPublicOpinion.org, April 2007. <http://www.worldpubliopinion.org/pipa/articles/brmiddleeastnafricara/346.php >

18 These color revolutions were inspired and advised by pacifist Gene Sharp and his Albert Einstein Institute (AEI, 1983) whose intent is to promote nonviolent tactics to overthrow any autocratic government. While by no means a direct tool of the US government's National Endowment for Democracy (NED), AEI has received NED grants and works with groups and individuals directly connected to the State Department. Given this powerful corporate and US government involvement, there can be no doubt that however well-intentioned, such 'nongovernmental' organizations coordinate their activities with, or at the very least, act as willing handmaidens to the postmodern imperial project.

19 He was hurriedly promoted following the coup. Sisi's only military combat experience is in suppressing Egyptians.

CHAPTER FOURTEEN

THE UMMAH IN THE TWENTY-FIRST CENTURY

The Rothschild-Clausewitz geopolitical 'laws'[1] underlie modern capitalism—economic control by banks and war as the bankers' ultimate weapon—both of which Islam rejects. This is not to deny a role for chrematistics (money-making) in social affairs, only it must be regulated and circumscribed, as it is a dangerous, even 'sin-full' practice. Rational management of economic resources requires rational tools, but they are tools in the hands of humans, not magic wands. They must be abetted by the willing cooperation and belief of the populations concerned, based on the social values revealed in the Quran, and incorporate human activity within the context of the larger natural world.

The US and the EU are multicultural, open to immigrants, and at least officially tolerant to Muslims; at the same time, they function according to these Rothschild-Clausewitz laws, making them both intolerant and warlike, i.e., *dar al-harb*, despite their pious claims to be protecting the world's human rights. Their legacy of imperialism lives on and must be confronted.

A new modernity must incorporate both revelation and reason, morality and materialism, and use of *ijtihad* in its jihad against US imperialism. This *ijtihad*-jihad process is in a sense similar to but more comprehensive than Marxian praxis insofar as it emphasizes:

- social unity rather than class struggle
- the family and worship rather than material poduction
- evolution rather than revolution.

Left secularists dismiss Islam as having 'run its course'—they ignore Foucault's startling and prescient embrace of the Iranian revolution and his call for a "political spirituality", finding the inherent social conservatism of Islam distasteful. But their secular, radical discourse does not *inspire* the masses. Without an adequate map to follow, protest movements such as the spontaneous Occupy Wall Street in 2011, are easily absorbed. But the map of Islam—the principles and guidance—is already implanted via the Quran, traditions and sharia.

The force of Islam continues to re-emerge, nurtured by believers, both on the frontlines, and in the West by émigrés and converts, as well as by Christians and Jews who recognize how their own faiths have been compromised in the age of imperialism. Other religious traditions, including Buddhism and native religions, have looked at Islam anew and found continuity with it in the Perennialist School, based on the belief that all the world's great religions share the same origin and are, at root, based on the same metaphysical principles, rejecting post-Enlightenment modernity. This is in fact very similar to a core Islamic belief that prophets were sent to all peoples (To every people [was sent] a messenger 10:47), that the message of the prophets was always the same, and that the apparent division into religions arose from the corruptions of this message. The Perennialist Rene Guenon wrote: "The rational, material and secular worldview of modern science threatens to overwhelm the traditional human quest for the metaphysical and spiritual realities that underlie the grand design of the natural world." In line with Foucault and Garaudy, he saw Islam as the only tradition that could resist this onslaught.

Can Muslims move beyond the western economic straightjacket by repositioning traditional Islam into the center of life in all its aspects? Iran's theocratic Shia answer to western secularism will not be duplicated in the Arab world even in Shia-majority Iraq, but *theocentric* Islamic traditionalists have achieved power through fair western-style elections wherever they have been held. They will not be going away soon, and will increasingly work together, unless the imperialists once again succeed in *their* 'traditionalist' policies of 'divide and conquer'.

Number One on the agenda of all reformers and even of the Wahhabis is Wali Allah's call for greater literacy, which is essential to meaningful reform, and will contribute to Islam's long term renewal. Recent social psychology research showing that we are hardwired to be both social beings and religious ones 'rediscovers the wheel' for Muslims, and hints at a reconciliation of the divine with science based on principles other than materialism.[2]

Also essential to the success of the Islamic project today is recognition of the important difference between the forces at the heart of Great Game II—capitalism and communism—the latter based on social justice, banning of interest, speculation and exploitation, though flawed by its militant secularism. The Muslim Central Asian states, after several decades of state repression of religion, became far more prosperous than their neocolonial Muslim neighbors, and voted overwhelmingly to keep the Soviet Union intact. A reformed communism could arguably have accommodated a genuine revival of Islam there. This includes in Afghanistan, where the 1978 socialist 'revolution' was instigated by Afghan socialists and was only reluctantly supported by Moscow, and where any thought of building a socialist or an Islamic society was lost in the US-led insurgency and subsequent invasion.

The spontaneous upsurge of Islamic fervor embodied in both the al-Qaeda-type jihad and its alternative, the Arab Spring, shows that we are now closer to a 'global Islamic movement', though to date, one that is far from united. The persecution of Muslims in Egypt following the 2013 coup acted to unite both Sunni and Shia, alerting the world to the continued danger from the imperial order.[3] The movement can't be stifled: when the lawful quest for political power is denied, as in Egypt after the coup, Muslims either hunker down and continue their grassroots organizing, or join the jihadists (in Syria, Iraq and Sinai).

The need for unity of the ummah, for Sunni-Shia convergence, in confronting imperialism and providing an alternative approach to the violent al-Qaeda-types has never been clearer. Iran's Islamic revolution remains as bellwether, even though attempts to emulate it have not yet succeeded. The only Islamic successes in achieving such a convergence recently have been Hizbullah and Hamas, where Sunni-Shia differences have been minimized. Hizbullah leader Hassan Nasrallah stresses that the current turmoil in the Middle East region was a political, not sectarian conflict, saying:

I address all Shias in the region: You need to

understand that Sunnis are not our enemies. We are not at war with Sunnis. We are both, together, at war with extremist groups like the Islamic State of Iraq and Syria.[4]

Nasrallah backed Hizbullah's main Christian ally, Michel Aoun, in Lebanon's presidential election. In a 2008 poll, he was the most popular leader in the Arab world, followed by Assad and Ahmadinejad.[5]

Muslim-Christian-Jewish Understanding

Even the imperialists are beginning to recognize that Islam must be given a chance to rule, if only in order to sap the following of the violent alternative. Among anti-imperialists, this means going a step further and recognizing that for them to successfully resist imperialism, they must find ways to work with Islamic proponents. While reaching out to non-Islamic movements is not central to Siddiqui's pre-9/11 analysis, his call for new revolutionary thinking by Muslims, based on the Quran and life of the Prophet while taking into account the historical context, leads logically to this.

What are the historical paradigms established by the Prophet Muhammad for relating to non-Muslims? New Muslim and Christian scholarship is beginning to explore this source. In particular, Zafar Bangash's *Power Manifestations of the Sirah*, focusing on Prophet Muhammad's letters, treaties and new social conventions. Another is John Morrow's *The Covenants of the Prophet Muhammad with the Christians of the World* (2013), offering a new way for Christians to understand the ethos of early Islam, based on the covenants established by the founder of Islam with Christians of the time. These covenants may, in fact, constitute a third foundational source of Islamic guidance (along with the Quran and hadiths) as it concerns the establishment of peaceful and equitable relations with non-Muslims under Islamic governance. The covenants state that Muslims are not to attack peaceful Christian communities, but defend them "until the End of the World", appealing to all Muslims to condemn the violence against Christians in the Middle East in the name of Prophet Muhammad himself. The "Covenants Initiative" addressed in Morrow's book, is a movement by Muslims in support of Christians under attack. The Egyptian MB's defense of Coptic Christians in the face of Salafist persecution confirms their adherence to this important solidarity with "People of the Book".

At the same time, when Christians side with the secularists/ imperialists, they must face the music. It depends on context: what the various People of the Book are actually doing. The Prophet Muhammad did not turn against Jewish tribes until they broke their contract which pledged their fealty to the Islamic state in Medina. Clearly if contemporary Christian groups decide to function as fifth columns for the enemy in Islamic-led states, this cannot be allowed.

These studies provide yet further evidence that Islamic values are compatible with European values. This fundamental truth has been obscured by the fact that historically, while Christians and Jews lived side-by-side in Europe, and Muslims, Christians and Jews lived side-by-side in the Middle East, Muslims and European Christians rarely crossed paths, and became enemies as a result of historical rivalry,[6] the legacy of the Crusades, the enmity of Roman Catholic clerics, and the propaganda serving British imperialism. But with the rise of capitalism and as a reaction to Nazism, the cultural construct "Judeo-Christian heritage" entered the English language in the 1940s, to be used by Zionists and the imperial elite in their 'clash of civilizations' platform targeting Islam. It is a concept which has been useful to a largely Christian empire where Jewish elites play a powerful role, but is rejected by serious scholars, both Christian and Jewish. Talmudic scholar Jacob Neusner calls this so-called Judeo-Christian heritage a "secular myth favored by people who are not really believers themselves". American scholars such as Richard Bulliet actually argue for the use of "Islamo-Christian" to characterize western civilization.

This is the intent behind the Pope's call for dialogue with ISIS/IS. In an attempt to counter yet the latest the rush to war by the West, Pope Francis called for dialogue: "The door is always open." In his first trip to a majority-Muslim country, Turkey, he said interreligious dialogue, rather than military action was necessary to end the conflict in Syria/Iraq: "Fanaticism and fundamentalism, as well as irrational fears which foster misunderstanding and discrimination, need to be countered by the solidarity of all believers."[7]

Apart from the secular economic groupings such as NAM, the SCO and the BRICS, where Muslim critics of imperialism make common cause with non-Muslims, there are many attempts to bring Christians, Jews, Muslims and other believers together for understanding, though rarely action; most conferences end with no concrete action. There are Israelis and ex-Israelis, such as Israel Shamir, Gilad Atzmon, Ilan Pappe and Orthodox Jews such as Neturei Karta who embrace the Palestinian cause and reject the very concept of Israel as Jewish state. Clearly, if Muslims should be committing to the protection of Christians, as per the Covenant Initiative, it should also work the other way around.

Postmaterialism

There is much to learn from the West, not only in what *not* to do. Egypt will only achieve some return of its stolen wealth if it takes a page from Ecuador's experience.

President Rafael Correa fought off the IMF and cut Ecuador's debt in half legally, identifying loans which were knowingly provided to corrupt officials and wasted, and renegotiating Ecuador's foreign debt using the "odious debt" procedure.[8]

The rise of "postmaterialism" in the West since the 1970s represents a new morality reacting against consumerism, in line with the essence of Islam.[9]

There is much for the West to learn from the Islam. The Islamic resurgence of 2011 has added fuel to mass political actions such as Boycott, Divestment and Sanctions (BDS), and the Occupy Wall Street and 99% movement sprang up shortly after the Arab Spring began in 2011, bringing Arab activists in direct touch with their western counterparts, and enabling western activists to be inspired by movements launched by peoples who were previously viewed as distant and incomprehensible.

Both the Islamic and socialist alternatives depend on grassroots organizing ("Think global, act local") to provide a truly democratic alternative to the nation state, long compromised by its ties with global capitalism (and now in the process of being undone by it). This would enable principled cooperation between the ummah and a loosely-knit political organization including secularists (read here: all people concerned with reviving the nonmaterial side of human life, and with social justice). This is not so radical, as the meaning of "Think global, act local" is world unity in spirit and decentralization in practice, parallel to the original intent of the caliphate.

There are various names attached to modern developments in the ummah—neo-secularism (Turkey's Erdogan prefers this term) and neo-Islam, even New Age Islam. Whether they represent attempts to engage pragmatically and hence more effectively in gradualist long term processes of change with respect to existing power relations on the ground, remains to be seen. As for Muslims in non-Muslim majority societies, they can enter into political coalitions with non-Muslims on areas of agreement such as peace and social justice, developing new forms of religiosity using social media/ satellite TV, challenging secularists in the cultural sphere through support for more 'halal' programming.[10] For Muslims, there is always the danger of straying from the intent of the Quran, of subtly undermining Islam by chipping away at it—indeed, this is well understood by Muslims as part of the western program to disempower Islam—which underlines the importance of education and *ijtihad*.

Muslims 'abroad' work with both Muslim and non-Muslim groups in international peace and ecology movements, promote interfaith dialogue, and even support genuine democratic development in Muslim majority countries—'Islamic democracy'—such as the American Muslim Council's support for Tunisia's political process through its Tunisian branch of the Center for the Study of Islam and Democracy. CSID organized workshops on democracy and Islam in 2013. So far, Tunisia has escaped the harsh fate of the MB in Egypt, though Tunisia's parliamentary and presidential elections in October/ November 2014 were inconclusive, and Tunisia will not be able to forge a new Islamic path on its own. Such interaction between Muslims 'abroad' and in traditionally Muslim countries will be increasingly important as both communities grow in strength and demonstrate that 'Islam is the solution' in society. However most western NGOs are by definition (and indeed, funding) embedded in western capitalism, and as much a danger as a support in moving towards a new political-economic dispensation, including pseudo-NGOs such as the US government-funded National Endowment for Democracy, which are blatant fronts for undermining genuine democracy in both Muslim and non-Muslim countries.

The best-known western critic of Islamists, Olivier Roy, argues that with the "deterritorization" of the ummah in an era of migration, political Islam has become passé, that both liberal and "neo-fundamentalist"[11] Muslims in the West are *de facto* secularists,[12] forced either to assimilate or to withdraw from mainstream western social activity. For Roy, even Saudi Arabia's rigid neo-fundamentalism, where religious practice is focused on observances and where politics is carried out in conformity with the secularist US empire, confirms this irony. 'Secularist' is clearly a slippery concept, as seen by its defense by both Erbakan against the Turkish military and by Roy as implicit to the Saudi Wahhabis.

For secularist Roy, 'there is no alternative'; the experience of Iran merely confirms that "political Islam has failed", that *realpolitik* there takes precedence over religion, that corruption, nepotism and hypocrisy are endemic to Iran's public life, that those dissenting clerics who reject Ayatollah Khomeini's *vilayat-e faqih* in fact want to save Islam from the inherent corruption of politics, and create a space for true religious practice, once again emphasizing the inevitability of secularist political domination in the life of this world (dunya). Ervand Abrahamian and Roy dismiss the Iranian revolution as "the last of the leftist, Third Worldist and anti-imperialist revolutions, carried out under an Islamic cloak."[13]

But there is life in the Iranian revolution yet, as its unwavering defiance of empire shows, and its ability to adjust its path through debate and an electoral system.

Also, Muslims in the West are not fated to assimilate. Tariq Ramadan advocates "integration without assimilation",[14] active participation by Muslims in electoral politics while maintaining allegiance to the principles of Islam, including modesty in dress. Ramadan rightly bemoans the dumbing down inherent in electoral politics, since even given honest balloting the timing of social reforms does not correspond to electoral political schedules.[15]

In Muslim countries, this confirms the necessity of supplementing electoral politics with something like the MB/ Hamas/ Hizbullah long-term grassroots institution-building/ social welfare strategy, to be ready for the next moment for genuine revolutionary change, as happened in 1978–1979 in Iran, and in 2010–2013 in Tunisia and Egypt. Capitalism cannot deliver an adequate life for the masses and meet their spiritual needs. The return of Islam to the center of Muslims' existence is inevitable, but must be prepared for.

> Surely never will Allah change the condition of a people until they change it themselves (with their own souls). But when Allah wills a people's punishment, there can be no turning it back, nor will they find, besides Him, any to protect." (13:11)

At the same time, the experience of Iran, as with earlier anti-imperialist revolutions in Russia in 1917 and Cuba in 1959, shows that revolution requires a breakdown of the existing order and a strong principled leader, a kind of mahdi, who can catalyze the people and steel them for the difficult birth of the new order. This means both patience and decisiveness, seizing the moment when it presents itself.

The rise of right-wing, anti-immigrant parties has led several European countries to impose policies restricting Islamic dress, mosque-building and reunification of families through immigration, a direct denial of personal freedom.

The struggle to oppose these violations attracts all people who support personal freedom and nondiscrimination. It also pushes otherwise apolitical Muslims to form associations, join political parties and engage in other aspects of civic life, promoting their positive integration into the political life of these secular societies, giving full meaning to the abstract promise of religious liberty. As then-Turkish Foreign Minister Ahmet Davutoglu argues, "A city with different cultural artifacts in its silhouette produces more and more pluralistic citizens."[16]

Christian fundamentalists would find that Muslims are their best allies on cultural issues such as gay marriage, prostitution and cultural restrictions to limit denigration of religion and to promote spiritual values in popular culture. All the more reason for western Muslims to promote Islamo-Christian civilization by joining in political life, however flawed it is in the West. The *Charlie Hebdo* tragedy or possible false flag operation in France in January 2015[17] shows the urgent need for a press code that makes religious defamation illegal.[18] This is something that appeals to Christians too.

The ability to govern one's life based on the Quran means that sharia must be at least permitted as a choice by consenting parties, even if the secular society has its own legal system. It is heartening to note that sharia has begun to seep into western legal systems (though not without loud protests by a tiny minority of Islamophobes). The US federal arbitration law, passed by Congress in 1925, allows religious tribunals, and their judgments are given force of law by state and federal courts. Recent attempts to outlaw sharia (notably a referendum in Oklahoma) failed on First Amendment appeals. After all, US Jews have had their *beth din* religious courts for more than a century, and there are now Christian conciliators for those Christians who prefer canon law to the secular law of the land. US courts "have been positively encouraging [its] use since the 1980s" for inheritance, business, and matrimonial disputes, "sorted out by Islamic scholars according to the sharia. The precepts of Islamic law, like those of other religious codes, therefore have judicial force in the US already."[19]

Are we in the home stretch for a re-emerging Islamic civilization? Mass opinion in the West prevented an invasion of Iran, and the end of the sanctions regime against it may be in sight. The Saudi monarchy faces continuing pressure, both external and internal, to open up its political process to popular rule, and to end its alliance with imperialism. Though the US was able to mobilize a massive response to 9/11, its economy continues to falter and its wars have never been more unpopular, as the pain and dysfunction of empire will inevitably force a greater realism into popular understanding of imperial policy.

The 2013 Egyptian coup looks like a desperate last-ditch move to brand Egypt's body politic indelibly with secularism. But the sands of time shift. By banning the MB, confiscating their property. torturing and murdering its members, the secularists only dug themselves deeper into a hole. The fact that even arch-imperialists like Kagan realize that Islamic civilization is inevitably re-emerging, and that the West had better find a way of dealing with it, is heartening. It is also a window of opportunity for the truest expression of Islam.

The MB's greatest sin for the secularists was their refusal to abandon the legacy of the ummah, their yearning to unite Muslims beyond the confines of nationalism. But this is on the contrary proof of their authenticity. They have no quasi-imperial baggage *a la* Turkish Muslims, whose Islam is clouded with a possible interest in reviving the leading role of Turkey in a throwback to the Ottoman Caliphate.

Humanity's real enemies have never been clearer. At the same time, terrorism and a prolonged armed insurgency is not the way to achieve victory, as the cumulative post-9/11 tragedies and now the tragic civil war spreading from Syria to Iraq demonstrate. The triumph of Islam will come only with patient and vigorous analysis and organizing, and patient pursuit of socio-economic justice. Muslims believe this, and there is no reason after 14 centuries, during which Islam has only continued to gain adherents, to believe otherwise.

Endnotes

1   Mayer Rothschild's "Give me control of a nation's money and I care not who makes its laws," and Carl Clausewitz's "War is the continuation of policy by other means." Together, they point to the underlying western economic and political dynamic: dominance of banks in controlling economic affairs (as opposed to governments acting in the popular interest) which has created a world where economics is forced to serve their particular needs (speculation, interest and exorbitant profits), and the politics which promotes the interests of banks—war. This is the thesis of *Postmodern Imperialism*.

2   See endnote 34.

3   Not only Iranian leaders, but IS leader Baghdadi denounced the Egyptian coup against the MB. Interview with *Let Us Build Pakistan*, 3 July 2014. <http://informationclearinghouse.info/article39058.htm>

4   Addressing supporters in Beirut on the religious festival of Ashura, November 5 2014.

5   ABC/BBC poll in 2008, cited in Khaled Hroub, *Political Islam: Context versus Ideology*, SAQI, 2010, 215.

6   The historic rivalry is also theological, as Islam asserts that the Trinity /Jesus as God is untenable, and Islamic monotheism is the corrective. This strikes at the heart of organized Christianity, which from the start has dismissed Islam as a Christian heresy (i.e., to be eradicated), a much more uncompromising position than Islam takes with respect to Christianity.

7   Sebnem Arsu, "In Turkey, Pope Francis Advocates Dialogue in Battling 'Fanatacism'" *New York Times*, November 29 2014.

8   Through the referendum process enshrined in the 2008 constitution

(along with rights of Nature), Ecuador's government has the political authority to take on major vested interests and powerful lobbies. A new law in July 2010 increased the government's share in oil revenues from 13% to 87%. The government managed a dramatic increase in direct tax receipts (mainly corporate taxes). Ecuador now has the highest proportion of public investment to GDP (10%) in Latin America, even as social spending has doubled since 2006. Jayati Ghosh, "Could Ecuador be the most radical and exciting place on Earth?" *Guardian*, 19 January 2012. After the election of President Morsi, negotiations with the IMF included a request for over $1 billion reduction in Egypt's debt based on the "odious debt" precedent. *Al-Ahram Online*, 7 January 2013.

9   Postmaterialism assumes an ongoing transformation of individuals and society, which liberates them from the stress of materialistic needs. From 1980–1990 the share of "pure postmaterialists" (Inglehart Index) increased from 13 to 31% in West Germany. After the economic and social stress caused by German reunification in 1990 it dropped to 23% in 1992. (German General Social Survey) The question then arises: Will anti-materialism per se survive austerity without a religious foundation?

10 Chamkhi, Tarek, "Neo Islamism Post Arab Spring", Australian Political Science Association, 2013.

11 "A closed, scripturalist and conservative view of Islam that rejects the national and statist dimension in favor of the ummah, the universal community of all Muslims, based on sharia." Roy, *Globalised Islam*, 1. I see no need for the 'neo', and find neo-Wahhabi more precise to describe the Wahhab-inspired Salafi militants which Bin Laden grouped as al-Qaeda.

12 Roy, *Globalised Islam*, 91.

13 Ibid., 59.

14 Ibid., 276.

15 Tariq Ramadan, *Radical Reform: Islamic Ethics and Liberation*, UK: Oxford University Press, 2009, 288.

16 Ramadan argues that the secular state notion was brought into existence by Protestants and Jews in order to make space for themselves in face of the power of the Catholic Church, and that therefore in western societies, multicultural secularism *protects* freedom of religion of Muslims. Acceptance by western Muslims of living under the rule of the secular state does not mean that they should seek invisibility in the society, but rather participate in it actively, and contribute to its improvement as Muslims, demonstrating the value of Islam. (Tariq Ramadan, Lecture, Islamic Institute of Toronto, December 2012.)

17	See endnote 15.
18	The European Convention on Human Rights, article 10(2) guarantees the right to freedom of expression and information, subject to certain restrictions that are "in accordance with law" and "necessary in a democratic society". The exercise of these freedoms, since it carries with it duties and responsibilities, may be subject to such formalities, conditions, restrictions or penalties as are prescribed by law and are necessary in a democratic society, in the interests of national security, territorial integrity or public safety, for the prevention of disorder or crime, for the protection of health or morals, for the protection of the reputation or rights of others, or for maintaining the authority and impartiality of the judiciary.
19	Muftis near Birmingham UK set up the "Muslim Arbitration Tribunal to offer consenting parties the right to have their commercial and family disputes resolved according to Islamic law, for a small fee." Sadakat Kadri, *Heaven on Earth: A Journey Through Sharia Law from the Deserts of Ancient Arabia to the Streets of the Modern Muslim World*, USA: Farrar, Straus and Giroux, 2012, 279.

BIBLIOGRAPHY

Algar, Hamid, *Islam and Revolution: Writings and Declarations of Imam Khomeini*, Berkeley CA: Mizan Press, 1981.

_____*The Roots of the Islamic Revolution*, UK: Open Press, 1983.

al-Asi, Muhammad, *The Ascendant Qur'an: Realigning Man to the Divine Power Culture*, UK: Institute of Contemporary Islamic Thought (ICIT), 2008.

Bangash, Zafar, *Power Manifestations of the Sirah*, Canada: ICIT, 2011.

Bayat, Asef, *Making Islam Democratic: Social Movements and the Post-Islamist Turn*, USA: Stanford University Press, 2007.

Behdad, Sohrab and Nomani, Farhad (eds), *Islam and the Everyday World: Public policy dilemmas*, USA: Routledge, 2006.

Peter Bergen, *Manhunt: The Ten-Year Search or Bin Laden from 9/11 to Abbottabad*, Doubleday, 2012.

Calvert, John, *Sayyid Qutb and the Origins of Radical Islamism*, USA: Columbia University Press, 2010.

Chamkhi, Tarek, "Neo Islamism Post Arab Spring", Australian Political Science Association, 2013. <http://www.auspsa.org.au/sites/default/files/neo_islamism_post_arab_spring_tarek_chamkhi.pdf>

Coll, Steve, *Ghost Wars: The Secret History of the CIA, Afghanistan and Bin Laden from the Soviet Invasion to September 10, 2011*, Penguin, 2004.

Crooke, Alastair, *Resistance: The Essence of the Islamist Revolution*, Pluto Press, 2009.

Eaton, Gai, *Islam and the Destiny of Man*, UK: Islamic Texts Society, 1994.

Eickelman, Dale and Piscatori, James, *Muslim Politics*, USA: Princeton University Press, 1996.

Esposito, John and Voll, John, *Makers of Contemporary Islam*, UK: Oxford University Press, 2001.

Fouda, Yosri and Fielding, Nick, *Masterminds of Terror: The Truth Behind the Most Devastating Terrorist Attack the World Has Ever Seen*, Arcade, 2003.

Fowler, Robert, *A Season in Hell: My 130 Days in the Sahara with al-Qaeda*, USA: HarperCollins, 2011.

Fuller, Graham, *The Future of Political Islam*, Palgrave Macmillan, 2003.

Hamid, Shadi, *Temptations of Power: Islamists and Illiberal Democracy in a New Middle East*, Oxford University Press, 2014.

Hroub, Khaled, *Political Islam: Context vsersus Ideology*, SAQI, 2010.

Jalal, Ayesha, *Partisans of Allah: Jihad in South Asia*, USA: Harvard University Press, 2008.

Johnsen, Gregory, *The Last Refuge: Yemen, al-Qaeda, and America's War in Arabia*, USA: Norton, 2013.

Kadri, Sadakat, *Heaven on Earth: A Journey Through Sharia Law from the Deserts of Ancient Arabia to the Streets of the Modern Muslim World*, USA: Farrar, Straus and Giroux, 2012.

Kaplan, Robert, Soldiers *of God: With Islamic Warriors in Afghanistan and Pakistan*, Vintage, 2001,

Kazmi, Zaheer and Deol, Jeevan (eds), *Contextualising Jihadi Thought*, Oxford University Press, 2012. <https://www.academia.edu/2613689/Contextualising_Jihadi_Thought_edited_with_Jeevan_Deol >

Kean, Thomas and Hamilton, Lee, *The 9/11 Commission Report*, 2004. <http://www.9-11commission.gov/report/911Report.pdf>.

Jim Lacey, editor, *The Canons of Jihad: Terrorists' Strategy for Defeating America*, 2008.

_____*A Terrorist's Call to Global Jihad: Deciphering Abu Musab Al-Suri's Islamic Jihad Manifesto*, 2008.

_____with Mark E. Stout, Jessica M. Huckabey and John R. Schindler *The Terrorist Perspectives Project: Strategic and Operational Views of Al-Qaida and Associated Movements*, 2008.

Lieberman, Matthew, *Social: Why Our Brains Are Wired to Connect*, Crown, 2013.

Miller, John and Stone, Michael, with Chris Mitchell, *The Cell: Inside the 9/11 Plot, and Why the FBI and CIA failed to Stop It*, Hyperion, 2002.

Miniter, Richard, *Mastermind: The Many Faces of the 9/11 Architect, Khalid Shaikh Mohammed*, Sentinel, 2011.

Moaddel, M., *Islamic Modernism, Nationalism and Fundamentalism: Episode and Discourse*, USA: University of Chicago Press, 2005.

Morrow, John, *The Covenants of the Prophet Muhammad with the Christians of the World*, USA: Angelico Press, 2013.

Nasiri, Omar, *Inside the Jihad: My Life with Al Qaeda, A Spy's Story*, Introduction by Gordon Corera, UK: Perseus, 2006.

Nasr, Seyyed Hossein, *Islam in the Modern World: Challenged by the West, Threatened by fundamentalism, Keeping faith with Tradition*, USA: Harper One, 2010.

Qutb, Sayyid, *Milestones*, Birmingham UK: Maktaba [1964]

ar-Rahman Koya, Abdar (Ed), *Imam Khomeini: Life, Thought and Legacy*, Kuala Lumpur: Islamic Book Trust, 2009.

Ramadan, Tariq, *Western Muslims and the Future of Islam*, UK: Oxford University Press, 2004.

_____*Radical Reform: Islamic Ethics and Liberation*, UK: Oxford University Press, 2009.

Rashid, Muhammad, *The caliphate or the great imamate*, Cairo: Matbaat al-Manar bi-Misr, 1934,

Roy, Olivier, *Globalised Islam: The Search for a New Ummah*, Hurst, 2004.

_____Interview with Columbia University Press, 2013. <https://cup.columbia.edu/static/Interview-roy-olivier-globalized>

Ruthven, Malise, *Fundamentalism: The Search for Meaning*, UK: Oxford University Press, 2003.

Scheuer, Michael, *Imperial Hubris: Why the West is Losing the War on Terror*, USA: Potomac, 2004.

_____*Osama Bin Laden*, Oxford University Press, 2011.

Siddiqui, Kalim, *Stages of Islamic Revolution*, UK: Open Press, 1996.

_____*In Pursuit of the Power of Islam: Major Writings of Kalim Siddiqui*, edited by Zafar Bangash, UK: The Open Press, 1996.

Sivan, Emmanuel, *Radical Islam: Medieval Theology and Modern Politics*, USA: Yale University Press, 1990.

Storm, Morten, with Cruickshank, Paul and Lister, Tim, *Agent Storm: My Life Inside al Qaeda and the CIA*, Atlantic Monthly Press, 2014.

Suskind, Ron, *The One Percent Doctrine: Deep Inside America's Pursuit of Its Enemies Since 9/11*, Simon & Schuster, 2006.

al-Suri, Abu Musab, "A Call to a Global Islamic Resistance", 2005.

Tenet, George, *At the Center of the Storm: My Years at the CIA*, New York: Harper Collins, 2007.

Walberg, Eric, *Postmodern Imperialism*, USA: Clarity Press, 2011.

_____*From Postmodernism to Postsecularism: Re-emerging Islamic Civilization*, USA: Clarity Press, 2013.

Woodward, Paul, "ISIS and the strategy of managed savagery", http://

warincontext.org/, 3 July 2014.

Wright, Lawrence, *The Looming Tower: Al-Qaeda and the Road to 9/11*, USA: Knopf, 2006.

_____ "The Master Plan: For the new theorists of jihad, Al Qaeda is just the beginning", *New Yorker*, 11 September 2006. <http://www.newyorker.com/archive/2006/09/11/060911fa_fact3?currentPage=all>

al-Zawahiri, Ayman, *Knights Under the Prophet's Banner: Meditations of the Jihadist Movement* , 2001. translation in *al-Sharq al-Wasat* <https://azelin.files.wordpress.com/2010/11/6759609-knights-under-the-prophet-banner.pdf>

INDEX

9/11 13, 14, 26, 157-168, 183, 200, 286
1920 Revolution Brigades 258

A

Abbas, Mahmoud 205, 210
Abbasid 71, 251-252
Abdel-Rahman, Omar 90, 96, 114-115, 118
Abduh, Muhammad 65, 257
Abdullah, King 54, 66
Abdullah, Abdullah 201
Abdulaziz, King 91, 253-256
Abrahamian, Ervand 283
Abu Bakr 90, 148, 251
Abyssinia 81
accommodationists 23-24, 44, 91, 95-96, 99, 152, 187, 240, 242
Aden 93
adl (justice) 43
al-Adli, Habib 167
Affan, Uthman ibn 251
al-Afghani, Jamal al-Din 23, 65, 69, 132, 257
Afghanistan 10, 53, 77, 79, 92, 96, 99, 101, 106-109, 116-117, 123, 125, 127, 129, 132, 139-144, 159-160, 164, 167, 169-172, 189, 197-201, 206, 239-240, 260, 269, 277
AFRICOM 172
Ahmadi Muslims 188
Ahmed, Lt. Gen. Mahmud 161-162
Ahmedinejad, Mahmoud 236, 238, 240, 267, 278
Aisha 251
AKP (Justice and Development Party), Turkey 191-193, 212, 262
Al-Jazeera TV 186, 231, 262
Alawites 192
Albania 263
Alevi 189
Algar, Hamid 68
Algeria 20, 61, 78, 93, 112, 114, 123, 142, 150, 151, 168, 172, 209, 217, 223
Ali, cousin of Muhammad 55
Ali, Muhammad (Egypt) 42,

Aliriza, Bulent 193
Allah, Wali 276
Allende, Salvador 230, 237
Alliance of Civilizations 192
American Muslim Council 282
animism 220
Aoun, Michel 278
AQAP (al-Qaeda in the Arab Peninsula) 173, 259
AQI (al-Qaeda in Iraq) 201-202
AQIM (al-Qaeda in the Islamic Maghreb) 168, 174, 219
al-Aqsa Mosque 130
Arab League 213, 265, 267
Arab nationalism 41, 43, 47, 64, 74, 79, 84, 112, 124
Arab Spring 50, 78, 84, 142, 152, 167, 210, 214, 217, 223, 235, 254, 277, 281
Arafat, Yasser 63
Armed Islamic Groups 93, 114, 143, 151
art 114, 184
al-Assad, Bashar 186, 192, 204, 233, 258-259, 271, 278
assimilationists 17, 24, 79, 106, 184
Atta, Mohammed 159, 161-163
Atzmon, Gilad 280
Australia 203
Avnery, Uri 259
Awqaf (religious endowments) 61
al-Azhar University 40, 49, 124
Azzam, Sheikh Abdullah Yusuf 36, 96, 106-109, 111, 116, 123, 125-126, 132, 139

B

Baath Party (Iraq) 22, 202, 258
Baath Party (Syria) 22
Badie, Mohammed 231-232
Baghdad 148, 201-202
al-Baghdadi, Abu Bakr 201-205, 255
al-Baghdadi, Abu Omar 202
Bahrain 79, 241, 265, 270
Bakiyev, Kumanbek 270
Bali 168
Balkans 192, 263

Bamiyan 199
Bandar, Prince 161, 163
Bangash, Zafar 72, 80-81, 278
Bangladesh 112, 190
Banisadr, Abolhassan 73
banking 18, 185, 192
al-Banna, Hassan 42-46, 96, 129
ElBaradei, Mohamed 224-225, 230
al-Bashir, Omar 114, 220
Basij/Baseej Forces 60, 74
Basnan, Osama 161-164
al-Bayoumi, Omar 161-162, 164
Bazargan, Mehdi 73
Bedouin 90, 256
Belgrade 267
Belgium 203
Belhadj, Abdelhakim 222
el-Beltagi, Mohammed & Asmaa 231-232
Ben Ali, Zine al-Abidine 214, 216, 235
Benkirane, Abdelilah 218-219
Berber 218
bid'a 48,
Bin Bazz, Grand Mufti Abd al-Aziz 107
Bin Laden, Osama 12, 50, 78, 92-93, 97-99, 107-110, 111-120, 123-126, 132-134, 139-142, 144, 152, 157-168, 172, 185, 198-200, 202, 211, 221, 256, 258
blowback 26-27,
Boko Haram 169
Bosnia 74, 77-78, 100, 106, 109, 126, 132, 139,142, 166, 169, 192
Boston Marathon bombing 171
de Botton, Alain 35
Bouazizi, Mohamed 214
Bourguiba, Habib 214, 216
Boycott, Divestment and Sanctions (BDS) 281
Brazil 268
BRIC(S) economic bloc 240, 244, 268, 280
Britain 16–17, 143, 150, 152, 173, 186, 205, 228, 231, 255, 256-257
British Empire 17, 41, 43, 58, 91, 100, 188, 259, 279
Brookings Institute 233
Buddhism 199, 252, 275
Building and Development Party, Egypt 167
Bulliet, Richard 280
Bush, George W. 119, 131, 160, 165, 171, 238
Bushehr nuclear facility 62
Byzantine empire 82-83, 252

C

Caid Sebsi, Beji 216-217
Cairo University 124
Caliphate (see also Umayyad, also ummah, Abbasid) 16, 19, 37, 54-55, 90, 146, 149, 166, 186, 190, 201-205, 208, 243, 251-265, 268-272
Call to Global Islamic Resistance 144, 147
Canada 72, 94, 170, 203
capitalism 10, 20, 24-25, 34, 46, 49-50, 64, 94, 96, 134, 187, 191, 205, 238, 252-253, 274, 276, 279, 281, 284
Carlos the Jackal 114, 115
Carter Center 232
Catholicism 16, 91, 94, 252, 279
Caucasus 109, 169, 192
Center for the Study of Islam & Democracy 282
Central Asia 109, 145, 164, 254, 261, 277
Chad 172
Charlie Hebdo 16, 285
Chavez, Hugo 228, 269
Chechnya 97, 100, 126, 132, 142, 169, 203
Chile 228, 230, 232, 234
China 19, 22, 34, 97, 99, 149, 240, 254, 268
Christianity 11, 44, 80, 82, 89, 98, 169, 188, 206-208, 220-221, 223, 225, 227, 252, 254, 262-263, 275, 278-280, 284-285
Churchill, Winston 170
CIA 11, 62, 111, 159, 162-164, 198, 237, 259
Clarke, Richard 165
Clausewitz 'law' 274
Clinton, Bill 119, 221
Coll, Steve 163
colonialism, European 16-19, 22, 53, 69
color revolutions 223, 229, 234, 236, 242
communism, communists 38, 47, 74, 142, 167, 190, 197, 234-235, 239, 242, 276-277
Congress for the Republic 215
Constitution of Medina 81-82
Constitutional Democratic Rally 217
Correa, Rafael 281
Côte d'Ivoire 169
Covenants of the Prophet Muhammed with the Christians of the World 278-279
Crescent International (Toronto) 72

Crusades 117-118, 133, 141, 166, 279
Cuba 19, 235, 240, 269, 284
Cutting the Fuse: The Explosion of Global Suicide Terrorism and How to Stop It 170
Cyprus 193

D

D-8 – see Developing Eight
dan Fodio caliphate 169
Dannenberg, Robert 10
dar al-harb 98, 118, 147, 274
dar al-islam 147
Davutloglu, Ahmet 192, 240, 260, 262-263, 285
dawa (proselytizing) 38, 43, 48, 187
Denmark 203
Developing Eight, D-8 190
Dhahran Air Base 184
dhimmi (poll tax on non-Muslims) 38, 73, 91
Dictators on Watch: A Democratic Path for the Arab World 215
Dilipak, Abdurrahman 261
al-Din, Muhiya 128
Doha 186, 262
Dostum 200
Druze 207

E

Ecuador 281
Egger, Vernon 256
Egypt 14, 18-21, 40-54, 61, 64-66, 73, 79, 83, 93, 95, 98, 108, 112, 116, 123-128, 132-133, 141-142, 152, 158, 167-168, 171, 183, 190, 209, 211, 213, 223-234, 241-242, 244, 260, 263, 267-271, 277, 279-281, 284-286
Egyptian Islamic Group 128
Egyptian Islamic Jihad 48, 114, 116, 125, 132-134
Egyptian Islamic Society 48, 114-117, 125, 132-133, 167
Elibiary, Mohammed 243
Enlightenment 276
Ennahda Movement 216
equity 130,
Erbakan, Necmeddin 190, 283
Erdogan, Recep Tayyip 191-193, 263, 281
el-Erian, Essam 21,
Eritrea 109, 139
Europe, European Union (EU) 17, 41, 72, 82, 112, 141, 149, 158, 165, 213, 217, 222, 233, 262-263, 284
Evident Sacriliges of the Saudi State 118

F

Fahd, King 112-113
al-Fahd, Nasir bin Hamad 131
Faisal, King 185
al-Faisal, Turki 119
Fallujah 94, 201
Fanon, Franz 58
Faraj, Abdus Salam 126
fard ayn (individual duty) 37, 107, 125
fard kifaya (collective duty) 98, 107
Farouq, King 44
Fatah 212
Fatima (daughter of the Prophet) 251
fatwa 36, 49, 99, 107-108, 116-119, 130-133, 160, 166
Fayyad, Salam 210
FBI 115, 161-162, 164, 170
Federal Aviation Administration 164
Feldman, James 170
fiqh (law) 55,
Finland 203
Foucault, Michel 33-34, 36, 38, 270, 276
Fouda, Yosri 159
Fowler, Robert 94
France, French 17, 23, 34, 94, 100, 115, 140, 143, 150-151, 168, 203, 214, 217, 255, 285
Frances, Pope 280
Franks, Gen. Tommy 170
Frankfurt School 33-34,
Freedom and Justice Party (FJP), Egypt 222, 227
Fukuyama, Francis 36,
Fuller, Graham 239-240

G

al-Gaddafi, Muamar 125, 174, 186, 221-222, 271
al-Gaddafi, Saif al-Islam 222
Gandhi, Mahatma 58
Garaudy, Roger 34, 276
Gaza 172, 191, 208-214, 269
Georgia 269
Germany 11, 17, 44, 151, 158, 170, 263
Ghana 267
Ghani, Ashraf 200
Ghariani, Mohamed 216
al-Ghazali, Muhammad 42,
al-Ghoul, Asmaa 214
Ghost Wars: The Secret History of the CIA, Afghanistan, and Bin Lain, from the

Soviet Invasion to September 10, 2001 163
GIA – see Armed Islamic Groups
Graham, Sen. Bob 161-162
Great Game I 16-17, 20
Great Game II 17-21, 152, 276
Great Game III 21-24, 33, 69, 157
Greece 263
Green Book 221
Green Revolution 65, 270
Guenon, Rene 276
Guinea 169
Gul, Abdullah 191
Gulf Cooperation Council (GCC) 186, 218, 265-266
Gulf states 63, 91, 117, 173, 183-187, 192, 261, 271

H

Habermas, Jurgen 33-34
hadd (hudud) 184,
al-Haddad, Gehad 225
Haifa, Princess 161, 163
hajj 62-63, 82
Hamad, Ghazi 212
Hamad, Sheikh (Qatar) 43, 185-186
Hamas (Palestinian resistance) 14, 27-28, 99, 109, 114, 167, 172, 187, 207-214, 244, 269, 277, 284
Hamza, Abu 150
Hanafi school of jurisprudence 252
Haniyeh, Ismail 209, 211
ul-Haq, Gen. Zia 189
Haqqani 125
haram 129
Hassan, Abdel Meguid Ahmed 46
Hashemites 255-256
Hassan II 217
Havel, Vaclav 50
Hazara 199
al-Hazmi, Nawaf 162
Hejaz 255
Hekmatyar 125, 198
Hejaz 185
Hidden Imam 72
hijab 212
al-Hijji, Abdulaziz 161, 163-164
hijra 81, 98
Hinduism 100, 188, 252
Hizb ut-Tahrir (HuT) 257-258, 266
Hizbullah 11, 14, 27, 115, 207-209, 212-213, 244, 277-278, 284
al-Hodeibi, Murshid Hassan 49,
Hosseini, Diako 264
al-Houthis 204
hudud/huddud penalties 95, 220
Hukumat-e Islami 56
Hussein (Mecca) 255
Hussein, Fouad 148, 150, 203
Hussein, Saddam 56, 98-99, 110, 112-113, 202, 257

I

ibada 89
Ibadi 221
IBTimes 162
ijma (consensus) 48
ijtihad 37, 41, 43, 55, 58, 90, 91, 123, 220, 254, 274, 282
Ikhwan 91, 255-256, 258
imam 54-57,
IMF 18, 20, 51, 229, 281
Imperial Hubris 97
In the Line of Fire 164
India 17, 23, 26, 68, 78, 97, 117, 188-189, 240, 254, 260-261, 267-268
Indonesia 22, 93, 168, 188, 190, 203, 244, 267
Inside the Jihad: My Life with Al Qaeda: A Spy's Story 150
International Atomic Energy Agency 238
International Criminal Court 205
International Islamic News Agency 185
International Islamic University 109
Inter-Services Intelligence (ISI) 111, 119, 126, 161, 164
Intifada 209
Iran 13, 18, 20, 33, 35, 53-65, 73-74, 77, 79, 96-99, 106, 114, 141, 150, 152, 189-190, 192, 207, 213, 221-224, 226, 229, 223, 234-245, 254, 264-271, 276-277, 283-285
Iraq 13, 15, 22, 28, 56-57, 64, 73, 79, 93, 97, 99, 112-113, 118, 128, 134, 140-141, 145-150, 160, 167, 169-171, 201-206, 235, 269, 277
Iraqi Islamic Army 258
Ireland 203, 222
irfan (gnosis) 55
ISIS/IS 13, 14, 26, 141, 146, 148, 150, 168, 171, 173, 200-205, 208, 211, 217, 255-260, 264-265, 268
Islamabad – see Pakistan
Islamic Alliance 167
Islamic Awakening 235
Islamic Dawa Party 257
Islamic Development Bank 185, 266
Islamic Endowment Ministry 212
Islamic Fighting Group 222
Islamic Government 56-57

Islamic Jihad (Egypt) – see Egyptian Islamic Jihad
Islamic Salvation Front (Algeria) 143, 172
Islamic Society (Egypt) – see Egyptian Islamic Society
Islamophobia 69, 79
Israel 17, 28, 50, 63, 95. 97, 99, 100, 108, 129, 146, 149, 151, 159-160, 165, 173, 188, 190-191, 204-206, 209-213, 226, 229, 233, 235, 239, 242, 260, 266, 280
Istanbul (Constantinople) 263,
Italy 158

J

Jabhat al-Nusra (al-Nusra Front) 173, 202
jahili system 48, 124
jahiliya (ignorance) 48, 49
Jamaat-e Islami (Pakistan) 69, 74
Jamal alNimeiri dictatorship 114
Jarrah, Ziad 159, 163
Jasmine Revolution 270
Jebali, Nahda Hamadi 214
Jews/Judaism 11, 80,-82, 89, 118, 205, 240, 254, 263, 275, 280, 285
jihad 36-37, 42, 47-48, 79, 93, 95, 98, 107-108, 117-119, 126, 140, 143-146, 149, 151-152, 163, 166, 169, 185, 189, 200, 203, 208, 255
"Jihad Against Jews and Crusaders" 166
Jihad, The Neglected Duty 126
Jinnah, Muhammad Ali 188
jizya (protection tax) 206
Johnsen, Gregory 95
"Join the Caravan" tract 109
Joint Intelligence Committee Inquiry 161
Jordan 112, 145, 158, 165, 168, 186, 202, 210, 218-219, 257, 263, 270
juhl (ignorance) 49
jumah khutbah (Friday sermon) 61
Jund Ansar Allah (Army of Supporters of Allah) 210
Jundallah 64
Justice and Construction Party (Libya) 222
Justice and Development Party, Morocco (see also AKP, Turkey) 218

K

Kaaba 108, 140
Kagan, Robert 233-234, 286
Kaplan, Robert 10-11,
al-Karim, Muhammed Abd 185
Karzai, Hamid 200

Kashmir 26, 77, 97, 100, 109, 117, 169, 189
Kazakhstan 266, 268
Kemal, Mustafa (Ataturk) 20, 188, 190, 252
Kemalist 50, 53, 190
Kenya 101, 117, 118, 128, 133, 158, 166, 168
Kerry, John 172
khalifah (steward) 71
Khameni, Ayatollah Ali 236, 238
Kharijites 90-91, 95, 97, 139
al-Khattab, Umar ibn 251
Khatami, Muhummad 236, 238
Khawarij 129
khilafa (governance) 54, 72, 243
Khilafat Movement 257
Khobar Towers, Riyadh 93
Khomeini, Ayatollah Ruhollah 20, 48, 50, 54-60, 224, 283
kidnapping 100-
King Abdulaziz University 111
King Saud University 124
Kissinger, Henry 113
Knights Under the Prophet's Banner: Meditations of the Jihadist Movement 90
Kosovo 78, 100, 166, 169, 222
kufr, kuffar 59, 98, 118, 147
Kulthum, Um 251
Kurds 192-193, 259, 261, 264
Kuwait 61, 110-115, 140, 265
Kyrgyzstan 223, 229, 266, 268-270

L

laicite 143
law 23-24,
Leaders of Change summit, Istanbul 262
Lebanon 100, 114, 127, 173, 207-208, 241, 263, 278
Lenin, Vladimir 24, 49, 205
Levant 17, 173, 202
LHOP 165-166
Liberia 169
al-Libi, Ibn al-Sheikh 172
Libya 112, 123, 125, 166, 172, 174, 186, 206, 216, 221-223, 258, 263, 269, 271
London 168
Luxor massacre 116, 128, 132-133, 166

M

Macaulay, Lord 19
Mahar, Ahmed 44

Mahdi, Imam 23, 55, 72, 112
Mahdi Army 257,
Mahmood, Sultan Bashiruddin 130
Majlis (Iranian parliament) 55
Majlis al-Shura 211
Maktab al-Khidamat (Office of Services, MAK) 109, 116
Malaysia 188, 190, 192, 268
Mali 78, 166, 172
al-Maliki, Nour 233, 257
Management of Savagery: The Most Critical Stage Through Which the Ummah Will Pass 146-147
Mansour, Adly 231
Manufactured Crisis: The Untold Story of the Iran Nuclear Scare 238
Al-Maqdisi, Abu Mohammed, Maqsid (maqasid) 90, 118
marja (religious figure) 55
Marmara 191
al-Marouani, Mohamed 219
Marx, Karl 24, 74
Marzouki, Moncef 214
Marxism 75
Maspero, Egypt 225
al-Masri, Abu Ayyub 202
Massoud, Ahmad 109, 117, 125-126, 132, 165, 198, 201
materialism 36,
Maududi, Abul Ala 47, 65, 74
Mauritania 53, 172
McCain, Sen. John 233
Mecca 39, 70, 81, 130, 152, 255, 264
Medina 71, 73, 81, 152, 255, 264, 279
Mashaal, Khalied 212
Meshal, Khalied 211
MI6 164
al-Mihdhar, Khalid 162
Milestones 47, 49, 74
"Milli Gorus" 190
Mindanao 109
Mir, Hamid 130
mizan 43
Mohammed, Khalid Sheikh 12, 159-160, 162, 268
Mohammed VI, King 217-218
Mongols 23, 90-91,
Morocco 145, 186, 203, 215-220, 270
Morrow, John 278-279
Morsi, Mohamed 51, 75, 83, 210, 226-234, 266
Mossad 159, 204, 238
Mosul 174, 202-204, 255
Mossadeq, Mohammad 237
Mubarak, Gamal 223
Mubarak, Hosni 51, 76, 116, 129, 171, 214, 223, 227, 235
Muhammad (Prophet) 36–37, 55, 70, 80, 89, 90, 93, 148, 152, 166, 251, 268, 278-279
mujahid(een) 11, 79, 90, 99, 107, 111, 113, 129, 143, 146, 198
Mujahideen Shura Council 202
mujtahideen (Islamic jurists) 72,
Al-Mulathameeen Brigade 168
munharif (deviant) 49
Musharraf, Pervez 161, 164
music 114, 184, 199
Muslim Brotherhood (MB) Egypt 12, 40-52, 64-66, 74-76, 96, 107, 116-117, 124, 128, 141, 150, 152, 167-168, 171, 186, 193, 210-212, 224-234, 242, 260, 282, 286
Muslim Brotherhood (other countries) 69, 185-186, 209, 214-217, 219-220, 222, 244, 284
Muslim Institute (London) 69
Muslim League (see as well World Muslim League) 188
Muslim Parliament (London) 70, 261
Muslim World League 185
muttaqi (pious, upright) 74
Muttawakil, Wakil Ahmed 165

N

Nagata, General 11, 13,
al-Nahda (Enhada, Tunisia) 214
naib (deputy) 72
Naji, Abu Bakr 146, 150, 203
Najibulah 198
Nasiri, Omar 150-151
Nasrallah, Sheikh Hassan 207, 277
Nasser, Gamal Abdel- 19-22, 44-47, 64-65, 75, 91, 96, 124, 214, 221, 224, 234, 267
Nasserist 65, 76, 125, 152
Natanz nuclear facility 62
National Democratic Party, Egypt 171
National Forces Alliance, Libya 222
National Salvation Front, Egypt 225
National Security Council 165
NATO 112, 172, 190-192, 206, 217, 221-222, 265
Nazism 279
NBC 203
NED (National Endowment for Democracy) 269, 282-283
Negus 81
Hehru, Jawaharlal 267
neo-caliphate 267
neo-Islam 280

neo-liberalism 96, 150
neo-Ottoman 262-263
neo-secularism 281
neo-Wahhabi 26, 70, 77-79, 89, 91-92, 96, 98, 99, 107, 132, 152, 166, 187, 197-198, 206, 242-243, 256, 258, 263, 265
New World Orser 269
Nepal 169
Neturei Karta 280
Neusner, Jacob 280
New Age Islam 280
Newsweek 163
New International Economic Order 267
New World Information and Communication Order 267
NGOs 199, 244, 269-270, 282
Nidaa Tounes 216
Nidal, Abu 114
Niger 172
Nigeria 23, 145, 158, 169, 172, 190
al-Nimeiri, Jamal 220
Nkrumah, Kwame 267
Nokrashi, Mahmud 44
Non-Aligned Movement 240-241, 266-267, 280
Non-Proliferation Treaty 238
Nonviolence Initiative 133
North American Free Trade Agreement 263
North Korea 19, 269
al-Nusra front – see Jabhat al-Nusra

O

Obama, Barack 131, 223-224, 234
Occupy Wall Street 275, 281
oil 97, 149, 183-184, 187, 204, 221, 236
Oman 265
Omar, Mullah (Afghan) 12, 119, 203
opium 199-200
Orange Revolution 269
Organization of Islamic Cooperation (OIC) 66, 71, 185, 241, 265, 267-268
Orientalism 69
Ottomans (see also Caliphate) 16, 19, 41, 47, 190, 205, 255-257
al-Oumma 219

P

pagans 82
Pakistan 19, 25, 53, 74, 78, 100, 107-108, 111-112, 114, 117, 126-127, 129, 133, 142, 145, 159, 161-164, 166, 169-171, 188-190, 198-199, 241, 268
Pakistani Muslim League 189
Palestine, Palestinians 44, 62, 63, 66, 75, 95, 97, 101, 107, 109, 112, 125-127, 132, 144, 158, 172, 188, 205-206, 231, 236-237, 257, 263, 280
Palestinian Authority 201, 212
Palestinian Liberation Organization (PLO) 63, 205, 207, 209, 212, 222
Pape, Robert 170
Pappe, Ilan 280
pax Islamica 252
Pearl, Daniel 162
Pentagon 164
People's Mojahedin of Iran 238
Perennialist School 275
Persia, Persians 23, 55, 58, 74, 82-83, 252, 257
Peru 125
Philippines 109, 139
pillars of Islam 38, 90
Pinochet, Augusto 228, 230, 234, 271
pollution 184
polygamy 184
Popular Democratic and Constitutional Movement 217
Porter, Gareth 238
Postmodernism to Postsecularism: Re-emerging Islamic Civilization 13
Powell, Colin 198
Power Manifestations of the Sirah 80-81, 278
Preachers Not Judges 49
Princeton University 69
psychology 37

Q

Qaddafi – see Gaddafi
al-Qadir, Abd 22,
al-Qaeda (see also AQAP, AQIM) 11, 13, 14, 48, 77, 94-97, 99, 101, 113-114, 116, 119, 123, 132-134, 139-145, 148, 152, 157-168, 172, 189, 192, 197-203, 210, 221, 238, 256, 258, 271, 277
al-Qaeda, philosophy/ strategy 89, 92, 148-149
al-Qaeda in Iraq 173
Qajar shahs 47,
al-Qamari, Issam 125
al-Qaradawi, Yusuf 101
Qatada, Abu 150,
Qatar 51, 185-187, 212, 265
Qatif 185

qist 43
Qods Force 60
Quran 37, 47, 70, 83-84, 98, 160, 199, 221, 252, 275, 278-279, 282, 285
Quraish, Qurashi 73, 82-83
al-Quds (Jerusalem) 56, 75, 265
Qutb, Sayyid 46-50, 53, 56-57, 65, 74, 77-78, 91, 96-99, 107, 124
Qutb, Muhammad 75, 96

R

Rabbani, Barhanuddin 117, 125
Rafsanjani, Ali Akbar 238
Ramadan, Said 96
Ramadan, Tariq 283-284
Rana, Gen. Naseem 119
Reagan, Reaganomics 95-96, 99, 111, 115, 189
Revolutionary Guards 40, 74
riba (interest) 82
Rida, Rashid 49
Right to Protect (R2P) doctrine 206
Rightly Guided Caliphs 54-55, 90, 251
Rose Revolution 269
Rothschild 'law' 274
Rouhani, Hassan 237-238
Roy, Olivier 283
Ruqayya 251
Russia 54, 97, 109, 132, 205, 233-235, 239-240, 255, 268, 271, 284
Riyadh 93, 113, 124, 138, 185-186

S

Sabahi, Hamdeen 224, 232
Sadat, Anwar 21, 64, 95-96, 98, 116, 124-126, 129, 214, 227, 234
sadaqa (charity) 82
Sadiki, Larbi 231
al-Sadr, Mohammad Baqir 57, 207, 259
al-Sadr, Muqta 257
Safavid 54,
Sajwa 185
Saladin 93
Salafi Nur Party 167
Salafism 23-24, 49, 54, 75, 79, 89-93, 99, 126, 141, 152, 185-186, 192, 211, 215, 219, 227, 230, 252, 260, 279
Salehi, Ali Akbar 241
Sampson, William 95
al-Saud, Prince Turki bin Faisal 119, 163
Saudi Arabia 21, 25-26, 53, 75, 91, 93, 95, 96, 98, 99, 107-108, 111-113, 118-119, 128-129, 133, 140-144, 159-166, 173, 183-187, 192, 198-199, 204-205, 210, 222-223, 226, 228, 233, 241, 255-261, 264-266, 271, 283, 285
Saudi cooperation with imperialists 183-185, 188
Sayyaf 125, 198
Scheuer, Michael 92, 96-97, 140
SCO (Shanghai Cooperation Organization) 244, 268, 280
secularism, secularists 20-24, 35, 42, 48, 50-51, 64-65, 74-75, 79, 91, 93, 96, 98, 106, 108, 112, 115, 123-124, 129, 143, 146, 153, 169-172, 186, 188, 190, 197, 203, 210, 214-217, 221, 224-230, 236, 254-255, 258, 260, 264-269, 274, 277, 285
Serbia 223, 269
al-Shabab 169
Shafii school of jurisprudence 128,
Shah Mohammad Reza Pahlavi 20, 55-56, 62, 98
al-Sham 173
Shamir, Israel 280
sharia (see also hadd, fiqh) 25, 37, 42, 47-49, 53, 57, 84, 92, 94, 98, 114, 183, 185, 189, 198, 203-204, 220, 229, 239, 252, 260, 275, 285
Shariati, Ali 58,
Sharif, Nawaz 189
Sharm al-Shaykh 129
Sharon, Ariel 209
Shayma 128
al-Shehri, Marwan and Walid 163
Sheikh, Ahmed Omar 162, 164-165
Shia 20, 54, 90, 100, 134, 173, 184-185, 188, 199, 201-204, 207, 239, 241-242, 252, 257-258, 276
Shia vs Sunni 23, 54-55, 61, 65, 71-72, 114, 134, 141, 145, 148, 160, 199-206, 222, 243, 257-258, 261, 265, 268, 277-278
al-Shibh, Yusuf bin 159-160
Shura Council, Egypt 229
Siddiqui, Kalim 68-73, 75-80, 240, 260, 278
Sidqui, Atif 128
Sierra Leone 169
Silk Road 21,
Simsek, Mehmet 191
Sinai 14, 95, 229, 277
Sirah (life of the Prophet) 80, 83
el-Sisi, Abdel Fattah 20, 54, 77, 172, 210, 228-234, 271
Social Justice in Islam 46
socialism 19-21, 24, 33, 41, 45, 47, 50, 64-65, 96, 106, 108, 124, 126, 143,

152, 184, 189, 191, 187, 221, 224, 228, 232, 236-237, 253-254, 277, 281
Somalia 109, 128, 139-140, 169
South Africa 268
South Asia Terrorism Portal 168-169
South Lebanon Army 207
Soviet Union 10, 17, 19-22, 36, 64, 74, 77, 96, 99, 106-109, 111, 113-114, 123, 125-127, 164, 169, 189, 198, 235, 237, 242, 253, 266-267, 277
Spain 109, 192
Sri Lanka 100, 169
Stages of Islamic Revolution 73
Stalin 259
Status of Forces Agreement (Iran-US) 55
Stevens, Chris 221
Storm, Morten 259
Sudan 21, 23, 53, 112-115, 119, 125, 163, 166, 198, 220
Suez Canal 229
Sufism 42, 219
suicide 100-102
Sukarno 267
Sunnah literature 80, 83
Sunni (see also Shia vs Sunni) 20, 54, 71, 101, 107, 148, 150, 188-189, 201, 205, 207, 256-257, 259
Suri 172
al-Suri, Abu Musab 140, 143-145, 150
Sykes-Picot Agreement 255
Syria 13, 21, 22, 26, 28, 54, 64, 78, 79, 112, 141, 144, 148-149, 166, 169, 171, 173, 186, 192, 201-202, 206-207, 213, 217, 220, 229, 233, 241, 258, 262-264, 269, 271, 277, 280

T

Tablighi Jamaat dawa society 162,
taghuti 60
Tahrir Square 270
Tajik, Tajikistan 198, 201, 266, 268
takfirism 49, 89, 98, 126, 131-132, 134, 172
Takkatol 215
Talib, Ali ibn Abi 251
Taliban 10, 12, 14, 79, 101, 114, 117, 119, 129, 132, 142, 144-145, 159, 164-167, 198-203, 206, 222, 260
Talmud 280
Tamarod, Egypt 229-230
Tamils 100
Tantawi, Hohamed Hussein 226
Tanzania 101, 117, 119, 133, 166
taqlid 79

taqwa (piety) 74
Taymiya, Ibn 23, 44, 47, 90-91, 98, 123
Tehreek e-Taliban (TTP) 203
Tel Aviv 214
Tenet, George 11-12, 165
terrorism 13, 14, 26-28, 58-59, 75, 91, 93-94, 107, 114, 118, 132, 141, 157-174
terrorism, European 11, 38, 78
al-Thani, Prince Sheikh Hamad Khalifa 185
al-Thani, Tamim bin Hamd 186
Thatcherism 96, 253
Tikrit 174
The Times 191
Times of India 161
Timurid 90
Tito, Josip Broz 267
torture 12, 94-95, 172, 185
Touchent, Ali 151
Treaty of Hudaybiya 82
Truth and Reconciliation Commissions 216-217, 220 243-244
Tudeh Party 75
Tulip Revolution 269
Tunisia 73-74, 112, 171, 203, 209, 214-220, 235, 243, 270, 282, 284
Turabi, Hassan al- 114, 220
Turkestan 261
Turkey 149, 158, 171, 184, 186-193, 203, 212-213, 229, 233, 244, 253-254-255, 259-262, 268, 271, 280, 283, 286-287

U

Uganda 128
Ukraine 269-270
ulama 23, 41, 49, 54-55, 58, 61, 68, 71, 152, 220, 227, 235, 257
Umayyad 71, 251
Umm al-Qura University 75
ummah (community) 20, 26, 28, 37, 43, 47, 63, 68, 71, 79, 99, 113, 139, 190, 243, 253, 257, 281, 283, 285
United Arab Emirates (UAE) 61, 161, 166, 199, 210, 265
United Kingdom – see Britain
United Nations 18, 63, 165, 192, 204, 213, 237, 267
United States, Middle East policy (see also Great Games II & III) 10, 54, 55, 62-64, 91, 108, 111-112, 115-116, 128-134, 139, 144, 148, 150, 152, 158-159, 164, 169, 171, 173, 186-189, 192-193, 198-201, 204, 208-209, 213, 222-223, 226, 228-

233, 239, 242, 256, 258-261, 265-269, 271
United States, Muslims in 145, 152, 203, 274, 285
University of London 69
Unocal 164
usra (family) 43
USS Cole 93, 128, 133, 170
USS The Sullivans 128
USSR – see Soviet Union
Uzbekistan 266, 268
USS The Sullivans

V

Venezuela 228, 240, 269
Vietnam 94, 213
vilayat/velayat-e faqih political theory 56, 72, 74, 283
Virtue Committee 212

W

Wafd Party 64, 76
al-Wahhab, Muhammad ibn Abd 23, 91, 123, 163, 255
Wahhabism 23, 26, 40-41, 79, 89, 98, 107, 112, 116, 131, 134, 141-142, 152, 160, 183-189, 242-243, 256, 264-265, 276
Wali Allah, Shah 23, 71
War on Terror 27-28, 131, 139
Wars of Apostasy 90, 148
al-Watan Party 222
Weissman, Steven 234
women 56, 71, 114, 184, 198-199, 212, 215, 220, 239
World Bank (WB) 18, 200
World Islamic Front for the Jihad Against Jews and Crusaders 118, 133, 141
World Muslim League 266, 268
World Trade Center 115, 128, 133, 157, 160, 167
World War II 17, 131, 188, 221
Wretched of the Earth 58
al-Wuhayshi, Nasser/Nasir 173, 259

X

Xinjiang 97

Y

Yemen 20, 95, 112, 115, 123, 145, 166, 169, 173, 197, 204, 217, 259, 265, 270

Yousef, Ahmed 212
Yousef, Ramzi Ahmed 11, 115
Youssef, Ahmed 28, 99
Yugoslavia (see also Bosnia, Kosovo) 169, 263, 267

Z

Zahar, Mahmoud 213
zakat 90, 148
Zanjubar 'emirate' 95
Zapatero 192
al-Zarqawi, Abu Musab 134, 202-203
Al-Zarqawi: The Second Generation of Al Quaeda 148
al-Zawahiri, Ayman 90, 92, 117, 123-134, 139, 141, 144, 146, 160, 168, 172-173, 202
al-Zawahiri, Rabia 124
Zionism, Zionists 46, 53, 56, 59, 69, 126, 188, 240, 279
Zitouni, Djamel 151
Zoroastrianism 252
Zuhri, Sami Abu 27